Journeys
HOME

The soft, spellbinding moorland atop the Brecon Beacons mountains in Britain

Contents

Foreword 6

A Buddhist monk burns incense of the ages in the ruins of Cambodia's revered Angkor Wat complex.

Foreword

By Dr. Spencer Wells, National Geographic
Explorer-in-Residence and head of the Genographic Project

Home. It conjures up memories of family and friends, warm fires, the smell of familiar foods cooking in the kitchen. Safety and security, a sense of *belonging*. Home is, in many ways, as much a state of mind as a geographic location. But for most of us, home also connotes a particular place, one that we return to after a journey.

This makes sense. Humans are a peripatetic species, having emerged from Africa (everyone's ultimate homeland, as Donovan Webster explores in his story inside) only in the past 60,000 years or so—or only 2,000 human generations, to put it another way. In that relatively short period of time we have scattered to the far corners of the Earth, occupying every continent. We had reached places as far afield as Asturias, Australia, and Argentina by around 15,000 years ago. Over time, our sense of connection to people and place created distinctive cultures, languages, and appearances. But much of what we consider to be our defining set of group characteristics—our heritage, if you will—has arisen during a relatively recent period of time, a few hundred to perhaps a couple of thousand years.

Heritage has a powerful pull on those of us who live in immigrant countries, missing as we are the sense of connection to place and community that our ancestors took for granted. Although we may never have been there, the attraction of returning to an older place, one that we may know about only through vague family reminiscences, can be intense.

The stories in this book reveal insights into the various meanings of home for 26 powerful writers. One theme that runs through all of them is a sense of home—a sense of belonging. Whether it's Andrew McCarthy's experiences in Ireland, his ancestral homeland, or Nawuth Keat's return to the Cambodia he fled as a child, there is a familial—almost a genetic—connection to place.

So sit back, relax, and enjoy a world tour to the homelands of the authors included in this moving book. And start to plan your own journey home—something we can all identify with.

Author Andrew McCarthy connects with the Irish hills of his forebears on a rugged trek to Carrauntoohil, Ireland's highest peak.

...ess P..ll

A young man wanders into his past and creates a new future.

BY ANDREW McCARTHY

Several miles from the [████████████] land, outside the market town of Listowel, along county road 555, just before the half dozen shops that compose the village of Duagh, a path was cut into the overgrowth and slashed up into the hillside. I almost missed it. There was no street sign, no markings of any kind. High hedges bound the single

lane—brambles brushed both sides of the car as I went. Occasionally there was a break in the wild growth, and green fields speckled with brown and white cows came into view.

This was the townland of Lacca West. The vista in this part of north Kerry was surprisingly vast, and looked out toward Ballybunion and the Atlantic—America beyond. The road tracked the hills for so long without a house in sight that I became convinced I'd come the wrong way. But with no way to turn the car, I drove on. Then ahead, on my left, a small yellow cottage dating from the 19th century, with two square windows set deep in thick walls, commanded an expansive view out over the valley below. Standing on the three-step cement stoop and spilling down into the drive were two dozen people— old women, strapping men, young kids. I'd never seen any of them before. This was my family.

The vast landscape of Ireland's County Kerry

Striking images of the past, including Ballycarbery Castle, dot County Kerry.

TRACING GENEALOGY, SEARCHING FOR ROOTS, has a long tradition—and has become big business. Information gathering that was once a painstaking, sometimes needle-in-a-haystack ordeal, with false leads culminating in frustrating dead ends, or hours spent sifting through crumbling church r⬛⬛⬛⬛ musty basements, has become often as si⬛⬛ few mouse clicks.

My own relationship to my Irish heritag⬛ always been one of casual pride and affect⬛ uninformed, identification. With a name li⬛ thy, I was quickly stamped as someone wh⬛ Ireland as home, if only a distant one—unt⬛ in Dublin, almost by accident, in the summ⬛

I had been lingering with little intent in⬛ when a friend with the nickname of "Seve,"⬛ surname of O'Connell, suggested we hop ⬛ Dublin for the weekend.

"Why not?" I answered. I was a young ⬛ no strings attached—or so I thought.

But when I stepped off the gangway on⬛ mac at the Dublin airport, impulsively, I d⬛⬛⬛ my knees and kissed the ground. Until that moment

I had no idea that I held any special attachment to the land of my ancestors, but the gesture felt instinctual. I was somehow "home."

We rented a car and were handed an 11-by-16-inch map of the entire country as our guide. Needless to

storefront haberdashery that my memory will never

erase. The shelves were overburdened; the smell was of new wool and fresh leather. Fishing tackle cluttered one corner. I picked up an Irish tweed cap and slipped it on. When I glanced in the small square mirror dangling by a thin chain from a single nail, I saw the map of Ireland written in my face. I kept that cap for 20 years, and still miss it. Seve disappeared behind a heavy curtain and stepped out a few minutes later wearing a pair of stiff, high-waisted trousers with suspenders. I laughed, but the heavily wrinkled woman behind the cluttered counter looked us up and down.

"You came in here looking like a couple of dandies," she sang in a lilting brogue, her head nodding with approval, "and you're walking out of here a pair of gentlemen."

It would take more than a cap and a pair of slacks to make gentlemen out of us on that trip. We sampled the Jameson in nearly every pub we came across—and broke into song along with the locals in a few (I was dubbed *O'Andy* in one pub after my solo rendition of "Heartbreak Hotel"). And if the name "McCarthy" or "O'Connell" appeared above the door at any watering hole, we set up shop and made a host of new friends.

>
> We sampled the Jameson in nearly every pub we came across—and **broke into song along with the locals in a few.**

Ireland in the 1980s was in the midst of a terrible recession. These were the days long before the Celtic Tiger economic boom remade the country. We often found folks who rented us their spare room for a few pounds a night to bring in extra money. One evening I sat squished on a narrow sofa with a family of five watching the Rose of Tralee beauty contest on a scratchy television beneath lace curtains, groaning in disappointment along with the rest when the girl from down the road (whom I'd never met) wasn't selected. It was a typical Irish August by the sea, and often we shivered under too-thin blankets on bad mattresses—and woke happy.

Eventually we drifted north, staying close to the coast. But wherever else in Ireland we went, I now carried with me the idea that I was a "Cork man"—an independent, strong lot. And everywhere we went we were welcome, our names our calling cards. In North Kerry, at Ballybunion Golf Club, we were told there was a local tournament on and no tee times available, until Seve leaned close to the burly man across the counter and said, "You mean two men with names like McCarthy and O'Connell, who've come all the way from America, can't get in a round of golf?"

The large man fixed us in a hard stare, and then said in a thick Kerry accent we could barely decipher, "You're a pair of chancers, aren't you?"

Like so many of the local Irish sayings, we had no idea what this one meant—but the look in the man's eye made his meaning clear. We just smiled.

"Go on then," his glare gave way to a grin, then to the shake of his mighty head and a wave of his meaty hand, "step up to number one and give it a lashing." (Little did I know then that I would return to the hills around Ballybunion more than a quarter century later on a very different mission.)

In County Clare, a place where I was to spend a great deal of time

Ireland's Atlantic-rimmed Ballybunion Golf Club

meet strangers, maybe play a bad round of golf, find somewhere to sleep, and drift on. We went places we had never been before—up to Sligo and Donegal, and some spots we returned to year after year. And there were people with whom we were sure to reconnect.

On one of our last trips together, Seve and I found ourselves near Ennistymon and thought of the Aherns. We decided to stop in and check up on them. Tommy had been elderly and frail when he escorted me into his golf club years earlier.

The travel agency was no longer operational—it had barely been functioning when we were there the first time—but the sign was still above the faded green door, the stained glass even more yellowed. Mrs. Ahern seemed tiny now. She smiled at us vaguely, but she was gracious and warm. Tommy had died a few years back; she was alone now. We shared a cup of tea, and then another. She talked of her husband and how she missed him. We laughed a little when she told a few

> ## 66
> We squinted through the sun reflecting off the ocean, out toward the Aran Islands . . . and **the wide world beyond.**
> ## 99

stories about his beloved golf club. When she looked tired, we left. At the door she reached up and took each into her pipe cleaner–thin arms and embraced first one and then the other with surprising force.

"Do you think she even remembered who we were?" I asked my friend as we walked away.

"I don't think it matters," he said softly, and we walked to our car in silence.

OCCASIONALLY I EVEN WENT OVER TO IRELAND ALONE, without Seve. By then I had become somewhat estranged from my family back home, and perhaps I was looking for some kind of connection, even a theoretical one. And so Ireland became *my* place. I felt more comfortable there, more like myself, than just about anywhere else.

Whether in Dublin or New York, when people asked what part of Ireland my people hailed from, "Cork" was always my answer. Yet I had no idea

On his first visit a quarter century ago, the author dangled his legs over the Cliffs of Moher.

Ireland's remote Dingle Peninsula
"is on the way to nothing."

was encased in the bubble of work and saw and did little else. Six months later I returned for the film's premiere, to a festival in the west, in the university town of Galway, a place where I had fond memories. It was there that Ireland took me by the hand, asserted itself once and for all into my life, and turned my world upside down.

In the lobby of what was then the Great Southern Hotel on Eyre Square, I met my future wife. A Dublin girl. The meeting lasted no more than a few minutes, but whatever it is that happens when two people meet and decide in an instant to change everything about their lives happened to us. There was nothing to do but acknowledge it.

As much of a go-it-alone guy as I had become, my new wife was that much more the opposite. Nothing could be as important to her as family—her people and their legacy mattered deeply. My wife's Irish clan was a boisterous Dublin brood that hauled me into the center of their chaotic, take-no-prisoners, full-throttled kind of love.

We quickly had a daughter, to go with the son from my first marriage. We bought a home in Dublin near my wife's family and began spending part of the year there. A land that had for me always been

> "
> **Kerry men are known to be the brunt of Irish jokes** in the same way that 'blonds' sometimes are in the States.
> "

an escape, a place shrouded in the gauzy glow of romance, became a three-dimensional, eyes-wide-open world, crowded with responsibilities and a mortgage—and family obligations.

I had spent a lifetime crafting insulation from my own family—I loved them all, and yet it seemed that my life existed outside of them. And here I was now, smack in the middle of a boundaryless Irish clan spilling over with good intentions and the love of Sunday dinner.

Even though I didn't really know exactly where my people came from, my mother-in-law, who was from West Cork, claimed me as one of her own (in fact, her maiden name was McCarthy!). My father-in-law was from the adjacent county of Kerry.

The Republic of Ireland is divided into 26 different counties (Northern Ireland is divided into six), each with its own fierce pride, with (sometimes) affectionate rivalry existing between neighboring counties. Inside my in-laws' home, such a Cork-Kerry rivalry thrived, especially during hurling and Gaelic football matches. Kerry men are known to be the brunt of Irish jokes in the same way that "blonds" sometimes are in the States—and Kerry was not spared that indignity inside my in-laws' home. It seemed that Kerry always got the worst of it.

"Why is it," I asked my Irish family one evening when we were all gathered around the table, "that everyone always makes fun of Kerry men?"

My mother-in-law paused. "Well now, Andrew, my love . . ." she smiled a Cheshire grin and would say no more.

My brothers-in-law rolled their collective eyes.

"Do you really need to ask?" one said, nodding toward his father.

"Envy!" my father-in-law barked. "We're the envy of the land, Andrew!" he grinned proudly.

"Yes, that's it exactly, my darling," my mother-in-law said in her lilting

Music infuses Irish life, including as bait for ice cream money in Longford.

A ferry from Dunquin links the Dingle Peninsula to Ireland's even remoter, nearby Great Blasket Island.

brogue, the grin still fixed firmly on her West Cork face. Clearly, this was a woman who knew the secret to a long and successful marriage.

Being a presumptive Cork man, my allegiances in the Cork-Kerry battle were clear.

"Did you hear the one about the Kerry man and the nun?" I began.

NO MATTER HOW MUCH MY WIFE tried to convince me that roots and continuity were not only important, but among the most valuable things in life, I resisted. Maybe it's the American notion of always looking forward, the idea that what's in the rearview mirror doesn't matter. After all, hadn't the belief in Manifest Destiny forged who we Americans are as a people? Where we're going, not where we're from—isn't that what's important?

Then one day last year without warning, I received an email. It came from a woman in Dunmanway, Ireland, whom I'd never met or heard of, never knew existed. A gathering of the McCarthy clan was being planned in Cork, the message said. There would be a gala dinner and music (she was looking for a harpist to round out her ensemble). Over the course of the

three-day weekend, visits were planned to historic McCarthy sites—castles and such—with lectures and presentations from experts and historians concerning all things McCarthy. And, of course, there would be ample time each evening in the McCarthy Pub in town for McCarthy socializing and bonding. *Would I like to attend?* the email inquired.

How this woman, who gave her name as Michelle, got my email address I had no clue. Even more surprising: The idea of attending intrigued me.

That I didn't simply delete an email with the subject line *McCarthy Clan Gathering* speaks to the encroaching influence my wife's thinking has had over me during the decade we've been together. Surprising myself, I responded quickly.

"The weekend sounds amazing," I wrote. (What a display of enthusiasm! Did I mean that?) Although I wasn't sure exactly where my family came from, I went on, I had always assumed it to be Cork. I would do my best to juggle my plans and attend, I concluded.

Michelle wrote back quickly. Anything she could do to facilitate my homecoming, she'd be more than happy to arrange. She wrapped up her message with an afterthought: If I ever had the desire to get more

The frigid Atlantic waters of Dingle, Ireland, are perfect—for horses.

specific and trace my own particular roots, she knew the people to ask. "They have helped lots of McCarthys," she assured me.

Work, however, prevented me from attending, and time passed. Life caught me up, the way life does, and I forgot about the whole thing. Then one day I was looking through old emails and accidentally came upon Michelle's correspondence.

I reached out. *Was it still possible to take her up on her offer of assistance?* I inquired. Might she put me in touch with the people who could help me trace my clan?

There was no earthshaking moment of commitment, no decisive declaration to my wife, "Yes, honey, you're right! It does matter where we come from! Our past informs our future, just like you've always said, and finally I'm ready to listen!"—as much as she might have liked or deserved such an admission. It was more simply a feeling of "Why not?"

> ❝
> The only thing I took away from my DNA trace was that **there was a good chance I was related to Billy the Kid.**
> ❞

Michelle, who seemed to live on her email, responded with the names of two men—one, Nigel McCarthy, who lived in England, was an amateur genealogist, and the other, David Butler, the head of genealogy at University College Cork and University of Limerick. I reached out. Both men responded with assurances that they would like to help, but that the first steps lay with me.

I was told to gather as much information on my father's lineage as possible. That didn't take long. There wasn't much. The only member of my father's family who had any clues at all was his sister.

Some years ago she had been on jury duty and with time to kill, went looking for records at the courthouse. What her digging produced was a photocopy of an old marriage registry stating that in Jersey City, New Jersey, on August 19, 1885, laborer John McCarthy, "born 1857(?)" in Ireland, son of Cornelius McCarthy and Mary Nolan, married Catherine O'Brian, born in Ireland "in 1857(?)," at St Joseph's Church. There was no indication where they met, or if John's parents, my great-great-grandparents, ever left Ireland. Catherine's parents were also listed, as were the witnesses to the marriage and the pastor who performed the ceremony. My aunt also knew that John and Catherine had three children, Cornelius, Johanna, and my grandfather John, born July 10, 1890. There was no other information.

My aunt suggested that my great-grandfather was from Cork, and that Catherine was from Clare, but when I pressed her on how she knew this, she confessed, "That's where most McCarthys and O'Brians come from." Then she added, "And that's enough for me."

For my search, I had decided to work primarily with Nigel, perhaps because he was a namesake, and to rely on David for corroboration—if I got that far. Without much optimism, I forwarded the little I had to Nigel.

He took the scant information and suggested I do a DNA test to see if it would

Connections

Among the more obvious things to say about Ireland is that to begin to understand a particular town, you need to spend some time in its pubs. If the half dozen bars I frequented during my stay were any indication, Dingle, a town on the peninsula of the same name where I embraced the search for my Kerry identity, was a proud, happy, and diverse place.

To name a few of those pubs:

• **Mac Cartig** (the old Irish spelling of McCarthy), on Goat Street, has the feeling of a warm and welcoming old living room.

• Over on Main Street, **Curran's** has a poet's thoughtful vibe.

• And when you want to raise the roof, the place to go is **Dick Mack's.**
—Andrew McCarthy

A song at Dick Mack's pub in Dingle

provide any tangible results. The report that came back—labeled in codes like SNP R-DF5 and R-CTS365 to explain the findings—was complete double Dutch to me, even after Nigel's explanation. The only thing I took away from my DNA trace was that there was a good chance I was related to Billy the Kid, as well as a member of the Wild Bunch and Jesse James. At least my fascination with the Wild West had been explained.

Then came news.

And the news was a shock.

Nigel had located my people, he was almost positive. A few more *i*'s needed to be dotted and a few *t*'s crossed, but it looked very much as if—using the Catholic Church's baptism, marriage, and death records—my family could be traced back to the house of my great-great-grandfather, the place John was born and raised until he left for America. And that house, a farm, was located . . . in County Kerry.

Kerry? There must be some mistake, I told Nigel. "I'm a Cork man!" I insisted.

"Apparently not," he said simply.

How could this be? Yet when Nigel showed me the paperwork, there was no denying what was before me in black and white.

It was as if I awoke, after a lifetime of supporting the New York Yankees, to find that my people actually hailed from Boston, and I was actually meant to be a Red Sox fan.

What could be worse? Everything I'd been led to believe, everything I'd led *myself* to believe, for the past 25 years was suddenly revealed to be false. I was not from Cork at all, as I'd long boasted, but was, in fact, a Kerry man—the brunt of endless Irish jokes. Only this time, the joke was on me.

The news rocked my in-laws' home.

"It can't be!" my mother-in-law wailed in mock horror. "Say it isn't so, Andrew, my love!"

"I knew it all along!" my father-in-law shouted. "A Kerry man! What news!"

I pressed Nigel to double-check, and asked David to have a look as well. But the facts bore out Nigel's claim. I was from the townland of Lacca West in North Kerry, a few miles south of Listowel, in the Catholic parish of Duagh. Not only that, but Nigel had identified 14 of my great-grandfather's brothers and sisters, and tracked a fair number of their marriages. Add to this, he had ascertained, from the 1852 Griffiths Valuation map, the exact location of the old homestead—most probably, he suggested, in ruin now.

I grew greedy. *Could he trace things back even farther?* I asked.

It appeared likely that my great-great-grandfather's father (Cornelius) also resided on the farm in Lacca West. But, Nigel told me, because of the stranglehold placed on Catholic life by the British at the time, earlier church records were not possible.

No matter. If it was true that Nigel had been able to locate the homesite, I'd be able to go and walk the land that my great-grandfather had walked before he left Ireland for good and came to America. The idea suddenly thrilled me.

But there was work that needed to happen first.

I had been a Cork man for all these years, or so I'd thought. If I was to embrace my new heritage, some changes in attitude were going to need to happen. Of course I had been to Kerry, I'd passed by the lakes of Killarney, I'd been to Ballybunion to play golf all those years before on my first trip, and I had driven the famous Ring of Kerry, but I'd somehow never paid the place much attention. My affections for counties Clare to the north and Cork to the south had relegated Kerry to drive-through status.

I had some serious mental adjustments to make. Something had to be done. I would need to get to know my home county, I concluded, before I walked my homeland.

The best course of action, I decided, would be to get an overview of the situation—from atop the highest mountain in Ireland.

CARRAUNTOOHIL IS TUCKED INTO THE HEART of the Macgillycuddy's Reeks Range in south-central Kerry, just beyond the borders of Killarney National Park, Ireland's first such protected land. The area has long been one of the country's premier tourist destinations—for that reason alone, I always gave it a wide birth. But tourist destinations become popular for a reason, and in a land of wild and rugged green spaces, Killarney was among the most audacious. Grand blue lakes reflect jagged mountains bulging up under restless skies.

One of Ireland's many ancient "ring" forts, Cahergall Stone Fort was actually a home cum animal corral.

Traditional Irish music and *craic* rule at Sheehan's Pub in Killarney.

The postcard-ready town of Killarney anchors the area. At Quills on High Street—where a sign in the window announced "trace your ancestry"—I purchased a warm Aran sweater I was told I would need for my hike up Carrauntoohil. At only 3,406 feet, I had assumed the trek to the top would be little more than a stroll, but local knowledge warned otherwise. Everyone from the store clerk to my father in-law ("People die up there, Andrew. Are you sure you're fit enough?") warned of the perils of the Macgillycuddy's Reeks. I dismissed this notion, assuming it to be little more than local Kerry braggadocio. After all, if I knew just one thing about Kerry folk, it was that in a land of prodigious talkers, they were among the absolute mightiest.

This seemed to hold true for John Guerin as well, the guide I enlisted after being assured the walk was far too treacherous to undertake alone.

"People who dismiss these mountains on the basis of altitude can find a lot of trouble," John promised me. Born a few miles away in the Kerry village of Beaufort, he had been hiking these mountains his entire life. During boom times of the Celtic Tiger, John rode the wave, purchasing several houses, and like so many Irish, he swelled with grand schemes. When it all went to hell, John, and far too many like him, lost a lot. These days he contents himself by spending much of his time deep in the land.

"We've come back to the bone and honestly, I think that's a good thing," he said, summing up what I've heard so many Irish say since the bubble burst.

We hiked past mountain lakes and beneath recently sheered sheep clinging to ledges above us. We passed outcrops with names like Hag's Tooth Ridge and avoided the Devil's Ladder in favor of the scramble up Brother O'Shea's Gully (named after the monk who lost his life sliding down its steep pitch). The sun shined. John waxed on about the attributes of Kerry men: "There's a sharp humor, a sense of irony, even more than in the other Atlantic counties. There's a cynicism in the humor, to be sure."

Hearty pub fare— bacon and cabbage

North along the Ring, just outside the town of Cahersiveen, I came upon another McCarthy castle, this one grander in scale and dating from the 16th century. In its shadow a woman with a small dog herded two dozen head of cattle and set them walking down the center of the road. I stepped into the derelict castle, a good portion of its walls covered in ivy. Perched on a promontory by the River Ferta, the view from high up was the most strategic and expansive for miles around. It seemed us McCarthys had an eye for real estate.

Then I headed to the Dingle Peninsula.

Stretching 30 miles out into the Atlantic, Dingle is one of several Gaeltacht (predominantly Irish speaking) regions in Ireland. It is remote, insular. You don't get to Dingle by accident; it is on the way to nothing—but itself. I had never been.

The narrow roads grew narrower. The wind was ripping off Inch Beach, a mile-long stretch of flat sand. Wildflowers—yellow, white, purple, and orange—littered the sides of the road. In the village of Ballyferriter, I saw nothing written in English. From every shop window, only Gaelic called out to passersby. Halfway out, the town of Dingle, with a population under 2,000, is the center of life. And Dingle buzzes.

> **"**
> In the village of Ballyferriter, I saw nothing written in English . . . **only Gaelic called out to passersby.**
> **"**

"There's a cracking mix of people in Dingle," local painter Carol Cronin assured me as we stood among her ethereal paintings of the sea in her gallery on Green Street. Born in Wicklow, Carol found her way to Dingle when she came to visit her sister who was here studying Irish. "Everything was fizzing. I suddenly didn't care what was happening in the rest of the world."

When she heard my last name and learned of my quest, Carol directed me around the corner to Goat Street, to see Tom McCarthy. "You can't miss him, he'll be the man behind the tap."

The old Irish spelling of McCarthy is "Mac Cartig," and it was painted this way above the door to the nearby pub. The gent behind the bar, a slightly elfin looking man with salt-and-pepper hair, was, as Carol promised, Tom McCarthy—a seventh-generation barkeep. "My father and his father and his father . . ." and he kept waving his hand in a outwardly circular motion. "Paying rent to the Protestant rector way back when."

I asked about the Irish spelling of our name on the door. "*Mac* means 'son' in Irish," he leaned over the well-worn bar. "We are the sons of kings."

At that moment, a gruff man pushing a handcart piled high with kegs of Guinness barged through the door. "I've got work to do now, Andrew," Tom said. "There should be some good *craic* in here tonight. Come back later, I'll buy you a pint."

And I did just that. As promised, the room was swarming. A pub quiz was in full swing. Groups of four and five were hunkered over their drinks fighting for the answers to trivia questions. It was clearly more an excuse for socializing and bending an elbow than knowing how many no. 1 hits the Chieftains had recorded.

After an hour I walked out into the Dingle night. Very low clouds raced across black sky, but air on the ground was still and cool. Around the corner was Dick Mack's. The sign out front read, "Pub and

Artist Carol Cronin paints the waterscapes of Ireland in her Dingle studio.

Tom McCarthy, a seventh-generation Dingle barkeep

a flash was up on a wobbling stool. He let rip a passionate, if unpolished, rendition of the Irish national anthem—hand over his heart. For a few moments the two men sang over each other, battling, without looking at one another. But soon the Welshman acquiesced and stepped off the bar. As Cirnan finished, he climbed down to roof-raising adulation.

A few doors away, on Main Street, soft-spoken, professorial-looking James Curran drew a smooth pint at the low-key pub that bore his name. A grandfather clock kept time beside an autographed photo of Robert Mitchum—acquired when Mitchum was in town filming *Ryan's Daughter* in 1969. Groups of twos and threes chatted among themselves, until a young man behind me began singing—unaccompanied—a soulful, lonely lament. He turned out to be the Irish singer-songwriter Damien Dempsey. "Just down for a bit of the craic," he told me.

I retuned to Curran's the next day because James had told me his father, who ran the pub before him, used to lend money to folks who were headed to America. James was in possession of their repayment letters and I was curious for a look. As sun shone through the window, he retrieved several overflowing notebooks from beneath the bar.

A letter sent from Brooklyn on November 5, 1929, was typical. "Enclosed you will find 3 pounds. It isn't much, but it will lessen the amount. I will send the rest later on, please God." Another, from a woman named Kathleen Moran and dated November 28, 1928, read, "I like this country very much, of course it isn't all sunshine, at all, like the locals in Ireland think, one meets with plenty of hard knocks. I know I have myself in the short time I am here. The worst is there are so many classes of people and one must try and get

One of the old letters belonging to James Curran

Haberdashery." Inside, the wall to the left was lined with shelves of scattered rubber boots and shoes; a few tweed caps hung from hooks. There was a thin coating of dust on all of it. To the right, an ancient wooden bar lined the wall. The bottles piled behind it to the ceiling were being grabbed and poured with lightning speed to service the throng. Two semiprivate drinking areas known as snugs, one beside the door, another at the far end of the bar, resembled nothing so much as confessionals. A few Tiffany-style lamps were suspended from above. The light switches were the old-school variety, visible wires climbing the walls. Jugs hung from pegs by the windows that were tinted yellow and bathed everything happening in a golden hue of memory. Conversation, which needed to be shouted over the din, was easy, considering the closest human was crammed in a few inches away.

Cirnan O'Brian had just sailed his boat down from Galway and was beginning to tell me about it . . . when a young fella who looked like a footballer climbed up on the bar, his head inches from an exposed lightbulb. He began to sing a melodious rendition of the Welsh national anthem. Impossibly, the crowd grew silent.

As we listened, Cirnan leaned closer to me: "Those Welsh can sing, I'll give them that."

The Welshman continued, gathering confidence, and volume.

Suddenly I heard Cirnan growl, "Not in my house he doesn't. Not in Kerry!" He shoved past me and in wise to all of them. Enclosed you will find 7 pounds ten shillings, please send on a receipt..." In still another, dated April 1919, Catherine Guihan boasted that she "wasn't afraid of those devils" at Ellis Island. "... They put a big card in front of my eyes, and thanks be to God, I was able to read it. They asked if I was ever out of home, I said that I was, they said I was a smart lady..." The letter went on to say, "... I am trying to pick up the American accent." Many of the letters were in Gaelic.

I didn't find any correspondence from any McCarthys, but the letters brought home to me in a way more real than ever what a massive, mysterious journey to America it must have been for so many, including my own great-grandfather.

The excitement I felt in Dingle, the sense of discovery, and rediscovery, reminded me of my first visit to Ireland, so many years earlier. So with renewed passion and regard for the land of my forefathers, I raced north.

Past Tralee, the drama of the Kerry landscape became considerably subtler. The untamed mountains gave way to rolling hills, and became almost flat in places. I found myself relaxing as the vistas opened. The gently undulating land felt familiar to me in a way that similar-looking parts of Ireland had long felt familiar. Perhaps there had always been a knowing of my place—even before there was a knowledge of it.

I pulled into the market town of Listowel and made my way to the hotel on the square. A ragged-looking Clydesdale pulling a two-wheeled trap crossed my path.

NIGEL MCCARTHY HAD DONE THE LABORIOUS RESEARCH locating my clan, but when I needed a man on the ground, Ger Greaney stepped up. A Kerry man, Ger had a passion for the past, a detective's relentlessness, and a flair for the dramatic. We had spoken several times while I was still back in America, and he said he would have more news when we met.

He was waiting in the lobby of my hotel, documents in hand. With his

> So with renewed passion and regard for the land of my forefathers, **I raced north.**

glasses and a Kerry man's biting wit, Ger struck me as a friendly, if sarcastic, librarian.

And he had news. I had originally intended to simply walk the land of my great-grandfather, and perhaps visit the site of what I was sure would be the ruins of the old homestead—if it could even be found.

It could indeed be found, Ger assured me. In fact, the house still stood, and was inhabited by my second cousin, once removed (meaning that my great-grandfather John, who had come over to America, and grandfather of the woman now living in the house, had been brothers). She was home now, awaiting my visit.

Excitement and trepidation swept over me.

My once frosty relationship with my family back home had certainly softened over the years (thanks in no small part to my wife), but I still found myself keeping a distance more often than not. My own children had, of course, burst my heart open and made me begin to look at the idea of legacy, or at least care about what happened in the future in a way I had never considered before their birth. Yet the idea that I was now about to bridge the gap across the Atlantic that had been carved open more than 100 years earlier seemed almost comical. I was, to say the very least, an unlikely ambassador.

A rare quiet moment at Dingle's Dick Mack's pub

A journey's end: Andrew McCarthy (center, in the green jersey) meets his Irish side, the McCarthys.

With butterflies in my stomach, I got behind the wheel.

A few miles out of town, just before the few shops and homes of Duagh, an unmarked, narrow lane veered up into the hillside. The road doubled back and tracked the hill as it climbed. It went on too long; I had made a wrong turn. I looked for a place to turn around, and then I saw them.

Standing on the stoop of a small yellow home that looked out over the valley below were two dozen other members of what turned out to be my family.

A roar went up as I disembarked. A gray-haired woman with mischievous eyes behind large glasses stepped up and shook my hand, then embraced me. This was Nell Fitzgerald, my second cousin once removed. She introduced me to her sister (another second cousin once removed), Mary Somers. Nell's daughter Mary, my third cousin, introduced me to her husband, who presented me with a Kerry football jersey. When I put it on, all hell broke loose. An endless round of embraces from more cousins and husbands and wives of cousins and children followed. Dozens, hundreds, of photos were taken. Inside we crammed into the small living room, a photo of the Virgin Mary framed on the wall. Above the door

hung the McCarthy and Fitzgerald family crests. I squeezed between Nell and her sister Mary on the sofa. We scoured the family tree Ger had wisely provided me. Tea was served. We ate cheese sandwiches and fairy cakes. The children ran in and out of the house. Everyone had questions for me, about my life, about my father—would he be able to come over?

"Can you dance at all?" Nell wanted to know. "The McCarthys was great dancers. My grandfather used to turn a bucket over and get up on it and dance a jig."

Among my relations were a nurse, an army sergeant, a quantity surveyor, and various laborers. Some of the men had been forced to commute to England for work and returned home on weekends.

At one point, a cousin sang a beautiful ballad as the boisterous room fell silent.

The day wore on. We went outside and took more photos. We strolled down the lane to the remains of the O'Brian house—long ago two of the McCarthy boys had married two of the O'Brian sisters. There were more hugs, and as I finally drove away, I saw two dozen of my family members waving in my rearview mirror.

The next morning I awoke in a quiet mood. The reunion had been joyful, but chaotic. Amid all the revelry, I felt I hadn't taken in as much as I would have liked. After breakfast I drove back toward what was my great-grandfathe[████]. The sky was without clouds. T[███]ally warm, yet a thin stream of [███████] chimney of the yellow house. I thought to knock on the door, but didn't want to arrive unannounced and empty-handed. I also wanted time alone in this place.

I walked down the lane. Wildflowers shimmied in the breeze. Ferns grew in the shade. A small white butterfly flittered past. I'd never been much of a sentimentalist, but I couldn't help but think of my great-grandfather walking this same lane, how many times? What must he have thought as he looked out across his family's 55 acres, out toward the Atlantic—his future waiting on its distant shore. I knew the anxieties and trepidations I'd felt before voyages and major events—could anything I'd experienced compare with an Irish country boy's excitements and fears about setting off on what he must have known was a one-way journey?

Just ahead of me a single magpie was flushed from the bushes—*one for sorrow*, as the nursery rhyme goes.

The meeting with relations I'd never known had left me with mixed feelings. I'd always felt slightly alone in a crowd, and this visit was no exception. Still, the gathering felt important. It was the kind of active connecting I'd always run so far from in the past. Their generosity had touched me deeply.

The relationship with my family back in the States [o]ften felt complex. Perhaps this strange home-[comi]ng to a home I never knew existed was an oppor-[tunity] to step out from under an imagined weight I'd [l]abored beneath. The visit felt suddenly significant in a way I would not have imagined—or been ready for—at an earlier point in my life.

As I looked down over the valley below, across to the sea and beyond, toward America, a second magpie darted across my path—*two for joy*.

It was time to go home.

Actor, director, and award-winning travel writer **ANDREW MCCARTHY** is an editor at large at *National Geographic Traveler* magazine.

Creating new memories and sharing old ones with newfound family in Duagh, Ireland

GET TO KNOW IRELAND

• CONNECT
Embark on a digital scavenger hunt. Discover artifacts representing more than 7,000 years of Irish history with the interactive **Ireland in 100 Objects** (*100objects.ie*) app or e-book. Many of the items, including a 1950s emigrant's suitcase, are housed in three **National Museum of Ireland** (*museum.ie*) locations (two in Dublin and one in County Mayo).

• CELEBRATE
Boston tops the list of the most Irish-American cities, but head to Milwaukee to join in what's billed as the "world's largest celebration of Irish music and culture." Held the third weekend in August, the four-day **Milwaukee Irish Fest** (*irishfest.com*) includes more than 100 entertainment acts on 16 stages, traditional *céilí* dance performances, and *currach* (Irish boat) races.

• COOK
Guinness and potatoes may get all the glory, but the true taste of Ireland is simple brown bread— the go-to accompaniment for any Irish meal. Native Dubliner and world-renowned chef Cathal Armstrong shares his family's brown bread recipe and many others in his debut cookbook, *My Irish Table: Recipes from the Homeland and Restaurant Eve* (Ten Speed Press, 2014).

Traveling the Truth

A white descendant discovers his African slave roots.

BY JOE MOZINGO

The heart of Angola: the Congo River

rolled down a sliver of red dirt road, weeds and sticks cracking under our tires, in search of an old slave port that was on no modern map. My guide and translator, a British expat named Paul, asked the two young boys showing us the way if they knew of any land mines.

This remote track made me nervous. It was exactly where the travel advisories warned visitors not to go in Angola, a country riddled with live anti-tank mines after three decades of civil war.

"No," the boys say, hesitantly.

"They say there aren't any," Paul confirmed.

This was not convincing.

We bumped along farther through the forest until the road fell away entirely into a gully. It didn't seem like the path led toward water, much less any substantial inlet, but we set down it on foot.

The sun was getting low, washing the high palm trees in ocher light. A man harnessed high in the fronds tapping palm wine watched us as we passed beneath.

We came to a small marker erected by the local church, inscribed in Portuguese, "In Memory of the First Baptized," with the date, April 3, 1491. It referred to the first slaves to be taken from here to Europe before the transatlantic trade began. *We must be going in the right direction*, I thought, as we descended into mangrove jungle.

We were outside the town of Soyo, hiking to what I hoped was an estuary of the Congo River, just about five miles from its mouth on the Atlantic. I had envisioned finding old stone docks and iron slave pens, perhaps strangled in roots like some ancient Khmer ruin. Even if I discovered that, I did not know what it would mean; I had no checklist to mark off, no tangible objective or end point to this journey. I was on a quest that was more than anything an act of imagination, if not insanity, given the cost and time it had taken me to get here.

I was looking for the man who gave me the name Mozingo, my African ancestor, a slave who landed in Jamestown, in colonial Virginia. I had been chasing his ghost for over a decade, ever since I came upon a handwritten court record from October 5, 1672, granting "Edward Mozingo, a Negro Man" freedom after 28 years of servitude. A great irony lies at the core of my origin story: I am white.

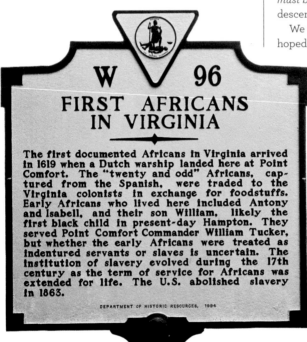

W 96
FIRST AFRICANS IN VIRGINIA

The first documented Africans in Virginia arrived in 1619 when a Dutch warship landed here at Point Comfort. The "twenty and odd" Africans, captured from the Spanish, were traded to the Virginia colonists in exchange for foodstuffs. Early Africans who lived here included Antony and Isabell, and their son William, likely the first black child in present-day Hampton. They served Point Comfort Commander William Tucker, but whether the early Africans were treated as indentured servants or slaves is uncertain. The institution of slavery evolved during the 17th century as the term of service for Africans was extended for life. The U.S. abolished slavery in 1865.

DEPARTMENT OF HISTORIC RESOURCES, 1994

America's first Africans, including the author's ancestor, arrived in Point Comfort, Virginia.

Dancing in the streets: a Sunday break by the beach on Angola's Ilha de Luanda

SINCE THAT DAY, I had learned much about Edward Mozingo's life, through research online and in libraries, courthouses, and historical societies throughout Virginia. He married a white English woman during a brief period in colonial America when that could legally happen. And he became a modestly successful tobacco farmer in the Northern Neck of Virginia. I found that more than 300 years later, his white and black descendants had long lost track of his story and were wondering where they got this funny name. The white ones insisted, sometimes virulently, they were Italian or French or Hungarian or Portuguese—basically from anywhere but Africa. I grew up being told we were "probably" Italian, until I was later notified that we were Basque. For some, the reality, had they

known it, wouldn't have sat well at their Ku Klux Klan meetings, a disturbing truth I learned about past generations of Mozingo men in Indiana and North Carolina. The black Mozingos found the story hard to grasp at first too, but most came to embrace it.

No matter how hard Mozingos tried to obscure it, the truth lies here in Angola, this troubled country on the coast of central Africa, which once lost torrents of enslaved people to the Americas. I just hoped I could find it.

In the year Edward likely set off across the Middle Passage, 4,336 slaves were documented as being taken from Angola, out of 6,858 from all of Africa.

I had spent days driving through the battered nation, starting in the capital city of Luanda. I drank espresso at a yacht club across the bay from the arc of beach where the slave pens once stood. I pictured the desperate captives staring up at the stone fort on the point as they waited to be hauled off in one of the wretched ships they called *tumbeiros,* floating tombs. Luanda was the crucible of the slave trade in Africa. Slaves arrived in caravans from the inland kingdoms and were marched through the cobblestone streets, past churches and the red-tiled porticos of homes and shops.

Now glass-and-steel skyscrapers were rising on a wave of oil wealth. The history of the mass slave trade that started in Europe's first African colony was not just faded, it was invisible. No one talked about it. Few historians visited here. Wealthy Angolans were waterskiing in the seminal spot of one of human history's great evils.

We drove north into the former Kingdom of Kongo, a place once ruled by Mozingas, my name as it was recorded in the 17th century. War had completely depopulated the coastal savannah, leaving lone stands of thorny trees and fan palms, almost black in the midday sun. On the highway—a rutted, bombed-out road with axle-breaking chunks of pavement—we went 50 miles at a time without seeing a single person.

We arrived at the provincial capital, M'banza Kongo, where the Kongo rulers once held court. All that remained of the great kingdom were the stone walls of the Catholic cathedral built in 1549 for King Mozinga's son, Afonso. The son reigned as Europeans siphoned slaves by the thousands to build new colonies in Cuba, Hispaniola, Puerto Rico, Mexico, and Brazil. While Afonso was complicit in selling enemies, criminals, and misfits to the Portuguese traders, he was outraged when the Europeans began kidnapping his loyal subjects. He complained to the king of Portugal about "thieves of men without conscience."

I knew I couldn't find records of my ancestor here like I could with my other forebears in Ireland or France. I would not see the school he went to or the church he attended, or pour through baptismal records, or meet long-lost cousins with oral histories.

But I needed to have a sense of where Edward came from, beyond the wild phantasms most of us in the West harbor about sub-Saharan Africa. This part of the "dark continent," where the slaves came from, had never felt like a real place in my mind, and our

A joyful moment in Congo

Tapping for palm wine near the Angolan slave port outside the town of Soyo

exotica has allowed us to dehumanize its people. I needed to go there, breathe its air, meet its citizens—to cross a mental breach that made it difficult to fathom my family's story—for Edward to be real.

We continued on to Soyo, and I swam in the Congo River on a bright afternoon with a yellow butterfly fluttering overhead. The water was translucent orange, glinting with flecks of pyrite and leaf matter. It had none of the primordial menace of Joseph Conrad—the "immense snake uncoiled"—or most journalistic accounts of the region. A lifeguard made sure no one swam too far out in the current. I almost got a citation.

I stroked out to a sandbar where little waves broke, and I sat down, gazing out to where the great river emptied into the Atlantic. The cold ocean water in the tropical air made strange mirage formations on the horizon. You could almost see the shapes of tumbeiros in some of them. I wondered what the day was like in 1643 or 1644 when Edward sailed off as a boy of probably 11 years old. Did he think the white people lived in these wretched boats, these "hollow places," as one former slave described them?

ABOUT ONE IN FIVE CAPTIVES died on the journey across the Middle Passage. The stench and disease was unimaginable. When the slaves were still within sight of the coast, they were shackled together on the floor below deck. If they couldn't make it to one of the buckets used as a latrine, they just relieved themselves

where they laid. The most emaciated slaves couldn't rise off the bare planks, and the rocking of the ship wore parts of their flesh away to the bone.

We headed into the bush looking for the old port and found the boys to guide us. The path ended at a clear stream. Paul said he'd wait there. The boys and I trudged down into the stream as it got deeper and joined more streams in a tidal swamp.

The boys laughed as they attempted to spear a crab with a stick near an old dugout canoe decaying in the mangrove roots. Edward would have been about their age when he left Africa. Maybe he was caught when he was out exploring, hunting, and playing around with a gang of friends. There were so many ways to become enslaved in 17th-century Angola. I suspected he might have been a prisoner of war caught during an internal conflict between the Kingdom of Kongo and the state of Soyo, which had seceded.

As we followed the canals, the forest closed in. It didn't feel like the path was leading us to a port where slave ships could have embarked. We crossed a sulfurous mudflat that slurped at our feet and had the boys in hysterics.

"Onde porto?" I asked. "Where's the port?"

They all pointed down. "Here?" I said.

Connections

This document exploded my family's myths about our origins and launched my quest to discover our true history.

The handwritten entry from October 5, 1672, recorded the Jamestown colonial court ruling that freed Edward Mozingo, a "Negro man," after 28 years of servitude.

The piece of paper survived by pure miracle. Many colonial records were lost in three separate fires, including at the courthouse in Richmond, Virginia, gutted during the Civil War. Luckily, the brittle, frayed record somehow survived. I found it at the Virginia Historical Society in Richmond. —Joe Mozingo

The port can't be here, I thought; no ship could get here. I started down the channel, the water rising above my knees.

The boys just stood there, studying the crazy white man from the mudflat.

"Porto aqui?" I yelled back to them again. "Is the port here?"

"Sim, sim, sim, aqui," they said. "Yes, yes, yes, here."

Maybe they were right. Maybe silt long ago filled in the port. The sun was setting in the northwest, and the mosquitoes were swirling around me. I knew I had to stop. When you journey into the past, you always want to go farther. You'll never get to your destination and you'll never be sated, just as you'll never fully understand your roots as they spin off into infinity. I began to feel lost, defeated. But then I took in the warm light and had the rushing feeling that my presence redeemed something here, resurrected the horror and struggle

> *The port can't be here,* I thought; no ship could get here. **I started down the channel.**

Edward endured for us so long ago. Now his descendants would know the tribulations that brought them forth.

THREE DAYS LATER I was walking along the beach of another river, in Virginia. The heat of the day did the same strange things to the James River as it did to the Congo. It looked like the middle of the channel was roiling with giant fish.

The year Edward Mozingo arrived here, a fifth of the entire settlement was killed in an Indian attack. Disease and starvation was rampant. Virginia's reputation in England was as a human "slaughterhouse." The average survival rate upon arrival in the early days was a few years. At one point, the Virginia Company began rounding up orphans in the streets of London because few others would go. The English were gradually taking more Indian land and using indentured labor to farm tobacco.

The author's family has lived and died in Virginia's Northern Neck since the 1600s.

Fewer than 300 Africans were in the colony when Edward landed on the banks, and no formal system of slavery had been set up yet. Certainly some were treated as slaves. Others became indentured servants and worked along poor English and Irish immigrants in the fields. Black and white workers cut tobacco together, drank together, gambled and ran off together. Black men had romantic relations with white women and even married them.

This was the social order Mozingo would find himself in. One of the colony's leaders and a grand planter, Col. John Walker, purchased him as an indentured servant. Edward learned carpentry and to play a fiddle.

When Walker died in 1668, Edward sued for his freedom. Amazingly, it appears that two of Walker's daughters testified for Edward in the main courthouse in Jamestown. Even more incredible, the court ruled against a member of the landed elite, and Edward Mozingo walked out a free man on October 5, 1672.

Edward went on to marry an Englishwoman, Margaret, who appeared to be from a family of fairly high station from Virginia's Northern Neck, where Edward and Margaret settled. They had a home on a creek called Pantico Run and raised two boys.

Along the river, I looked for the spot where Edward would have first seen freedom.

The only colonial building that remained intact was the church built in 1639, now restored. Would he have prayed here 33 years later, before his day in court?

Hunting around the "Back Streete" area, I came upon a sign noting the site of Swann's Tavern, where visitors to Jamestown usually stayed when they came

Author Joe Mozingo and his young Angolan guides

to the court and assembly. Would they have let a visiting "Negro" get a room? I continued west along the seawall, where wharves once teemed with the commerce of tobacco and slaves. At the east tip of the island, I found a book at an archaeological museum showing exactly where the courthouse had stood and the judges ruled. It was right where I was standing. The museum's door was the court's entrance.

Nearly three decades after he left the Congo, Edward walked out that door a free man. I followed him, imagining the exultation he must have felt as he took in this view, the slow brackish river, the pines on the low white banks fading off into a new continent his descendants would someday cross, chasing the American dream.

JOE MOZINGO is a projects reporter for the *Los Angeles Times* and author of *The Fiddler on Pantico Run: An African Warrior, His White Descendants, a Search for Family.*

GET TO KNOW ANGOLA

• EXPERIENCE
Short films, educational exhibits, and 17th-century artifacts depicting the experiences and contributions of the first known Africans in Virginia are woven into the deeply immersive **Jamestown Settlement** (*history isfun.org*) living history museum located in Williamsburg, adjacent to the original Jamestowne settlement site.

• TASTE
Angola's staple starch, the polenta-like *funje* (or *funge*) is made from one part finely ground cassava or corn flour, two parts boiling water, and a whole lot of steady, rapid stirring with a paddle-like, wooden stick. Funje is typically paired with chicken, fish, or greens, but there are more exotic options, including toasted grasshopper (*gafanhotos depalmeira*).

• VISIT
Artwork, artifacts, photographs, and audio recordings are part of the collections of the Smithsonian's new **National Museum of African American History and Culture** (*nmaahc.si.edu*) in Washington, D.C., scheduled to open in 2016. Exhibits and programs span the breadth of the African-American experience from the 17th century to the present.

The soft landscapes of Salta, Argentina, set the scene
for a road trip in search of distant family.

An Accident of History

The search for a name reveals a distant family.

BY ALEX BELLOS

I

t all started with a political assassination.

On November 14, 1909, an 18-year-old Jewish Ukrainian anarchist threw a homemade bomb at the national chief of police in Buenos Aires. The authorities responded to the attack by clamping down on immigration.

The crackdown created a rather devastating blow for

Chaim Bialistotski, my great-grandfather, a young Jewish Ukrainian who had just arrived in the port of Buenos Aires, hoping to immigrate, after the long transatlantic journey from the United Kingdom. Chaim looked far too subversive to be allowed in. He was forbidden from even stepping off the ship and was sent back to Europe, where he settled in London.

Chaim had sailed to Argentina to join his brother-in-law (of the same last name), Moshe Bialistotski, who had settled there a few years before. In order to disguise his Jewish Ukrainian name, Moshe changed it to Morris Bellos, which means "beautiful" in Spanish. On returning to London, Chaim adopted it too, thus founding the British branch of the Bellos family. In Argentina, the surname may have given the illusion of a Spanish ancestry, but not in the United Kingdom. Here most people think we're Greek.

One consequence of Chaim's failure to alight in Buenos Aires was that he never met his brother-in-law again. The Argentinian and British Belloses eventually lost all contact. When I was a boy, all we knew about their whereabouts came from a letter, received in the 1950s, that said they were now in Tucumán, a provincial capital 700 miles inland near the border with Chile and Bolivia. Included in the letter was a black-and-white photograph of Morris surrounded by his wife, their children, and grandchildren. As a child I remember staring at this picture and wondering who was who, whether any of them were still alive, and whether I would ever meet them. With the exception of a bald, round-faced man in a Latino mustache, the picture gave nothing away of its location: It was a middle-class Jewish family portrait that could have been taken in Budapest, Paris, or New York.

When I looked at the photograph, I also felt relief. I knew how lucky I was to have grown up in Britain, a fading power perhaps, but still at the center of the developed world. The state had paid my education all the way through Oxford University, and I was working as a reporter in London, a dynamic and exciting global city. Had there been no assassination in Buenos Aires in 1909, I would most probably be living in Tucumán, what I assumed was a peripheral city in a peripheral nation. Thank God, I told myself, that my great-grandfather was not allowed to disembark.

The Cathedral of San Miguel illuminates a night in Tucumán, Argentina.

Salta's Red Rock Canyon provides a dramatic backdrop for the author's solo search.

IN 1998 I DECIDED TO LIVE ABROAD. I chose Rio de Janeiro, Brazil, because my roommate had recently returned from a trip there and I liked the idea of living by the beach. Being in Rio also meant that I was a lot closer to Argentina, where I planned one day to rediscover my long-lost relatives.

Before I had time to properly think about how to find them, I was sent to Argentina to write a story on soccer. On my last day there I visited a branch of a telecommunications company full of booths and telephone directories. I found the one for Tucumán, and looked under Bellos. I was stunned: There were about a dozen names.

I made a note of the numbers and addresses of each. But rather than calling any of them or sending a letter, I decided to travel to Tucumán. I wanted the first reconnection of the two families to happen in person, rather than on the phone or through correspondence. It felt more epic that way. Plus it allowed

me to turn my fear that the names I had written down were from a completely different family into a meaningful adventure.

Still, my stint in Rio was over before I had time to organize the trip, and in 2003, I returned home to London.

Incredibly, a few months later I received a letter from Tucumán. They had found me before I had found them! The letter, from Hugo Osvaldo Bellos, said that he was the grandson of Morris Bellos. Were we possibly related?

My reaction was one of joy, tempered with the frustration that I had missed my chance to visit when I was there. Hugo had found my address on the Internet and sent the letter speculatively. This time, I decided that I would visit as soon as I could.

IN FACT, IT TOOK ME SEVERAL YEARS to find both the money and the time for a trip. I finally took off

Salta's sun-saturated facades

for the tourist city of Salta, about 150 miles north of Tucumán, for a story on the spectacular red-and-orange Quebrada de Humahuaca canyon.

After a few days in Salta, I was on my way. I drove to Cafayate, a small town famous for its vineyards that's halfway to Tucumán. I reached Cafayate in the afternoon after a drive down a stunning road through mountains and rocky scenery that at times looked like I was on Mars. My relative Hugo picked the location so I could meet his son Ariel, who is my age. It felt appropriate for the first encounter with my long-lost family to be of the same generation. I checked into the agreed-upon hotel and waited.

As I waited for Ariel to show, I started to feel nervous. Would we have anything to say to each other? I didn't even know what he looked like. But when he walked in, there was no mistaking: curly hair, lightly Semitic features, dressed in a T-shirt and jeans. We stared at each other for a second and then hugged. *"Primo!"* he said. "Cousin!"

Ariel and I headed straight into town to have a drink of the local Torrontés wine and catch up on half a century of family history. Ariel went on

a student exchange to Ohio when he was 18 and speaks good English. I bombarded him with questions. It was only toward the end of the evening that I realized I had barely spoken about myself. I was much more interested in learning about the Argentinian side of the family than he was about the British. Part of this may have been because I am a journalist and predisposed to asking questions and finding things out. But I also think it was because, as I discovered, there are many more Argentinian Belloses than there are British ones, and they all still live in Tucumán. For me, to find a new Bellos was exotic. For him, not so much.

The following day we drove to Tucumán. The city is important in Argentinian history as the place where the provinces declared their independence from Spain in 1816. It has a population of just under half a million people, making it the fifth largest city in the country, and is nicknamed the Garden of the Republic because it sits on very productive agricultural land. It boomed 100 years ago when the railway arrived and the sugarcane could be easily exported. It still is relatively wealthy, and many middle-class residents have weekend homes in the lush mountains that overlook it.

The city itself, however, is not pretty. Ariel drove us to his father's flat in the small commercial center, which consists of a few blocks of shops and galleries. When we got there, Hugo was waiting for us with his wife, Maria Helena, and we went across the road to have dinner in their Italian-themed restaurant, Il Postino. Alberto, another of Hugo's sons, joined us. Sitting next to Ariel and Alberto, I felt like a long-lost brother returning home.

BEFORE I VISITED MY ARGENTINE FAMILY, I had assumed that they would be poorer than the British side, simply because Argentina is poorer than Britain. I knew from my emails with Hugo that he ran a stationery store called Todolandia—"Everythingland." I imagined a small shop like the kind you might see in a provincial British town, often parodied in TV sitcoms.

> **"**
> Sitting next to
> Ariel and Alberto,
> **I felt like a
> long-lost brother
> returning home.**
> **"**

Yet Hugo was very successful. Todolandia had a prime location on Tucumán's Main Street. It was cavernous inside, and sold toys and books as well as stationery. An armed guard stood outside. The shop got so busy before the beginning of school that they had to take on extra staff. Business was so good, in fact, that Hugo opened Copytec, another store, on the other side of Main Street opposite Todolandia, that Ariel and Alberto ran.

Hugo told me the family story. When Morris moved to Argentina, he lived in Rosario, 200 miles inland from Buenos Aires, where he worked for the British Railways. He married and had two children, Isidoro and Sarita. When his wife died, probably as a result of a miscarriage or abortion, he asked the Jewish community to find him a new one. They found Rose in Tucumán, and she moved to Rosario. When Isidoro grew up, he also worked for the railways, but he was not politically allied to President Juan Perón, so

Argentina's river-sculpted Quebrada de Humahuaca canyon

there was no chance of promotion, and he decided to take his young family, including son Hugo, to live in Tucumán, at the end of the railway line and to his stepmother's hometown.

Hugo said his father was manic-depressive, with prolonged lows interspersed with huge highs. During one of these highs he bought a kiosk in a downtown shopping gallery. He called it Todolandia because it sold everything from umbrellas to hardware supplies. When Isidoro was unable to run it during a bout of depression, Hugo stepped in. A family friend gave Hugo administrative control of a workshop that made rubber stamps, and Hugo joined the businesses together. Soon Todolandia became *the* place in town for rubber stamps. In a highly bureaucratic country like Argentina, where documents endlessly need to be signed and stamped in triplicate, rubber stamps are an essential part of daily life. On the back of the profits from the stamps, Hugo was able to expand into other shops and live a comfortable life. He and his family wore Western-branded clothes, lived in good-size homes, drove high-end cars, and worked hard.

I compared Hugo's family to mine. We are typical descendants of the eastern European Jewish diaspora. My father is an academic, and I am a journalist. Hugo and his sons are small businessmen.

Connections

My relative Hugo Bellos owns a stationery store in Tucumán, Argentina, that produces rubber stamps, among other things. He was quite surprised I did not have my own personalized stamp, so he made me one as a gift. It looks like a pen, but the back comes off to show the ink pad and the stamp, which contains my name, email, and phone number. The prosperity of my South American relatives (above) is largely the result of rubber stamps like these, in high demand in Argentina. —Alex Bellos

A bestial immigrant: Ancient ancestors of llamas, like this one in Tucumán, originated in North America.

Yet there were differences that felt more significant. Hugo and his sons felt like a unit; they lived near one other, worked together, and spoke every day. My parents and two sisters are spread between three countries and four cities. I was both attracted to and alienated by the strength of their family ties.

The following day Hugo introduced me to the family of his younger sister, Graciela, at the home of one of her sons, where they were celebrating his daughter's first birthday. Plates of salad were on a big table, and barbecued beef was passed around. A normal Argentinian family get-together. I learned that Graciela's first husband had been kidnapped and killed by the dictatorship in 1978, and afterward she married his best friend, Negro. Her eldest son is a neurosurgeon, who spent seven years in Israel and was on duty when late Prime Minister Ariel Sharon was brought in after having a stroke. It was a lot of information to take in, especially since there were 11 Bellos descendants in the room and I was asking a lot of questions. The only time you get that many British Belloses together is at weddings and funerals!

I calculated that there are more than 20 surviving descendants of Morris Bellos, and they all live in Tucumán. Hugo took me on a drive to meet the family of his late brother, Mario. His daughter, Daniella, is a yoga teacher and lives with her four beautiful daughters. We also met his cousin, who is a chemistry professor at the local university. Hugo is the self-appointed family historian, and likes to keep links with all the branches, even though I could see that they all have such different lives that each member is in touch only with his or her immediate family.

On the plane home I scribbled down in a jotter as much as I could remember. "Wow! So many Belloses!" I wrote on the first line. The feeling that I brought home was the opposite one that I had when I arrived. I had shed the developed world arrogance that I was "lucky" that I had been born in Britain. My Argentine family had, on the whole, made a prosperous and happy life for themselves in Tucumán. So much so that none of them wanted to leave. With stunning scenery nearby, successful careers, and surrounded by loved ones, their quality of life, certainly, was in many ways better than mine.

ALEX BELLOS is the author of books on Brazil and popular science, including *Futebol: The Brazilian Way of Life, Here's Looking at Euclid,* and *The Grapes of Math.* He lives in London.

The author, Alex Bellos (right), shows off a custom rubber stamp at his relative's Tucumán shop.

GET TO KNOW ARGENTINA

• DANCE

During the two-week **Tango Buenos Aires Festival** (*tango-international.org*) each August, many of the Argentine capital city's major avenues are closed to traffic, creating open-air *milongas,* or tango salons, for couples to perform Argentina's sultry, signature dance, recognized by UNESCO as a distinct art form.

• DRINK

Sipping this herbal elixir through a shared *bombilla,* or metal straw, is a time-honored Argentine activity. *Maté,* made by steeping the yerba maté plant, is traditionally shared among friends from a single carved gourd. Taste and learn how to prepare authentic maté at **The Guayaki Mate Cafe** (*guayaki.com*) in Sebastopol, California.

• TOUR

Take a guided tour (in English, Tuesdays and Thursdays, 11 a.m.) of Buenos Aires' legendary mausoleum mini-city, **La Recoleta Cemetery** in Recoleta, to "meet" a veritable who's who of Argentine society—including Eva Peron and multiple Nobel Prize winners, former presidents, artists, and celebrities—interred in the ornately decorated marble tombs.

Change comes slowly in rural "Khmer's Land."

The Reluctant Traveler

Revisiting a brutal childhood to discover where home is

BY NAWUTH KEAT WITH MARTHA E. KENDALL

My childhood ended when I was nine years old. Khmer Rouge thugs attacked our village of Salatrave. They murdered my mother, my baby sister, my grandmother, my aunt, and uncle. I survived the three bullets they fired into me, but my world never recovered.

During the reign of terror, I was forced to slave in the rice fields all day, every day. Food supposedly went into the common pot, but when I wanted to eat, I was told there was nothing left. To survive, I caught fish, crabs, and eels with my hands, and I trapped and ate frogs, rats, and snakes. Hungry and scared, I endured this misery year after year, not knowing if my life would ever change. For a few months I hid out with my father in the jungle, but he sent me away just before the Khmer Rouge killed him.

My brother-in-law, Van Lan, and my sister, Chantha, planned our escape. They had an infant son and didn't want him to suffer the cruelty of the Khmer Rouge. One night our little group sneaked off. Van Lan and Chantha, their baby, plus my three brothers and I waited silently in the tall grass by day, and traveled as quietly as we could by night. The Khmer Rouge shot anyone they didn't like, anyone who seemed too smart, anyone who might be running away.

At the market in Cambodia's capital, Phnom Penh

The author, Nawuth Keat, discovers a new pride in his homeland at Cambodia's Angkor Wat temple complex.

We'd heard the Vietnamese had taken over the Cambodian city of Batambong about 12 miles away, so that was our destination. Van Lan knew we'd be caught if we followed the obvious route to get there, so we walked in circles and zigzagged, going anywhere to evade the Khmer Rouge.

After several days and nights of terrified hurrying and then hiding, we made it to Batambong. We were not alone. The city was filled with other hungry escapees, and we all needed to find a way to make a living.

On the outskirts of the city, the Khmer Rouge had burned farms and barns to starve "the enemy." We made use of any crops still growing. My older brother and I often walked from Batambong into the countryside. Avoiding any ditch or mound that might be hiding a land mine, we picked vegetables and fruits that had managed to grow in the abandoned fields. We walked so far that we were gone more than a day, and we slept on the ground under trees that lined the road. In our cart, we carried food

to our family, and we sold some, too. The trips were risky, but we were surviving.

Van Lan wanted to do more than just survive. Older and wiser than I, he said there was no future worth living in Cambodia. He and Chantha were determined to get themselves and their baby out. He told me I was the only family member brave enough and strong enough to escape with them—if I wanted to.

Did I dare? I was terrified to imagine the trip, and terrified to imagine staying behind.

I have never regretted my decision.

We walked barefoot across Cambodia, dodging bullets and land mines. I walked until I was too exhausted to move, and then walked some more. We kept to ourselves, afraid we might suddenly come upon Khmer Rouge who'd shoot us or a Vietnamese soldier who'd rob us.

We finally trekked to the border with Thailand, and then dashed across. There, my life became different, but not better. We were separated in the refugee camps and I couldn't have felt more alone. Officials said my bullet scars were a sickness, and for a year I failed one health inspection after another. When the scars never changed, the authorities finally let me go. I boarded a plane filled with refugees bound for San Francisco.

It was 1982. I was 18 years old.

WHEN I CAME HOME FROM WORK ONE DAY in 2013, my wife, Kelly, handed me an airplane ticket to Phnom Penh.

Kelly had also been a Cambodian refugee, but she did not endure the years of horror that I did. I came to the United States alone. She came with her mother, two sisters, and three brothers. She had once taken our daughter with her to visit Cambodia.

"This time," Kelly said, "you come with me."

I had no desire to return to the place where I'd suffered so much, but I love my wife.

> " We searched for the fields where we had lived and worked **during the worst years under the Khmer Rouge.** "

And so I went.

As our plane made its descent, flying low over palm trees by the airport in Phnom Penh, Kelly said, "Nawuth, I bet you've forgotten how hot it is here." She was right. We emerged from the airplane into an oven of soggy air that took my breath away. What else had I forgotten about my native country?

Van Lan met us at the airport. He and my sister Chantha had been sent from their refugee camp in Thailand to France, where they raised their son, Vibol. Then Chantha and Van Lan divorced. He returned to Cambodia to start a company in Phnom Penh that sells French perfume.

I am thankful that Van Lan still treats me like his younger brother. At my request, we searched for the fields where we had lived and worked during the worst years under the Khmer Rouge. He too had never gone back.

All in a day's work in Phnom Penh

Fit for kings: the Royal Palace
in Phnom Penh

After centuries, Buddhist monks still worship at Cambodia's Angkor Wat.

I was still haunted by the memory of how the Khmer Rouge, wielding their guns, had forced us out of our homes. They marched us into the countryside where they "allowed us" to build shacks to live in next to rice fields where they made us work. I dreaded returning to that site, but I felt compelled to see it.

Van Lan found the general area, and we drove a paved road until its end. Then we wandered on foot, asking directions now and then as we walked narrow dirt paths.

Van Lan finally said, "This is it."

There were no rice fields or shacks on the low levees. We saw a few vegetable gardens, but that was all.

"How do you know it's here?" I asked.

He pointed to a large tree and said, "Sometimes we'd rig up a tarp, tying it to this tree's branches, so we could cool off in the shade."

I vaguely recalled a big tree whose name I don't know in English. It grows wild in the jungle.

Sweating under the tropical sun, Van Lan and I walked over to it. I pulled a branch toward me, picked off a leaf, and stroked my finger across it. The surface felt like sandpaper. Ah. This is what I remembered—the roughness.

I thanked Van Lan for bringing me to that place, which I never want to see again.

Another day, Van Lan drove Kelly and me to my old village of Salatrave. At least, that's what the sign said. I closed my eyes and tried to call up my memory of the place. No trace remained that matched the images in my mind. I wanted to kneel at the spot in the field where my mother was shot and killed, but I couldn't. There was no field to be found. I did locate the land where my family's home used to be, but the house had been destroyed. Now all that's there is somebody's small, rickety shack.

I chatted with a few residents. "You're not from around here," they said. At first I was confused, because my wife and I still speak our native Cambodian without an accent and our clothing looked like that worn by prosperous locals. Then one of the truths about Cambodian society hit me. We stood out because we talked openly and kindly with these village people. As the rural poor, they were accustomed to being ignored or insulted by city folks. Where I live in California, people treat each other with courtesy, no matter their station in life.

Van Lan told me that bribery and insider connections determine who gets the few good jobs. Phnom Penh has a fine university, but a degree means nothing if a competing job applicant comes from the right family. The powerful flaunt their money, driving Range Rovers and wearing expensive jewelry. At the market, I watched people flee when the big bosses pulled in. If there was a line to buy lunch at a café, the wealthy cut in, no questions asked.

In the countryside, life hasn't changed much from when I was a child there 40 years ago. There's no electricity, the ramshackle houses have dirt floors, and few people own cars. I thought everyone would be interested in what life in America is like, but they didn't seem to care. They were where they were and that was that.

On our way to visit the city of Batambong, we drove the same route my brother and I had taken those many years ago to glean fruit and vegetables from abandoned fields. What had been a full day's walk took about 15 minutes in Van Lan's Lexus.

Connections

When I finally returned to Cambodia, I was stunned by the majesty of Angkor Wat, a temple that was built in the 12th century. At last I'd found something of substance, something enduring and worth preserving in my poor homeland. It must have been a grand civilization that created this masterpiece. I craned my neck to behold the temple, which rises from the center of a large complex of architectural ruins. My wife, Kelly, and I have hung a painting of Angkor Wat on our living room wall so we can admire this gem of our heritage every day. —Nawuth Keat with Martha E. Kendall

The calm face of Angkor Wat, the world's largest religious complex

Angkor Wat is a glittering survivor of a painful past.

"Where are the trees I slept under?" I wondered aloud. Van Lan said they'd been cut down to make room for the paved road.

He took me to visit my few surviving relatives. I hadn't seen my oldest sister, Chanya, for 35 years. She lives alone and has long been retired. Even though she is physically and emotionally frail, she spent almost every day with us during our monthlong stay. I was glad to see her, but we had little to say to each other. We lived worlds apart, and I could not build a bridge over the ocean that separated us.

We drove to the home of my mother's sister. I had to explain again and again to her who I was before she understood. Her very ill

Happier times: the author, fourth from the left, and his siblings

husband had been bedridden, she told me, for about five years. He could not speak and could barely gesture with his crippled hands. I gave my aunt $200 to help get whatever care for him they could. He died two weeks later.

WHEN I WAS A CHILD, nobody in our village ever saw a doctor. If people got sick, they either recovered, or they died. Most never saw a dentist either. I remember cringing as people moaned in agony with a toothache. If they were lucky, they could borrow enough money to take a bus to a city to find a dentist who would pull it out.

We didn't have access to health care, but some parents,

like mine, foun... ...education for their children. At the... ...rivileged to attend in Batambong, I le... ...ng-kor. It's a huge t... ...ex park revered by... ...and admired throughout Southeast Asia. We were taught that its central shrine, Angkor Wat, rivals the Taj Mahal and the pyramids in Egypt. My family had never visited it. On this trip, I made a point to go.

With joy, I explored everywhere. I climbed as high as I could up the temple. The jungle looked beautiful from the spires of Angkor Wat, and the culture that constructed such a monument rose in stature, too. At last I'd found something of substance, something enduring and worth preserving in my poor homeland.

BEFORE THE KHMER ROUGE TOOK OVER, I attended only four years of elementary school. Nine years later, as a new immigrant in the United States, I enrolled in high school. I graduated in three years and then studied at San Jose City College. I had dreamed of becoming a dentist and preventing the kind of suffering I'd seen in my village, but as a young man starting a family in California, I couldn't find a way to make that possible. I needed

> **"**
> I climbed as high as I could up the temple. **The jungle looked beautiful from the spires of Angkor Wat.**
> **"**

a better job than working in a doughnut shop and going to college part-time. So I earned a certificate as a machinist, and that training has allowed me to have a good career. Kelly and I also bought and operate a bagel shop. I don't mind working two jobs. I'm glad I'm free to earn a salary for my labors.

Kelly and I have raised three children in California. One son and his wife just had their first child. My other son works at an auto dealership. My youngest child, our daughter, hopes to become a dentist and is about to start college. I know that she can succeed. I feel privileged not only to be her father, but also to have given her a life where she has choices and the chance to fulfill her ambitions.

I left my country as a displaced Cambodian. I returned as an American.

Now that I'm back in the United States, I am very glad to be home.

NAWUTH KEAT and **MARTHA E. KENDALL** are co-authors of *Alive in the Killing Fields* (National Geographic, 2009), a memoir about how Keat survived and escaped the Khmer Rouge. Keat and his wife recently moved from California to Vidor, Texas.

GET TO KNOW CAMBODIA

• TOUR
Icon of Khmer civilization, northern Cambodia's Angkor Wat is one of the most famed temples in Southeast Asia. The 12th-century "temple mountain" (which appears on the national flag) was built as a spiritual home for the Hindu god Vishnu and is part of the sprawling, 154-square-mile **Angkor Archaeological Park** (*whc.unesco.org/en/list/668*), a UNESCO World Heritage site.

• LEARN
Learn about Khmer culture and the Cambodian genocide at the **Cambodian-American Heritage Museum and Killing Fields Memorial** at the Cambodian Association of Illinois, 2831 W. Lawrence Ave., Chicago, 773-878-7090.

• CELEBRATE
Known as the "Cambodian capital of the United States," Long Beach, California, is home

to the largest population of Cambodians outside Southeast Asia and the nation's first officially designated **Cambodia Town** (*cambodiatown.org*). As part of April's Bonn Chaul Chnam (Khmer New Year) celebration, the 1.2-mile-long ethnic enclave hosts the Cambodia Town Culture Festival featuring traditional Khmer dance and music performances and elaborate Cambodian wedding displays.

BRITISH COLUMBIA, CANADA

Sun and Shadows

A century later, a daughter visits the
landscapes of her artist father's life

BY JOYCE MAYNARD

Vancouver Island's coastal inspiration

T he sign caught my eye on a road trip a friend and I took some years ago through British Columbia: Forbidden Plateau.

The name was familiar. For as long as I could remember, I'd had a painting by that name hanging in my house. Painted by my father.

More than 20 years had passed since my father's death, 70 since he had painted that particular landscape.

"Let's turn back!" I said to my friend, who was driving. We did, but it was winter, the mountain steep, the trails that I wanted to hike impenetrable. At that moment I vowed to return one day. And I did.

I grew up in the United States, on the other side of the continent from British Columbia. But I always knew that my father—age 51 when I was born—had another life before the one he lived with my mother, my sister, and me.

Max Maynard was born in 1903 in India, the son of British missionaries. They had immigrated to Canada in 1912, when my father, and the province of British Columbia, was still young. My grandfather, Thomas Maynard, established a church following the doctrine of a small fundamentalist sect called the Plymouth Brethren. My grandfather and his group were so strict that my father once was severely punished for buying a paint box; my father's passion for painting remained.

The man I knew taught English at a small state university during the day. However, every evening

"Forbidden Plateau" by the author's father, Max Maynard

The place for a proper tea: the Fairmont Empress Hotel in Victoria, British Columbia

without fail, he climbed the stairs to our attic to work not at a desk but at an easel. The paintings he made there—often laboring late into the night—portrayed two very different landscapes. One I knew well. One not at all.

Most of the time, my father's work in that studio focused on the New Hampshire countryside: the fields and woods near our house, the narrow strip of coastline not far away. But another set of images haunted his nights in the studio: a vast, rugged territory where the trees grew taller and the coast was strewn with driftwood logs. Abandoned churches, desolate beaches, roads that seemed to lead into ever darker forests.

The New Hampshire landscapes held no mystery for me. Almost every Saturday of my growing-up years, times when other children I knew played sports or watched cartoons, my father and I rode our bikes into the countryside on sketching expeditions. At some spot along the way—seldom the most obviously scenic—we would stop and draw. As we worked on our sketches, he'd talk about art, discussing not

just how to represent an image on paper but how to see. Sometimes when we were ambling along, he'd stop and lift his walking stick to the sky. "Look at that cloud formation, chum," he'd say, with a passionate urgency. "See how the light hits that tree? That log? Do you see how the shadow of that barn falls on the field? Let's consider how to draw that cow."

But I'd never laid eyes on British Columbia. I only knew the province from the intriguing paintings that hung on our walls. So the idea came to travel there, my route mapped by my father's sketchbooks and paintings.

For eight full days I would give myself over to the landscape and my own thoughts. My starting point would be the place that held many of my father's works: the British Columbia Provincial Archives, in the capital city of Victoria.

SOME 100 YEARS FROM THE DAY my grandparents arrived in Victoria, the largest city on Vancouver Island, my plane touches down there. Victoria is a center for tourism now, a quaintly British throwback

Vancouver Island's Coast Trail

Inspiration for an artist and, now, his daughter along Vancouver Island's Coast Trail

long, beautiful fingers. The facing page showed a drawing of trees and the notation "made on a sketching trip with Evelyn, March 24, 1932." A few years after this my father left this woman. The drawings and one old photograph provided my only glimpse into that unknown chapter.

MY DESTINATION TODAY is the Coast Trail, which winds six miles along the shore of the Strait of Juan de Fuca, a particularly dramatic stretch of British Columbia's famously scenic coastline some 22 miles west of Victoria. I check out ancient petroglyphs on my way to the rocky headland of Creyke Point, overlooking a wild and stormy expanse of sea. Opening my sketch pad, I imagine how my father's eye would have broken down this rugged shoreline.

"First, just look. Draw nothing. Locate the center. Find where the light comes from and where it falls.

filled with double-decker buses and tea shops. Looming over the harbor sits the century-old Fairmont Empress Hotel, where reservations are taken for tea (brewed in a manner my father claimed few Americans ever master). Too poor to dine at the Empress, my father loved tea there and always wanted to bring me. We never got there.

After checking into my guesthouse, I head straight to the Provincial Archives, where I'd asked to see the Maynard collection. It turns out to consist of a handful of sketchbooks filled with my father's drawings—a few hundred images of British Columbia in the 1930s and '40s. Leafing through the pages with gloved hands, I jot down notes of places to see, all on Vancouver Island. I trace my route on a map that evening over a meal of wild salmon with my third cousins, relatives unknown to me until after my father's death. "Your father was part of a salon of young artists, writers, and poets in Victoria," one says. "In the early 1920s he showed them reproductions of works by a painter he felt they should know about, Pablo Picasso. He confessed his first glimpses of the images so excited him that he'd stayed up all night studying them."

I drive west to the resort coastal town of Sooke. In his late 20s my father married a young woman named Evelyn, who came from these parts. For a time the two lived around here, but I was 17 before I knew Evelyn existed. On my visit to the archives, I saw a drawing of her: an elegant young woman with

Connections

My father, Max Maynard, met famed Canadian artist Emily Carr in his 20s when he lived in Victoria. He was attending an art exhibition and declared that one particular painting was the only worthwhile thing in the show. It was Carr's work, and she was standing there, to hear him.

This began a sometimes stormy friendship, with the iconoclastic, modernist Carr in the role of fierce mentor, my father her protégé.

Later, my father would become a fierce mentor himself—to his students, and to my sister and me. I have never known another individual more passionate about looking at and making art than he was.
—Joyce Maynard

Find where shadows cut across light. Consider the movement of the forms—branches, rocks, clouds—and the way they intersect. See not only their shapes but the shapes created by the spaces around them. Don't be timid with your pencil. Move not only your fingers but your arm. Go right to the edges of your paper. And beyond them."

Next stop is a place called Whiffen Spit, sketched by my dad in the 1930s and '40s. In my father's renderings, Whiffen Spit at low tide is an empty stretch of sand and driftwood looking out on an unbroken horizon. I imagine he would have been surprised to find, as I do, an inn here: the Sooke Harbour House, with rooms in the $300 to $400 range—more money than a handful of his paintings would have sold for.

From here, I head north to the town of Lake Cowichan, an old logging hub where my father often

> **66**
>
> It is one of my father's gifts to me, I think: the lesson that **beauty can be found in unlikely places.**
>
> **99**

went sketching and where my minister grandfather settled near the end of his life in a houseboat he'd brought on shore and turned into a house of worship. Among the most prevalent images in my dad's early works were stumps of trees and fallen logs, strewn like giant pickup sticks on vast expanses of beach.

Lake Cowichan sits inland, only 63 miles north of Sooke, but making the journey as I did, along dirt logging roads, took several hours. Most tourists wouldn't choose this route, but I found the landscape, defined by trees and the cutting of trees, not only visually captivating but oddly moving. It is one of my father's gifts to me, I think: the lesson that beauty can be found in unlikely places. Those were the ones he favored, in fact.

In the town of Lake Cowichan I stop in the Kaatza Station Museum, which includes a re-creation of a local general store from the 1930s. I explain to the

An old painting of Vancouver Island by the author's father sparks a new curiosity.

Little has changed at the Old Stone Butter Church of Max Maynard's paintings.

woman in charge that my grandfather lived in this town long ago.

"I'll look him up," she says. Five minutes later she's back with a handful of documents—a news story dated December 14, 1939, is titled "Lake Cowichan Pastor Dies on Way Home." It appears my grandfather, then age 74, was returning from a visit with his congregation and took a shortcut, where it's believed that "toiling up the embankment had imposed an extra strain on his heart" and caused him to fall.

Among his survivors: five of his seven children, including my namesake, his daughter Joyce, who died not long afterward; and a son, Max, my father, whose address in the 1939 news article is listed as being somewhere in Los Angeles.

Los Angeles? I'd never heard about that chapter either.

Also in the stack of papers is a photo of my grandfather toward the end of his life, dapper in his suit. Though I'd not seen the picture before, the face

is utterly recognizable. It is the face of my father. Also—to a startling degree—the face of my younger son, born two years after his grandfather's death.

I MOVE ON, LOOKING FOR A PARTICULAR SPOT east of Duncan, a place my father returned to in his art: the Old Stone Butter Church, perched by Cowichan Bay on First Nations land. The church was founded in 1870 by missionaries and nicknamed for the butter manufacturing that helped fund it. When my father sketched it, in 1936, it had sat vacant for decades. I pull over at an opening in the brush that leads to the church. No sign points the way. I climb an untended path toward a clearing. Then there it is, in a field overlooking Cowichan Bay.

The church looks surprisingly unchanged from the image in my father's paintings. The stone structure remains solid, though the roof is open to the sky in places, and graffiti covers the walls. From a certain angle I can almost re-create the scene as it

A familiar sight and name at remote Forbidden Plateau

must have looked to my father. I squat down, imagining that young man with his sketchbook, and form the church's outline on my own pad. No more than that. Then I move on.

It's a function of travel that going out into the world can become the catalyst for an interior journey. In my case this journey evolved into a rumination on the passage of time—the poignancy of witnessing change against the backdrop of what endures. The natural world, one hopes, remains among the things that are timeless. Likewise, art endures. Parents pass their stories and beliefs to their children. Children may or may not pay attention to them. Some, like me, do so belatedly.

> **"**
> **It is seldom the happy story,** with the easy and obvious resolution, that I burn to examine.
> **"**

Maybe because it inspired my trip, I have left the Forbidden Plateau for last. I drive northwest from Duncan 110 miles to Mount Washington, a ski area that abuts the plateau. I set out from an abandoned ski lift. No trail here, just a sandy moraine of gravel, rock, and scrub climbing straight up the mountainside, hiking hard into the afternoon, passing no one. The sky looks threatening, and I consider turning back—but remind myself that 70 years ago my father scaled this same mountain, sketch pad in hand. If I don't keep on now, will I ever return?

Forbidden Plateau, when I finally reach it, offers no particularly dazzling scenery. A few trees dot

ONTARIO, CANADA

Secrets and Spirit

Caught between two strong women with a mysterious past

BY TIFFANY THORNTON

My grandmother was the love of my life. She was my confidant and my stability in a rather tumultuous childhood. My mother and I were at odds, not seeing eye to eye on much. My grandparents were my safe haven. I spent years on and off as a young girl and teenager living with my grandparents in Toronto.

My father left when I was a baby and got engaged to another woman while married to my mom. The deception created a deep heartache for my mother, yet she did her best as a single mom to provide for me, making sure we always somehow celebrated nature. Picnics in the park, hikes in the nearby ravine. She really tried to stretch the little money we had.

Gram's mother, the author's great-grandmother, at the Six Nations Reserve

My mom eventually met someone else, a cultured bohemian of sorts who loved to drink a little too much. When my sister came along, the heavy drinking escalated. I came home from school to police in the house and punched holes in the walls several times during those years. I begged Mom to leave so we could be happy, not fully cognizant of how afraid she must have felt to embark on yet another journey as a single mom with two young children. I could only feel my fear.

I always had a small bag packed so I could run away when the next blowout ensued. And I did, over and over again to Gram's house, which was quite the walk for a girl of ten or so.

Growing up, I knew only threads of my grandmother's story: She was a Native American, raised in a one-room shack on an Indian reserve where she went to the well for water. Her mother was a heavy drinker, with a temper she described as "being able to send steam up the chimney." All Gram ever knew about her father was that he was white and thought to be German; his affair with her mother was brief. My great-grandmother then married a Native American and had four more children. She was a woman I knew only from a few faded black-and-white photographs reflecting her tan dark skin and large round features, with a look of determination etched into her face.

The shimmering wheat fields of the sweeping Grand River Reserve in Ontario

Beyond that, my grandmother was aloof when it came to discussing her past. She would delve into it fleetingly, at times sharing brief excerpts of her life as a Mohawk Indian on the Six Nations Reserve near Brantford, Canada. Early on, I was curious about the part of my lineage that I was never really exposed to. I wanted to know more about our family's mysterious, and mystical, past.

ON SOME LEVEL I WAS ALWAYS aware of little things that Gram had around the house that were Indian. Paintings of girls and loons in the water by an Ojibwa artist lined the walls. The shelves displayed a coyote sculpture, a clay teepee, and dream catchers. Braided sweetgrass, considered the sacred hair of Mother Earth, filled each room; it was braided into three strands representing honesty, love, and

> My grandmother was aloof when it came to discussing her past . . . **I wanted to know more.**

kindness. Sometimes Gram would burn the tip and the sweet smell would waft through the house. Indians believe sweetgrass cleanses all negativity and attracts the good spirit.

Gram's sister managed the Native Canadian Centre in Toronto, and Gram worked in the gift shop part-time. On the odd occasion when Gram was terse with us, she always muttered a verse loudly in Mohawk, meaning we were being naughty. At times when the strong veneer would ebb away, I would catch a glimpse of her in her bedroom rocking one of the younger grandchildren on her knee and singing an old Mohawk tune. It was the same song she sang to me.

I grew up my whole life wanting to visit the reserve. Close family still lived there on their own land. My mother and her siblings

Family tradition: a powwow on the Canadian reservation of Gram's childhood home

of contention when discussed. Her face would contort into an angry grimace. "Why do we have to talk about this when there is nothing to say?" she would lament. I was fearful to keep persisting as I knew her temper could flare up when pushed.

Still, sometimes late into the evening when she was relaxing with a cold beer, Gram would soften and tell me little tales about life on the reserve. I relished the memories. She eventually went to live with her grandparents on a farm off the reservation and then finally to the big city of Toronto. The rest of her family stayed behind.

WHEN I WAS IN MY LATE 20S and after much persisting to see the land where my beloved Gram grew up, we finally went to visit. My great aunt and great uncle owned thousands of acres of land on the reserve that had been in his family for centuries.

When we arrived, a powwow was going on. Native dancers were dressed in vibrant costumes and adorned with intricate beading and headdresses covered with cascading feathers. The tribal drums echoed in the distance, and I felt a resonance with the land; I wanted to know my people. I was

spent several summers there as kids, wading in the Grand River. Everyone there except my mother, it seemed, all had dark hair, completely different from my fair-haired mother. Everyone, that is, except for a boy who was blond and described only as a "family friend."

Mom had always wondered about this boy. Whispers of family secrets would filter through the air over the years, with tongue-and-cheek inferences of some sort of deception that were quickly brushed aside. My mother always grappled with the notion that something was awry and sought out the truth, her suspicion at times creating a fury in her spirit that never subsided.

All the mystery surrounding the reserve I had never seen fueled my curiosity about it, and about my heritage. How must it have felt for Gram growing up there as an Elizabeth Taylor look-alike, with her deep blue eyes and soft dark curls that framed her perfectly proportioned features? Gram was the white girl with the Mohawk blood—a bastard, born in the 1930s. It was a sore subject and definite point

Connections

As a child, I remember the braided sweetgrass that filled each room of my grandmother's house in Toronto. Native Americans consider it the sacred hair of Mother Earth. They believe it cleanses all negativity and attracts the good spirit.

Now, I always keep some in my house too. And like Gram, I sometimes burn the tip and let the sweet smoke envelop me. It helps to connect me to the native roots that I am still uncovering.
—Tiffany Thornton

A river runs through it: the First Nations Reservation

introduced to all these new faces so different from my own. Great-aunts and uncles and cousins, wearing turquoise jewelry filled with beautiful stones, embraced me lovingly as Gram introduced me as "her best friend." Stories were exchanged and corn bread was broken. For a brief moment these people were truly a part of me.

Gram showed me what remained of the shack where she grew up. Only the foundation was still standing. Up into the field we walked, trekking through grass that reached above my knees until we finally came to an unmarked stone. It was my great-grandmother's grave site. We stood side by side as the sun beat down. I was finally

> 66
> The tribal drums echoed in the distance, and **I felt a resonance with the land.**
> 99

standing on the land where Gram was born and raised, sharing her history. I remember not wanting the day to end as we drove away with the sun setting behind us.

Before I knew it, things resumed the way they always had. The subject of Gram's past was not something you wanted to stir up. It was fine to wear Indian jewelry, ask about a word in Mohawk, or wear moccasins. But beyond that it could get uncomfortable. My grandmother feigned disinterest when my mother started learning Native drumming on her own. She did the same when my mother began digging around for old photos of her family, wanting to learn more about her family as part of a study she was doing with a Native group in town. My mother had always had an affinity with that side of herself: the Mohawk blood that she would boast about to her friends.

Yet my mom did not have the support or encouragement to foster that part of herself. A palpable tension always lingered between her and Gram, my mother yearning to find her place in the past and connect to it.

I felt split between the two pivotal people in my life, my Gram whom I adored and my mother the truth seeker who always drew me in with her passion. They were yin and yang, and I was smack dab in the middle, left questioning my loyalty.

WHEN MOM WAS DIAGNOSED WITH CANCER in her early 50s, we all knew she was not going

> ## I felt split between the two pivotal people in my life, my Gram whom I adored and my mother the truth seeker.

anywhere. She had too much fight in her. She wanted to map out her destiny and have a chance to work through her anger, much of which came from the fact that she felt she never fit in with her family.

But a second round of cancer proved to be more furious than even her tenacious spirit. Though never taking away her beauty, it began to ravage her body. During this time my mom yearned for her mother to comfort her. But Gram was not one to be overly demonstrative. Mom's illness stirred a painful internal process within Gram, not good for someone who had been diagnosed with heart problems years before.

During this time, my mother befriended a Native cousin of hers. Together they burned white sage, a Native tradition known as "smudging," meant to purify the mind, body, and spirit and purge bad

The calm of Grand River Reserve belies the conflicted memories of the author's grandmother.

The old Royal Chapel of the Mohawks stands
as a Canadian Indian symbol of endurance.

The author, Tiffany Thornton, with her beloved "Gram"

energy. My mother embraced her knowledge of medicinal plants and the healing ways of the Great Spirit, grasping onto her tribal past.

As her body weakened and just a few months before she died, her cousin casually asked her how she felt about having a brother she had never really gotten to know. When Gram was a teenager, she had a son—her first-born—with a city boy, she told my mother. Gram was sent away to give birth, and soon after gave the baby up to her aunt to raise on the reserve. The child, who had non-Native features of fair skin, blond hair,

and blue eyes, was never to know the truth about who his parents were, nor was my mother. This was the mysterious "family friend" of her childhood—her half brother. He died of cancer when he was in his late 50s.

My mother loved my grandfather, who she had been told was her father. But my mom began to wonder: Was her biological father actually that city boy with whom Gram had been enamored long ago? (He drowned in 1954 during Hurricane Hazel.) This, she believed, was the secret and source of all the family deception she had always known.

My mother wanted me to confront Gram with her revelation. She wanted me to confront Gram with what she believed were all the lies and deceptions, almost as if it were some sort of redemption.

I was again caught in the middle, as I loved them both. My family wanted me to be angry, to right the wrongs before it was to late, and to honor my mother's dying wish. Yet even among the anxieties and expectations that had somehow fallen on my shoulders, I found I could not do it. I felt deep empathy for my mother and the brother she never knew. But I also loved my grandmother, who made me warm when the world appeared cold.

Neither I nor anyone else mentioned our discovery to Gram. My mother passed away, and a deep ache settled in my grandmother. Her stoic eyes began to lose the shine that they had once emitted. As I had feared, her heart was heavy with the burden. Five months later she suffered a massive heart attack. In the hospital Gram was calm and collected, even when faced with the certainty that this was the final hour. She chatted away with family and even chuckled a bit.

Finally, she asked to be alone and if I could bring her some sweetgrass. I raced back to her place, gathered up a braid, and wrapped a silver and turquoise necklace around it. She was asleep when I brought it to her. A nurse later told me that Gram had woken up briefly in the wee hours of the morning before her heart finally gave out and had seen the sweetgrass. She said to the nurse, "Do you know what this is? It's sweetgrass. It helps you get to the other side." She clutched it tightly. The white girl with the Mohawk spirit had finally returned home.

I felt a sense of calm in my grief and a strange, almost unidentifiable empowerment. I walked back from the hospital, about a mile and a half, to Gram and Gramp's house as tears stung my eyes. When I arrived, I knew what I needed to find. There in Gram's room on her dresser was her favorite pair of silver, native earrings. I put them on without any trepidation; it was as though I was being guided. I stared at my reflection in the mirror, with the intricate feather earrings dangling. They felt like mine now.

Nova Scotia–based journalist and freelance writer **TIFFANY THORNTON** loves watching the written word evolve. She covers music, travel, and theater for a number of publications. Her website: *spinthemap.com*.

A 1940s Thanksgiving at Tiffany Thornton's great-great-grandmother's Toronto home

GET TO KNOW CANADA'S MOHAWK CULTURE

• **CELEBRATE**
Listen to the throbbing beat of the drums, watch over 400 native dancers in full regalia, and sample Native foods such as corn soup and fry bread at the annual **Grand River "Champion of Champions" Powwow** (*grpowwow.com*) held the fourth weekend in July at Ontario's Six Nations of the Grand River Reserve.

• **TOUR**
The Mohawk Institute in Brantford, Ontario, was the longest running of the church-run, federally funded Indian residential schools designed to assimilate aboriginal children into English-speaking Canadian culture. Attendance was mandatory, and from the 1830s until 1970, Six Nations of the Grand River Territory children lived there. Learn about the school and see Mohawk art at the **Woodland Cultural Centre** (*woodland-centre.on.ca*) housed in the former institute building.

• **READ**
The Mohawk tradition of iron-working began in the mid-1880s, when Native laborers were hired for a St. Lawrence River bridge construction project. Mohawk crews helped build multiple New York City skyscrapers including the World Trade Center twin towers and One World Trade Center, and are among those profiled in *High Steel: The Daring Men Who Built the World's Greatest Skyline* by Jim Rasenberger (Harper, 2004).

A Year of Living Differently

Discovering a new life in the old country

BY JENNIFER WILSON

...d, Jim, and their dog on a quiet meadow walk in Mrkopalj

computer screens, or driving to Target, viewing
those growing kids through rearview mirrors. When
we lost half our savings in the stock market crash,
it really got us thinking about an investment that
might truly last.

The grandmothers called and called.

One night in late summer of 2008, after a particularly good bottle of wine, Jim and I considered
something crazy. Could we just walk away from
the hamster wheel here in Des Moines? To spend
the last of that savings account on a family sab-
batical to Mrkopalj, a year of exploring, learning
new things, just loving each other in the wide,
wide world?

We could. We wanted to be that kind of family.
So we did.

OVER THE NEXT NINE MONTHS, we saved every
penny, sold our stuff, rented out the house, pro-

Magisterial Veliki Prstavci waterfalls emerge like
ribbons from Croatia's Plitvice Lakes.

Every time I look in the mirror, th[e] immigrant lady with the high ch[eek,] dark circles beneath like half pl[ums,] grab a towel and hold it under my chi[n in] a loud granny voice.

Other than those high-style moments, I'm a pretty standard-looking, 44-year-old, middle-aged mom. Sandy hair, pointy chin, a little pear-shaped. I'm the blur rushing past at swim practice; we're a few minutes late because we had Science Club. I've probably carpooled your kid to soccer.

But the brave old immigrant who got me here is always along for the ride—in appearance and in

[...] wanted to bring home [so]mething from Croatia [to] connect my great-[g]randmother's house to [m]ine. But when I finally [fo]und Jelena Iskra's [ad]dress, the lot was empty, [th]e house bulldozed.

Kicking through the rubble, my husband, [Ji]m, found an old kitchen tile, white with blue spirit. Ma[d]isies painted on it.

It wasn[t] "The glass has cracks. There's concrete on started t[o] the back," he said. "This is old. I would bet ing. Whe[n] money that this is original." Who am I [w]hen we walked off of the lot, I noticed

I knew n[o]thing. Atop the rubble of Jelena's family grandpa wi[th] a fountain of wildflowers sprouted that ended [ab]andon.

[I ke]p the tile on my desk to this day.

[—Jennif]er Wilson

In the end, it all circled back to the woman in the mirror.

The author learns about the medicinal flowers of her Croatian ancestors.

[Something] shifts inside of us when we see where we come from, when we unravel the eternal fabric of our extended families; we grow in resilience and understanding. Before we left the States, I only knew I wanted to go further than my mother, who'd pushed us kids away and fell into a whiskey bottle. I wanted connection.

In Mrkopalj, I began to see women who looked like me—the old lady in the mirror showed up everywhere. She became familiar. I passed gangs of kids, running free, scaling low mountains, climbing apple trees, scouring meadows for wild strawberries, looping distant orbits around their mothers— women I recognized. They embodied what I'd always wanted to be with my kids: free, yet together.

But the language barrier yawned like a great abyss between the women and me. Though Jim and I had taken language lessons, I only

The author's Croatian neighbors teach her how to make au... ...ovitica pastry.

those women tutored me. I eventually hired a translator, the town's beloved bartender, Stefanija, and spoke through her instead.

The lessons for Jim were more laid-back. He mostly kicked it all day with the kids. He'd spent the past few years crabby and maudlin from the desk job at the architecture firm where he worked. A pre-bedtime shift with Sam and Zadie was the extent of his parenting.

But in Mrkopalj, while I worked on a book about our journey, Jim's days were filled with cooking, planning road trips, and homeschooling Sam and Zadie. All these years I'd been the stay-at-home, writing through nap times and midnights, and now it was Jim's turn. Though he'd never admit it to me, I think he lost that saccharine ideal that the life of a stay-at-home is all sunshine and daylong jammies,

> "
> **All these yea**
> **I'd been the sta**
> **at-home,** writin
> through nap time
> and midnights, and
> now it was Jim's turn
> "

...gnized it for the real work that it is. Still, a ...sight was Jim, perched on the yard swing reading, the legs of our children dangling from nearby trees.

Of course, the men openly wondered why Jim was living the life of a Croatian woman. What did he do for a living? Why was he not doing it? Jim's position as a stay-at-home dad was the subject of much curiosity.

"So, you do not work, but your woman work?" Robert asked one day.

"While we're here, yeah," Jim said.

"This is a very good situation," the landlord mused, rubbing his ...nd clearly considering a ...a kept man. As he swigged ...ite wine and fizzy water ...all day, I could see his wife ...g in difficulty before my eyes.

mix he generally
Goranka's life inc...
The women in Mrk... worked, often multiple jobs,

Far from Des Moines: The Wilsons relocate and renew.

plus tended the house and the garden; many of their husbands drank with equal vigor.

Booze seemed to take as many men as war did.

OUR TIME IN CROATIA widened our lens on the world. It's easy to understand on a surface level that we're lucky to have had no major conflict on our turf in generations, but to live in a country that's spent the last 1,000 years in one war or another really drove the point home. We *felt* gratitude for our quiet state of Iowa, where many former Yugoslavians actually fled in the 1990s. Even our youngest Mrkopalj neighbors understood the hunger, fear, and loss of war—horrors that made the recession seem like less than a scrape.

Just trying to get a handle on Croatian history was like falling into a dark well. I was flabbergasted to learn that many Croatians sided with the Nazis and fascists in World War II, or the communists of the Soviet Union.

There were quieter lessons. Lessons about leaving a lighter footprint, and needing less. Though our frugality was self-imposed—the more we saved, the longer we stayed—Sam and Zadie learned that getting stuff was not to be expected. To this day, when Jim or I say we cannot do something because we don't have the money, there is no badgering. We've been in the chips, and we've not. We're fine either way; we know what lasts. The stories we tell from our journeys. The memory of the perfect empty beach. Hiking wilderness that feels primordial. Mrkopalj's self-sustaining backyard lifestyle, its people having seen good times and bad, and wanting to be less dependent on both.

Though Sam and Zadie were pretty young in Mrkopalj, when they have their own babies, we hope they'll remember to seek out meadows, and forests, and mountains to wander, when they want to connect with each other, to real things. They experienced in the village the freewheeling kid life that

I had growing up, that Jim had, and that our great-grandparents had. A life virtually lost to American children of this generation.

Sam and Zadie roamed the village with a cackling pack of school kids that soon began taking Zadie to biathlon practice—the ski-and-shoot winter competition with a dedicated training field at the edge of the woods.

"This is something Mrkopalj is known for," the village tourism director told me. "We produce many Olympic athletes. All parents in this village send their children to biathlon training."

Everyone in Mrkopalj could tick off the local Olympians, including Robert's niece, Petra Starčević, who'd competed in the 2006 Winter Olympics, the youngest Olympian in Torino. Our most beloved neighbors Mario and Jasminka sent their son, Jakov Fak, to carry the Croatian national flag in the 2010 Winter Olympics. Jakov won bronze and later dominated several world championships.

The athleticism clicked with Zadie, my slight and asthmatic daughter. Physical activities became her steam valve. When we watched Jakov in the 2014 Sochi Games, we waved the jersey he'd signed for us.

For Sam, it was Croatia's meat-centric culture that left its deepest mark. From our very first visit to a roadside barbecue joint, where a burly guy in a jumpsuit hauled out a pig trussed to a metal pipe, Sam has scorned meat, despite our enthusiastically carnivorous family.

Zadie, four, revels in the freedom of Croatian country life.

In Mrkopalj, I remembered where I came from, as a parent, as a daughter, as an American. I unraveled a nice section of that family fabric, and through it my own family found a kinship with those brave immigrant souls who crossed oceans for a better life.

If I forget, I just look in the mirror. There she is again. She's my great-grandmother, yes. But now she's also just me.

JENNIFER WILSON writes for *Esquire, National Geographic Traveler, Better Homes and Gardens,* and others. Her travelogue, *Running Away to Home,* received Best Nonfiction Book of 2011 from the American Society of Journalists and Authors.

GET TO KNOW CROATIA

• TASTE
For centuries, skilled craftsmen in Northern Croatia have deftly shaped, baked, and decorated *licitar* (gingerbread-like biscuit) hearts. A variety of wooden molds are used, but it is the licitar heart—always red and elaborately decorated with swirling patterns and small flowers made of icing—that is the traditional symbol of Zagreb and a keepsake for travelers to Croatia.

• LEARN
Spend three or four weeks in Dubrovnik learning Croatian. **The Croatian Centre for Mediterranean Studies** (*cms.unizg.hr*) hosts beginner-, intermediate-, and advanced-level language classes mid-July through mid-August. Lessons are four hours each day, leaving plenty of time to practice your pronunciation at the local *tržište* (market), *kafić* (coffeeshop), or one of the many *muzeji* (museums).

• CELEBRATE
Seattle's **CroatiaFest** (*croatia fest.org*) celebrates all things Croatian: *tamburitza* folk music played by fast-moving fingers on the lutelike *tambura;* the smooth vocal harmonies of traditional *klapa* (a cappella) groups; Croatian hymns sung at the festival's opening Mass; and the aromas—and tastes—of hot and fresh *burek* (meat-, cheese-, or spinach-filled pastries), baklava, and *kobasica* (Croatian sausage).

Along Havana's famed Malecón

Indefinite Voluntary Departure

After half a century, a lost childhood is reclaimed.

BY JUAN JOSÉ VALDÉS

O n the morning of August 10, 1961, I was awakened early and informed that I would be flying out of my country: Cuba. I recall that I carried precious possessions in each hand—my most prized toy train in one, a bagful of smaller playthings in the other.

When entering Havana airport's glass-enclosed waiting area, *la pecera* (the fishbowl), uniformed guards checked both my belongings and me. From the other side of the tear-stained walls stood my parents, watching my every move, guiding me with their eyes: *Follow the guards' instructions.* Surrounded only by children, I truly believed my mother and father would be joining me, entering through some magic door.

Time moved fast and we were shortly shepherded onto the tarmac. My parents had moved farther away.

I next saw them waving at their only child from the observation deck. They kept motioning not to look back. No simple thing for a kid who had always been surrounded by a large, doting family to comprehend.

I was seven.

As instructed, I sadly walked alone toward the plane, climbed the stairs, and boarded. The seats filled with unaccompanied children. Some were excited about the trip; others, like me, called out to parents who could neither see nor hear their pleas.

Author Juan José Valdés at age six in front of his Havana home

Music still infuses daily life in Havana.

After the short flight, I once again found myself on another tarmac, this time in Miami. I was led into a terminal where a customs official checked my passport and prominently stamped "INDEFINITE VOLUNTARY DEPARTURE."

One of the last to exit customs, I found myself looking for the family that would be taking care of me. They were nowhere in sight. So I sat alone in a lounge of a very alien place. Not until then did I realize that my toy train—my most prized possession—was no longer in my hands. I searched the lounge and retraced my steps back to customs, whose doors had long been shut.

I stopped several adults to explain my plight. No one understood what I was saying. Scared and disheartened, I made my way back to the lounge and found my temporary family waiting for me.

No doting family, this. I learned how to do things for myself, things that would have been normally done for me, like getting dressed or tying my shoes. School would have to wait until my parents arrived. I filled the days by reading books, watching television,

and occasionally going to a deserted park. Saturdays became the most special day of the week—the day I phoned my parents. A tearful "*¿Cuando vienen?* When are you coming?" would open and end every call.

Only years later would I learn why I was mysteriously spirited away from my home and forced to take those involuntary steps to a new life.

The author's Cuban passport

Traveling Cuba's countryside, the author recalls a last childhood vacation.

I was one of more than 14,000 Cuban children sent to the United States without their parents between 1960 and 1962. The mass exodus would eventually be known as Operacíon Pedro Pan: Operation Peter Pan. Its origins and purpose—possibly to destabilize the Cuban revolution—is to this day contested on both sides of the Straits of Florida. This program, run through the auspices of U.S. religious welfare services, would eventually resettle many of us across the United States.

In my case, I lived with friends of the family in Miami until my parents arrived three months later.

When I reunited with my parents at the airport, all I wanted to express was how happy I was to see them. I told them how much I had learned since I last saw them: I could now dress myself and tie my shoes. My mother shed tears, apologizing for what she had done. She vowed she would never leave me again.

Once reunited, we began our new American life. As with most newly arrived immigrants, those early days proved hard and jobs scarce. "Together, we can overcome anything" became our refrain.

I was tasked with three objectives: to study, get good grades, and, in keeping with the times, assimilate! All things Cuban were only to be found and expressed at home.

By the close of 1963, we had moved to the Washington, D.C., area, where my father restarted his career as a systems analyst and my mother established hers as a clerk.

Assimilating was hardest of all. English is difficult enough to learn, let alone to speak properly. In the 1960s, the Washington area, like most of the United States, had yet to witness an influx of Latinos. In the Washington suburbs, we were a rarity, if not an oddity. Those first few months in school proved to be challenging, not only because I looked so different from my classmates but, more importantly, because I sounded so very different as well.

Years passed. I assimilated (lost my accent), got (somewhat) good grades, obtained a degree in geography, secured my dream job as a cartographer at

National Geographic, married an Irish-German lass, and raised a family.

Busy as my life became, Cuba seemed never far away, especially when I visited my parents, who always lived nearby. On those days when the sky would be at its bluest, my mother would always make it a point to remind me, "It's bluer in Cuba."

IN 1999, NATIONAL GEOGRAPHIC EXPEDITIONS was granted a license to participate in a people-to-people exchange program that allowed Americans to travel to Cuba. So it was that two years later, on the eve of the 40th anniversary of my departure, I was asked to lead a group to tour the island.

I was both excited and apprehensive about the trip, most of all to walk off the plane and return to la pecera.

When we landed in Havana, we entered directly into an ultramodern building—no walk on the tarmac this time. The terminal I had expected to reenter had long ago been converted into a domestic one. Just

> ## 66
> As we exited [Cuban] customs into a sea of waiting people, . . . **I felt a sudden wave of emotion.**
> ## 99

as well. I quickly realized that I was not yet truly prepared to face my past.

As we exited customs into a sea of waiting people, I could no longer hide my feelings. I felt a sudden wave of emotion. Fellow Cubans there stared at me sympathetically. I would later be told that my reaction was common among expatriated Cubans returning home for the first time after many years of separation.

That evening, we registered at the historic Hotel Nacional. At the reception that followed, I walked the grounds with the group. A vaguely familiar path beckoned. It led me to a patio overlooking the Malecón (Havana's broad seaside esplanade). Striking as this view remains, the marble map of Cuba embedded on the patio floor entranced me more. I've been here before. My father later told me this map was one of my favorite stops when my parents brought me with them to dine at the hotel.

The days that followed took us to the Valle de Viñales, Trinidad, Cienfuegos, El Cobre, and Santiago—roughly the same places I had visited on the last

Havana's Hotel Nacional conjures treasured times.

Cuba's Museo Nacional de la Lucha Contra Bandidos
in Trinidad was formerly a church.

vacation with my parents before they sent me off. If time allowed, I made it a point to seek vaguely familiar paths at every stop. The *mogotes*—dome-shaped hills emerging from the flat valley floor—in Viñales proved to loom smaller than I had remembered, while the Caribbean looked just as blue and clear from a tower in Trinidad that I now had little time or stamina to climb. We drove by the Hotel Jagua in Cienfuegos where we had stayed and I remembered playing in its pool. Most importantly, I was finally able to stand on Cuban soil and gaze at the sky. Before departing, I took a minute to look up to heaven and tell my mother, you were so right—the sky is bluer!

It was then that tears began to flow, not so much for what had been forgotten, but for what had been remembered.

Still, I stuck mostly with my group. I only cautiously connected with a handful of Cubans. I did not have the confidence or fortitude to fully experience all that I had encountered.

The people-to-people program was suspended in 2003 and reinstated in 2011. I thought of Cuba often in those eight long years. An azure blue sky, the weaving hips of full-figured women, or the smell of strong coffee would bring memories of home flooding back.

RETURNING IN THE SPRING of 2012, older, if not wiser, I put my fears aside, or so I thought. I talked to every Cuban I could and danced with every Cuban

Connections

Railroad enthusiasts will recognize the numbers 4-6-4 as representing the wheel arrangement of a type of locomotive. A model of this engine— including mine—powered many a 1950s electric toy train set.

On the eve of my eighth birthday, this—my most prized possession—went missing. It took me 52 years to find it. Within those years, I thought, if not dreamed, of my locomotive. To fill the void, I took up collecting model trains. A collection larger than I could have ever imagined, it is prominently led by my 4-6-4. —Juan José Valdés

Once a vibrant center, Trinidad was a vacation stop for the Valdés family.

Havana's seaside Malecón esplanade remains a gathering place.

woman who gave me the chance—*bailar es olvidar penas* (to dance is to forget one's sorrows). And I drove to my childhood home in Havana.

I walked up to the front door of the house, where we had lived on the second floor. Though battered by time and politics, its interior might provide a glimpse of my past.

I summoned the courage to knock and an elderly gentleman appeared. I introduced myself in Spanish and asked permission to take pictures of my long-ago house. He welcomed me inside, but my legs would not allow me to enter. Emotions outweighed my bravado. This crossing would have to wait.

As I was taking photos, the man yelled to his neighbors: "There's a bald man with a gray beard at the door. He says he lived in this house as boy." Within seconds their front door opened, and when they saw me they yelled, "Juan José, where the hell have you been?" as if scolding me for coming home late for lunch. Despite the years, my old neighbors somehow recognized me, and I them.

In that instant, the years, and all they had brought, melted away. I was once again a seven-year-old boy

caught in the act who had to excuse himself for being late. I was almost home.

IN THE SPRING OF 2013, I returned to Cuba. On this, like all other trips, my goal was to introduce the group to as much of Cuba and its people as time allowed. Starting in Havana, we accidently drove by the office building where my had parents worked, just a few blocks from our hotel. In Cienfuegos, I was able to not only take a dip in the pool at the Hotel Jagua, as I had done 52 years earlier, but also spend several nights there.

Toward the end of the tour, I met up with David Montgomery, an American reporter who was doing a story on me. As we explored the city, we ran across a friend who had taken me to visit my old house a year earlier. He agreed to take us back.

Like the three musketeers, we set off in search of my unfulfilled past. This time, I took the elderly gentleman's offer and entered his house. As if time had stood still, I saw my grandmother's sewing machine and my aunt's beloved framed portraits of Spanish maidens hanging on the dining room wall. The once manicured backyard was but a ghost of its former self.

My next steps were to climb the stairs to my long-ago home. My legs did not fail me this time. There, I found additional pieces of my former life. Save for slightly different furniture, all remained as I had remembered: the living and dining rooms, the bathroom (immaculate and unchanged since my departure), and most of all, the patio where I had so often played with my toy trains.

As before, I was overwhelmed with memories. But as much and as long as I wanted to stay, I also had to accept that it was no longer my house or my home.

I made a pact with the owner: The next time I returned, I'd bring cake and candles so we can celebrate all those birthdays I missed in my long-ago home.

Later that afternoon, I reunited with my cousins Mayda and Miguel, whom I had reconnected with on the Internet but had not seen in 52 years. If the word "reminisce" could come to life, it would have been born in that one visit. We talked about childhood pranks, heard long-remembered music on the phonograph, and most importantly, I got to dance with Mayda—bailar es olvidar penas.

Later that day, Miguel presented me with my long-lost train, the one of my nightmares and of my dreams. He told me of its tale. It turned out my beloved toy had not been lost. My father had taken the train from me before entering la pecera. He charged his brother with taking care of it, telling him that someday I would return. Before his death, my uncle instructed my cousin to keep that promise. A promise fulfilled on the eve of my 60th birthday.

No words were needed to express how the two of us felt. My cousin had honored and fulfilled his father's wishes, and in my hands I finally held one of the dearest missing pieces of my life.

My friends saw me off at the airport the next day. This time, photographs attest to my "indefinite voluntary departure." Among them, one of a middle-aged man with a toy train in his hands. If you look at the picture in just the right way, you'll also see the beaming face of seven-year-old boy standing by his side.

JUAN JOSÉ VALDÉS is National Geographic Maps' geographer and the director of editorial and research.

This time, the author departs Cuba with his beloved train.

GET TO KNOW CUBA

• CELEBRATE
Calle Ocho, the main artery and cultural hub of Miami's Little Havana neighborhood, pulses to a passionate fusion of jazz, son montuno, bolero, trova, timba, hip-hop, and Afro-Cuban rhythms each March at the city's biggest block party: **Carnaval Miami on Calle Ocho** (carnaval miami.com).

• DRINK
With a can of Miami-roasted **Café Pilon** (cafepilon.com/en) or

Café Bustelo (cafebustelo .com/en) coffee, anyone can brew high-octane **cafécito** (Cuban-style espresso) at home. For café Cubano (Cuban coffee) connoisseurs, however, nothing compares to sipping the molasses-thick espresso from thimble-size cups at a Little Havana ventanita (walk-up coffee window).

• TOUR
Scheduled to open in early 2015, the new 15,000-square-foot home of Miami's nonprofit

Cuban Museum will showcase the work of nearly 250 Cuban diasporic artists, host Cuban films and live performances, and include historical exhibits related to the émigré community experience, such as **Operacíon Pedro Pan** (pedro pan.org), code name for the 1960–1962 Catholic Welfare project, when more than 14,000 unaccompanied Cuban children were sent to Miami, as well as the Freedom Flights and the Mariel boatlift.

The Mandolin's Story

The strains of a small instrument carry a son to his father's war-ravaged past in Prague.

BY JOSEPH HURKA

Prague's storied Charles Bridge: the ancient place of modern memories

When I was a boy, there was a mandolin in my home in Boxford, Massachusetts, that my father often played for me. I liked the instrument's bright, cheerful sound, and my father's happiness when he strummed old Bohemian tunes. Sometimes he put the green mandolin rope around my shoulders and showed me how to

work my fingers on the fret board. I remember his patience, and the way he would sing with me as I picked up a song.

The mandolin had, in the early part of the 20th century, been in my grandparents' home in Radnice (pronounced Rad-NEE-say), Czechoslovakia, a small village just southwest of Prague. There, it witnessed my family's history—my father and aunt growing up in the only democracy central Europe had ever known, and then the Nazi occupation, the Second World War, and the subsequent dark shadow of communism falling. The little mandolin stood vigil through many difficult years.

IN 1993, AT THE AGE OF 32, I flew in an SAS Fokker 50, a small propeller plane, on my first trip to the Czech nation. I thought of the mandolin, and of the stories my father had told me: Josef Hurka was 13 when the Nazis invaded his country, and shortly after the start of the war, he was put to work in a Nazi coal mine—part of what the Nazis called the *Totaleinsatz*, the total war effort. There he began to work with the Czech resistance, taping sticks of dynamite from the mine to his legs, beneath his trousers, and smuggling them past the guards at the end of the day.

After the war and after Czech Stalinists staged a coup in 1948, my father, by then an air force

Grand Prague Castle evokes a storied past.

Happier times in Prague subsume dark memories.

lieutenant, was arrested and charged with espionage for the West. He was innocent and, despite brutal interrogations in a series of communist prisons, he stuck to his story of the truth. Eventually, after eight months, he was released. He immediately went to work for a *Czech skupina,* an underground group funded by U.S. Intelligence, which ferried important democratic statesmen and their families to safety in Germany.

My father was shot in a communist ambush in 1950, escaped, and made his way to West Germany, where he worked with U.S. Intelligence until the late 1950s. In 1958, aged 33, he came to America; he took a job in the private sector as an engineer; he married, and with my mother, raised two sons.

My father was shot in a communist ambush in 1950, escaped, and made his way to West Germany.

While the communist regime remained in power, there was little chance of me seeing the land of my father. The Velvet Revolution of 1989 changed all that, and I was flying now to stay with my aunt Mira, my father's sister, in Prague. It was like stepping into the twilight zone—I had never imagined that the Iron Curtain would finally fall, and that I would get to explore this part of my history. My father, approaching 70 and struggling with heart complications, told me he was glad that I would see the Czech Republic—but that he had no great desire to return himself. I had the sense that his reluctance had more to do with his dark memories than his health.

Below us were the rolling hills of Bohemia, and we were surely descending. A stewardess announced over the intercom that we would soon arrive at Prague's Ruzyne (now Václav Havel) Airport.

HERE, WAITING BEYOND CUSTOMS, was Mira, 71, smiling at me, with snow-white hair and colorfully framed glasses. During communist years, when she worked as a draftswoman at the Tesla electronics company in Prague, Mira had been allowed to come visit us in America on 11 occasions—always with the understanding that if she did not return, her boss and his family would suffer the consequences. This was how the communist system kept citizens imprisoned even when traveling; the jobs, the lives of others you knew or loved were held in collateral. It was a joy, now, to see my aunt without the restrictions imposed by the former regime.

We dropped my suitcase off at Mira's flat, at 139 Vinohradská, and went together into a cool Prague spring evening. First by subway, then walking, we made our way to Charles Bridge; built in the 14th century, it is one of the most distinctive symbols of the city. The famous old lamps of Prague lit the bridge, and a river of tourists was streaming through. Groups of young people played guitars and tambourines and sang. The cobblestones beneath me were a burnished black, and I sensed the presence of ghosts in these stones: Generations of my family had walked here. There was a vibrant hum to the city around me, a feeling of something greater than a simple recognition of sights I'd seen on Mira's postcards. Prague had survived all these years, and here it was—bold and ancient and newly free, welcoming me along with the familial ghosts.

Long tourist barges, lit like diamonds, made their way down the Vltava River. The 30 ancient statues that line the sides of the bridge—of Christ on his cross and saints and Good King Wenceslas—looked down at us, some of them silhouettes against the city lights. Above, as if hovering in the sky, Prague Castle—the largest functioning castle in the world—was lit sharply against the violet night.

Over the next weeks, with Mira patiently telling me the history of family and friends, we made excursions all over the city. Prague was a city of contrasts—between dark and light, between the joy and dignity of a nation reborn in freedom, and memories of 51 years of totalitarianism. Because I'd grown up hearing the stories of Nazi and

The author, Joseph Hurka, tours Prague's Pankrác Prison, where his father was imprisoned during World War II.

Free and easy in Prague's Old Town Square

communist oppression, I had a real sense that many of these memories were personal.

I felt this especially strongly on one gray, flat day, as Mira and I walked beside a soiled concrete wall of Pankrác Prison, once a Gestapo facility, then for 40 years the primary political prison of the communists. In years of Czech-Stalinist rule, thousands—protestors, artists, resistance fighters, priests, intellectuals—saw the inside of these walls. Many were executed by hanging, and many were sent to hard labor camps, a slow death sentence. Here, the current President Havel, the dissident playwright, had been imprisoned, and had nearly died of pneumonia until international pressure demanded that he be released; here, in cell 64, my father had also been

I sensed the presence of ghosts ... **Generations of my family had walked here.**

held, in 1949. On the door of my father's cell a prisoner of the Nazis had once scratched, with a nail, *Believe in the future of your nation, and believe that your suffering is not in vain—1944*. Sometime later a prisoner of the communists had written, *But it sure as hell was in vain—1949*.

My father had told me that and other stories of Pankrác, but now, walking along this eastern wall, the despair the prisoners lived with—the battle to keep spirits alive—hit me. I imagined them in the exercise yard, watching coffins in hearses being driven out of the prison after hangings; I imagined how they must have braced themselves before interrogations. I could see the red Pankrác clock tower. During my father's time here the clock bell was silenced on the

One of Prague's indelible sights, the 14th-century Týn Church

Prague's medieval astronomical clock

nights before executions, to terrify the condemned in their last hours of life. My father was one of those facing the death penalty. Now, with the clock facing me, I understood the steadiness of nerves he needed in this concrete place—how every moment, for him and for others incarcerated here, must have been a struggle against terror and hopelessness.

My aunt and I looked at each other—both of us making an effort to hold back emotion.

ONE DAY, MIRA PAIRED ME UP with Jana Pazlarová, a childhood friend of hers, now a tour guide at the famous Old Town Hall. The Gothic structure is an icon of Prague, with its astronomical clock dating to the time of Columbus. Inside, Jana took me up the winding staircase to the Town Hall tower, 230 feet above the city, and we went onto the balcony, where she pointed out the sights. The day was sunlit and very windy, making us feel we were at the helm of a great ship. There was Prague Castle and threading up to it Nerudova Street, where a grand-uncle of mine once lived. Closer, by the Vltava, was the National Theatre with its shimmering blue, curved roof, where my grandmother, an actress, had performed long ago. Near the theater, I knew, ran Národní Avenue; there, on November 17, 1989, tens of thousands of citizens, including Mira and a young cousin of mine, Maruška Kublová, marched for freedom,

only to be stopped and set upon by communist thugs with truncheons—the beginning of the Velvet Revolution.

The dramatic, twin towers of Týn Church were directly across the Old Town Square, darkened with the ages. Below us, young people gathered on and around the statue of the 15th-century religious reformer Jan Hus, with his words carved in stone, to "defend the truth unto death." I looked out at this city of spires, thinking of how my father and Mira and other members of my family had stood up for truth in their time. I felt pride at this, and something growing in me that had started at Charles Bridge—a powerful sense of belonging: I had a part to play in this story, perhaps with my writing. Jana seemed to read my mood. She spread her arms before her, as if to offer the metropolis to me, and said, "Joe, *Prague*."

TWO WEEKS INTO MY NEARLY MONTHLONG VISIT, Mira and I took a train to the countryside,

Connections

I frequently look at this photograph of my father, Josef, and his sister, Mira, taken just before the Nazi invasion of Czechoslovakia. Mira is probably 16, Josef 13. Ahead of them lay many years of  oppression and separation, under Nazi and Communist rule.

In 1950 my father escaped and went to work for U.S. Intelligence in West Germany. Mira stayed in Prague. It would be 20 years before they saw each other again, in America. Mira died in 2002, my father in 2005. But they lived to witness the Velvet Revolution of 1989 that liberated their homeland. Their photo reminds me of how precious freedom is.
—Joseph Hurka

The author's search leads through the Bohemian countryside.

to my grandparents' village of Radnice. We walked through the streets with Hana Blechová, an old family friend who still lived in town. I could hear birds and the soft sound of the Radnice church bell on the hour; soon, we came up to my grandparents' former home at 145 Švehlova Street. "So," Mira said, "here it is."

The mortar of the old narrow structure, one in a row of tight, brownstone-like buildings, was gray and worn. Mira told me it had once been a clean lime green. Some empty, dented garbage cans sat in front now, and the cobblestones of the sidewalk and street were broken. Years of communism, Mira said, had taken their toll on the neighborhood.

We spoke of Christmases here, behind one of those upper windows—how my grandparents kept the room locked until Christmas Eve, so that the children could be astounded, all at once, when they came upstairs to see the sparkling tree and gifts. I remembered photographs of Mira and my father at that age, caught up in the magic.

Then Mira and Hana grew more serious as we talked about the war, and June 1942.

The Nazi leader in Prague, SS Gen. Reinhard Heydrich, a favorite of Hitler and the principal architect of the "Final Solution," had been assassinated by the Czech resistance late that May. The Nazis were barbaric in their fury, conducting a sweep of the entire country for the assassins. There were mass arrests, random murders, and family executions.

Nazi soldiers came to Radnice. A small group of them pounded on this door before me. Mira described it now.

"We were very lucky the troops were not SS," Mira said, referring to the elite Nazi guard. "These were Wehrmacht—regular army, and they

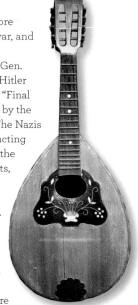

The Hurka mandolin

Another Uncertain Voyage

Retracing the steps of a lost family

BY JIM EAGLES

T
he Joiners Arms in the little village of Bloxham is a charming English pub, more than 500 years old, and normally I'd like nothing better than to order a pint of real ale, sit back, relax, and soak up the atmosphere.

But this morning I'm nervous and twitchy. Bloxham is the town my great-grandparents left in 1873 to make a new life for their young family in far-off New Zealand. I've just flown 11,386 miles to explore my roots, and I'm not sure what I'm going to find.

The waitress brings my wife, Chris, and me a couple of coffees—unfortunately it's too early for an ale—but I still cannot settle. I wander off into the pub's deserted restaurant. I've discovered from my research that it was once a separate cottage where my great-great-grandfather George lived out his declining years with his son, daughter-in-law, and grandchildren.

It seems quite roomy and I know there's an attic above so, by the standards of the time, the family would have been quite comfortable. But it's hard to sense their presence amid the lines of tables with their crisp white tablecloths, folded napkins, and neatly laid cutlery.

I wander back and sip my coffee while keeping a wary eye on new arrivals. We're due to meet up with a couple of long-lost relations, Nick Eagles and his partner, Tina, who are driving down from Leicester to meet us and the last remaining Eagles family member still living in Bloxham, Alison Eagles, and her husband, Martin Smith, who are taking time out from organizing a daughter's wedding.

What will they be like? It would be terrible if we didn't hit it off. A dour elderly couple stomp in and grumpily order coffees. Please don't let them be relations. They're not.

I should have had more confidence in our breeding. Nick and Tina, who arrive a few minutes later, are delightful. Alison and Martin, who turn up shortly afterward, are equally charming. We get on as though we've known each other all our lives.

Nick, the family historian, has information to share. We sip coffee, talk, and laugh, have lunch, talk, and laugh some more, just like old friends. Alison has arranged for the little Bloxham Village Museum to be opened especially for us and also leads a family tour of the village. It's marvelous—far more than I'd dreamed of when I started this quest back home in New Zealand only a few months earlier.

FOR SOME REASON I'D NEVER TAKEN MUCH INTEREST in the Eagles. I did a lot of research into one of my great-great-grandfathers, William Oliver, who was among the earliest settlers in New Zealand,

The Blo

The autumnal Oxfordshire of author Jim Eagles's great-great-grandfather George

got shipwrecked, built the first house in Devonport where I live, and was involved in a grisly murder.

But of the Eagles family I knew next to nothing. Perhaps that's because my father never spoke about his parents, and we rarely had anything to do with the wider family. I had never met my grandfather Jim, for whom I was named. My older cousin, Peter Eagles, who did meet him, got the impression that he was estranged from his family, who lived in the capital, Wellington. For some reason they didn't approve of my grandfather's marriage and move to Auckland. "They reckoned it was the worst thing he ever did to marry Elsie," Peter told me.

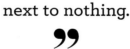

> ❝
> Of the Eagles family **I knew next to nothing.**
> ❞

My interest in the Eagles only really arose when I looked in a dictionary of surnames and found it came from the d'Aquila family, lords of L'Aigle in Normandy, who invaded England with William the Conqueror in 1066. There was also mention of the name being given to people with big noses— and my father had a famously big conk. I preferred the idea of being descended from a noble warrior.

Unfortunately, by the time this interest developed, my father was no longer around for me to question. Fortunately, the digital age makes tracing family history relatively easy.

For a start, I got a copy of old Jim's death certificate, which revealed that he was born in "Bloxham,

Jim Eagles's great-grandparents and their children set out from England for New Zealand in 1873.

At least, I thought, things went well for that part of the family thereafter, because I knew they were a prosperous lot—certainly more prosperous than poor old grandfather Jim's branch of the Eagle clan: On his death certificate he is described as a laborer. My father, his brother, and sister had a tough childhood.

But then, to my surprise, I heard from one of the Wellington Eagles, Neil, who told me I had it all wrong. Things had initially only gone from bad to worse for the Eagles. Soon after their arrival in New Zealand, he said, "they moved to Christchurch, where Francis leased a farm property near the Avon River. He farmed there for several years before all his property was devastated by two successive floods." In March 1887 Francis lost the farm, uprooted the family, and moved to Wellington, where he started working in a tannery.

This time, Neil said, they did prosper.

"He arrived there after 13 years in New Zealand with nothing. By 1895 he owned a two-story house on

Oxford, England" and had lived in New Zealand for 70 years. Goodness. I'd assumed he was born in New Zealand. It also showed that his parents were Francis and Sarah Eagles, so I got a copy of Francis' death certificate. This showed he, too, was born in Bloxham, son of George and Lucy Eagles.

Through Archives New Zealand I discovered that great-grandfather Francis, listed as a farmworker from Oxfordshire, arrived in Wellington with his family on the immigrant ship *Ocean Mail* on February 2, 1874. The ship's register showed he and Sarah brought four of their children, including grandfather Jim, and that the New Zealand Government paid their £50, 15s passage.

When I visited the national archives in Wellington, I was allowed to study their file on the *Ocean Mail*. It included a handwritten report on the voyage from the onboard surgeon that revealed the ship was supposed to leave London November 6, 1873, but was unseaworthy. When it did set sail two days later, he wrote, "she was by no means ready for sea."

The subsequent voyage was a troubled one, including an outbreak of scarlet fever that killed five of the 130 children on board, including grandfather Jim's brother, young Samuel Eagles. When the ship finally reached Wellington, the migrants were quarantined on board and had all their clothing and belongings disinfected before being allowed to disembark. I felt a prickling of tears in my eyes as I read these immaculately scripted words and thought of the anguish they represented.

Connections

This photo of my grandfather Jim is one of only two I have of my Eagle ancestors. Though I was named after him, I never met him. About all I know is that he became very fat and died after falling down the steps of Black Jack's Billiard Saloon in Devonport, New Zealand, shortly before I was born.

This photo shows Jim at his wedding to my grandmother Elsie Oliver. Unfortunately, the marriage "was the ruination of him," says my cousin Peter Eagles. It seems it was not a happy marriage and the cause of an estrangement between Jim and the rest of the Eagles family. —Jim Eagles

Ngaio Gorge Road and had entered into business as a coal merchant."

I was pleased to hear it, and not just because they were my great-grandparents. It must have taken a lot of courage for Francis and Sarah to leave all they knew and take their young children on a dangerous voyage to an unknown land on the other side of the world. They deserved success.

STILL, I NEEDED TO FIND OUT MORE ABOUT THEM. What was it that drove this young couple—and so many like them—to risk everything to make a new life?

Online English records allowed me to trace my grandfather Jim's birth, the marriage of his parents, the birth of my great-grandfather Francis, and from that the death, marriage, and birth of his father,

> ## Records allowed me to trace ... **eight generations of Eagles, all in Bloxham or the surrounding area.**

George, and so on back through eight generations of Eagles, all in Bloxham or the surrounding area, and all farmworkers.

Unfortunately, as far as I know, there are no letters or diaries from Francis or Sarah telling of their lives. But there is plenty of information about the lot of agricultural laborers in 19th-century England. It paints a uniformly depressing picture of a class of workers whose position plummeted from relatively comfortable at the birth of the century to disastrous by its end. Forces from mechanization to a surplus of labor caused by soldiers returning from the Napoleonic Wars conspired against farmers like my ancestors. This led to rioting in some rural areas and the passing of Poor Laws providing a vestige of relief to starving families.

Normandy's Bayeux Cathedral, onetime home of the famed tapestry

The author unravels a possible family mystery in the Bayeux Tapestry.

The agricultural crisis also sparked mass migration, to the cities to work in the new industries, and to the colonies.

That explained why Francis and Sarah embarked on their great adventure, but I was still intrigued to find out more about the life they left and, especially, the village of Bloxham, where the family had been centered for all those centuries. I wanted to see it for myself.

Chris and I had been planning a trip to England, so we decided to include a visit to Bloxham. During my research I had found a posting by Nick Eagles on one of the genealogical websites and discovered his great-great-great-grandfather George (the man who lived in the pub cottage) was my great-great-grandfather. Nick offered to come down to Bloxham to see us. He also put me in touch with Alison, and she, too, was eager to meet. As far as I could tell, I would be the first New Zealand Eagle to return to Bloxham and connect with the family since Francis left there in 1873.

> ❝
> ## As far as I could tell, I would be the first New Zealand Eagle to return to Bloxham ... since Francis left there in 1873.
> ❞

AS WE GOT CLOSER TO THE VILLAGE, I began to feel a little apprehensive. It seemed ridiculous, but I so wanted it to be somewhere nice. I needn't have worried. The surrounding countryside was picture-perfect with verdant fields, hemmed in by old stone walls, and dotted with picturesque farmhouses.

Then came the sign saying, "Welcome to Bloxham." Towering overhead was the elegant 14th-century spire of St. Mary's Anglican Church. On the left was a row of neat medieval cottages; on the right was the Joiners Arms, and I could see a section that had obviously once been a separate cottage. It was charming. I was very happy to have Bloxham as the place my ancestors came from.

Alison gave us a tour of places connected with the family that strengthened my connection to this lovely place. With the aid of a map, we found several weathered gravestones marking where my ancestors lie. She showed us around the church with its Norman arch, medieval wall paintings, stained-glass windows, and a 15th-century font where I imagined generations of Eagles having been christened.

We wandered the narrow streets, including what was once the aptly named Back Lane, where census records show several Eagles living from time to time. Today it rejoices in the name of King Street, and its old workers' cottages are sought-after homes, many complete with thatched roofs and windows glazed with thick antique glass. Alison pointed out a particularly attractive cottage her father had recalled visiting to get vegetables from his grandfather George.

The village museum, in the restored medieval courthouse, was fascinating to explore, with its displays of village life, many covering the period when Francis lived there. We even found a photo showing the Bloxham Methodist Church Band, with an Eagles as its leader and three others as members.

This place really did feel like home.

Of course, all too soon it had to end. Alison and Martin had to plan their daughter's wedding. Nick and Tina had to drive back to Leicester. And I had work commitments elsewhere.

Happily, we still had time for a relaxing pint. As we sat and chatted, enjoying easy companionship, I asked Nick if any of his family had big noses. Why, he wondered, was I asking such a peculiar question? I explained about the possible origins of the name "Eagles": We could be descended either from people with big noses or from Norman warlords.

"Ah," he said, with surprising enthusiasm, "I can tell you about that."

It turned out that a few years before, while researching the Eagles family online, he had been contacted by an Eagles in the United States keen to trace his family and who offered a free DNA test. "The DNA report showed that our ancestors came from Normandy about 1,000 years ago," he said. "Before that they were Vikings from somewhere in Finland."

Aha. Normandy. So we could indeed be descended from the lords of L'Aigle. It was good enough for me.

Not long afterward I happened to be in Normandy and took the opportunity to see the famed Bayeux Tapestry with its portrayal of the Norman Conquest. There, toward the end of the 230-foot wall hanging, I found a panel depicting one Engenulf de Aquila, also known as Engenulf de L'Aigle, my possible ancestor. Magnificent in his armor and sitting astride a black horse, he was shown just a bit late in bringing his sword down on an axe-wielding Saxon.

It turns out that Engenulf was the only Norman lord to lose his life in the invasion (though, fortunately for his descendants, a son survived him). I stared at the image in the tapestry. Goodness. What a big nose. We definitely must be related.

In 50 years as a journalist, mostly in New Zealand, **JIM EAGLES** has edited a range of publications from daily newspapers to, most recently, a weekly travel magazine.

GET TO KNOW RURAL ENGLAND

•LAUGH

Oh-so-Brit hilarity ensues every year, along with lots of live music, at **Bloxfest,** Bloxham's free street party *(bloxfest.org .uk)*. In addition to utterly British pirate panto (pantomime) featuring plenty of slapstick comedy, visitors will also find the event is big on parades, blacksmithing, live music, dance demonstrations, as well as face painting and other activities for the kids.

•TOUR

If the red horse-drawn fire wagon (sans horses) is parked outside, then you know that **Bloxham Village Museum** *(bloxhammuseum .com)* will be open to visitors that afternoon. Housed in a medieval stone courthouse, the small museum's collection of more than 5,000 artifacts—including antique tools, furniture, clothing, and photographs—records the history of the village and surrounding Oxfordshire.

•CELEBRATE

Enjoy a taste of country life as your ancestors knew it at the annual spring Village Fete in Reading, about an hour north of Bloxham. The family-friendly fest includes traditional Morris and stave dancing, cooking demonstrations, including lots of homemade biscuits, among other country treats. While you're there, check out the **Museum of English Rural Life** *(reading.ac.uk/merl)*.

The Never Ending Story

Uncovering an unknown past with little more than a few clicks and a trip

BY JOE YOGERST

A land left behind: pastoral Fulda, Germany

It started on a rainy afternoon in northern Germany. I was in Hamburg researching a story on the city's musical heritage—Bach to the Beatles—and had some time to kill between interviews. I asked the concierge where I could while away a few hours and he suggested the new BallinStadt Emigration Museum, only a few S-Bahn stops from the hotel.

Until that day I had really never thought much about my German ancestors. I knew my father's side of the family was 100 percent German, kinfolk who had migrated to America sometime during the 19th century. But that was about it. At that point, I didn't even know my grandmother's maiden name or where my forerunners lived in Germany. This genealogical apathy was passed down from my father, who had very little curiosity about his past, almost no contact with family members elsewhere in the United States, and little in the way of mementoes or documents that might have explained who the Yogersts were and where they came from.

All of that changed that afternoon in Hamburg.

Built on the exact spot where the emigration halls stood 100 years ago on Veddel Island, a place where five million hopeful souls left the Old World behind,

the museum delves into the lives of these migrants. It wasn't until I reached the final exhibit—a room full of family research computers—that my own backstory began to unfold. In little more than an hour of browsing the museum's online documents, I learned more about my German ancestors than during the rest of my life combined. Even though the spelling of my surname had changed over the centuries—from Jockerst to Joggerst to Jogerst to Yogerst—I was able to trace my family back eight generations, to the middle of the 18th century in the Ortenau region of southern Germany and a tiny village called Önsbach that lies between the Rhine River and the Black Forest.

The crucial date I came across was 1861. That's when my great-grandfather Leopold left sleepy Önsbach behind, boarded a steamer, and made his way to New York and the start of our American odyssey. But Ballin Stadt also yielded a mystery. I couldn't find a single thing about my grandmother Julia's lineage, not even her maiden name. I knew she was also German, but without more clues to her background my search for her story reached a dead end.

INSPIRED BY MY DISCOVERIES in Hamburg, I couldn't wait to find out more. Digging through the attic back home, I located a

Documents from Fulda bearing names of the ancestors of the author, Joe Yogerst

The author unravels his family history in the small streets surrounding Fulda's Dom.

box with items my father had left behind when he died in the 1990s, including a postcard showing the hilltop Frauenberg Monastery in Fulda, Germany. There was no way to know for sure, but perhaps Fulda was the key to my grandmother's side of the family.

In an effort to find living relatives, I scoured German online phone books for people with my last name (and its half dozen spelling variations) in the region between the Rhine and the Black Forest. Surprisingly I found none in Önsbach—my family had completely abandoned our *heimatdorf,* or home village. But there were half a dozen in nearby towns. Using online translation tools, I composed emails explaining my quest and sent them off cold to the names on my list.

Like most everyone else who catches the ancestry bug, I registered on several online genealogy websites and began a long and tedious search for more clues to my past. Browsing old U.S. Census forms,

I learned that my hunch about Fulda was spot-on: My grandmother was born in 1873 in "Fulda, Prussia," and her maiden name was Dorschel. I also found my grandparents' marriage certificate from 1892, listing Julia's parents as Bonifaz Dorschel and Anna Maria Binder—a very important detail in my effort to trace her.

Baerbel Johnson, a research consultant at Family-Search in Salt Lake City, helped me take the next step. With more than 20 years of genealogical detective work under her belt, Baerbel immediately began to think outside the box. Perhaps the immigration officer at Ellis Island had spelled my grandmother's name wrong? Sure enough, she came across a "Julia Durschel" from Fulda on the passenger list of a ship called the *Werra,* which docked in New York City on May 3, 1887. That would have made her 14 years old. No other family members were listed, but below her entry were the names of two teenage boys from the same town.

They had apparently made the transatlantic journey together.

While that discovery certainly solved one uncertainty, it conjured a completely different mystery: Why had my grandmother left her entire family behind in Germany at such a young age and traveled thousands of miles to a new land? With the online paper trail petering out, the only way to answer that question was traveling back to Germany.

"ARE YOU A STONEMASON?" was the first thing that Elmar Jogerst asked me. It seemed an odd opening for someone meeting a long-lost cousin for the first time. But then Elmar explained his curiosity. As far as he could trace back, nearly all of the males in his family had worked with stone, makers of buildings and public monuments, tombstones, and sculptures. And he wanted to know if the craft has also passed down through the ancestors who had gone to America.

Earlier in the day I'd dropped in at Elmar's workshop, strewn with all sorts of stonework and sculptures. Having just missed him, we decided to meet at a hotel bar in Offenburg, the closest big city (ten miles) to Önsbach. His palms cut and calloused, it was obvious that Elmar worked with his hands. And he was disappointed to learn that my only manual talent was mastering a computer keyboard. But the more we talked, the more we discovered we had in common.

Connections

The only toy my father kept from his childhood in Buffalo, New York, was a small felt-covered, wooden horse mounted on a small wooden platform with wheels. The tail is real horsehair, the mane made from rabbit fur. And there is a *Y* carved in the base, probably by a small pocketknife. My dad kept it on a shelf in his bedroom closet, and after his death I stowed it in my own attic. I had always assumed it was made in the United States around the turn of the 20th century. But further investigation revealed that felt horses were common in Germany at the time, a nicely crafted piece of folk art that was also functional. It's held up well for more than 100 years.
—Joe Yogerst

One of only two people who answered my emails, Elmar had immediately recognized our shared lineage. Our great-grandfathers (Leopold and Eduard) were brothers and apparently both had been stonemasons. Another brother from that generation had sired an entire line of carpenters. Another was an architect who designed train stations in Switzerland, so there were cousins there, too. And yet another brother, quite separate from my great-grandfather, had emigrated to America and fought for the North in the Civil War. It was that generation, born in the 1830s and '40s, that had scattered to the wind, seeking opportunity and sculpting new lives in other lands. Only Elmar's direct line had stayed in the Upper Rhine-Black Forest region.

Trying to discern why my kinfolk and so many other Germans had migrated around that time, I consulted Kurt Hochstuhl at the State Archive in Freiburg, where many of the documents on my

Fasnacht, the carnival before Lent

The author discovers his great-grandfather left the small town of Önsbach—and his homeland—for New York in 1861.

Önsbach ancestors are stored. "Mostly emigration had economic reasons," he told me. The advent of the industrial revolution severely altered traditional ways of life in the German countryside and made it increasingly difficult for German craftsmen and farmers to survive. Compounding the situation was a political system that hampered reform, and a society that discouraged equal opportunity and made upward mobility almost impossible.

The agricultural crises led to crop failures and famine. The consequences were especially strong in the Black Forest region, where many people decided that their only hope for economic and social advancement—and sometimes basic survival—was leaving the homeland, packing bags and heading off to distant lands. "The main direction to flee the

Önsbach unfolded as a hardworking farming burg surrounded by apple and cherry orchards.

unsatisfying situation was America," Hochstuhl continued. The irony is that the very thing that had precipitated the crises—the industrial revolution—also made it much easier (and cheaper) to reach the other side of the Atlantic. Newfangled steamships could make the passage faster and under much safer conditions than sailing vessels.

Suddenly it made perfect sense. My great-grandfather and his siblings had fled their homeland during an era of acute economic and political turmoil. In fact, it now seemed like remaining in rural Germany was the exception rather than the rule. Elmar's family was the outlier, not mine.

Önsbach unfolded as a hardworking farming burg surrounded by apple and cherry orchards, the streets muddy from tractor tires and the air suffused

Southern Germany's remote Önsbach, a village of Yogerst stonemasons through the centuries

with the aroma of fresh manure. From the town square I could see the snow-covered Black Forest on the eastern outskirts of the village; nine miles due west was the River Rhine. It was Fasnacht, the week before Lent, and the place was decorated with multicolored flags and banners, effigies of witches and other mythological creatures, and youngsters in costume getting ready for a carnival parade in a nearby town.

Even though my family had long ago abandoned Önsbach, they were not completely forgotten. A Jogerst had sculpted the sandstone Franco-Prussian War memorial on the main road. At least five of my ancestors were mentioned in *Familienbuch der Gemeinde Önsbach,* the town family register, in the tiny village museum. And I have to admit that I got goose bumps sitting in St. Josef's Church, knowing that scores of my ancestors were baptized, married, and eulogized within its whitewashed walls, and

that the patron saint of Önsbach was probably the origin of my own first name.

THREE HOURS NORTH VIA THE AUTOBAHN, on the other side of Frankfurt, was the other half of my German-American equation: Fulda. Lacking heavy industry, it was spared destruction during the Second World War, and the city center looks much as it would have in my grandmother's day, dominated by a hulking 18th-century baroque cathedral and the remains of Fulda abbey, once the largest Roman Catholic basilica north of the Alps. Hovering above the old town is Kloster Frauenberg, the monastery, with its distinctive red-tiled roof, virtually unchanged from the postcard I'd found in the attic back home.

I had been corresponding with Christina Reiche, chief researcher at Fulda's diocesan archives, for several months. And she had already hinted at what lay in store during my visit. A onetime Egyptologist who turned her detective skills to genealogical study, Dr. Reiche had uncovered an incredible cache of material on Julia Dorschel and kin.

"The Dorschels were a family of musicians here in Fulda," Dr. Reiche related, showing me articles and book passages on the town's 18th- and 19th-century musical heritage. "Both her father and grandfather were musicians, as were many of her uncles and cousins. Some of them were well-known composers. And as was the custom in those days, many of them traveled to other parts of Europe to perform. It is a very interesting family." And one that had remained a complete mystery to me until this time.

Juliana (to use her proper German name) was one of the seven children born to Bonifaz and Maria Anna Dorschel between 1864 and 1881. According to the parish records, three of her siblings died in infancy or childhood

from measles, pneumonia, and a heart defect. But that wasn't the only sign of hardship. Unlike the more prominent musicians in the family, Bonifaz Dorschel had never owned a home in Fulda; archive documents show that for his entire adult life he and the family migrated between rented accommodations in the warren of streets around the cathedral. As time went on, his musical career waned; in later documents he also listed himself as a "railway worker." In other words, by the 1880s, prospects were rather lean for the Dorschel clan. "Perhaps that's why your grandmother left home," Dr. Reiche suggested.

Or maybe not. Even in those days, under those conditions, I still wasn't clear why a 14-year-old girl would be allowed to voyage across the Atlantic without a single family member. To never come back, never see her mother and father, sister and brothers again. And there was still a mysterious five-year gap between Juliana's journey

> On the other side of Frankfurt . . . was **the other half of my German-American equation: Fulda.**

Fulda's City Palace, along with the rest of the town, was spared destruction during World War II.

Fulda's hulking baroque 18th-century cathedral remains a centerpiece of the town.

to America in 1887 and her marriage to my grandfather in 1892. There seemed to be no record whatsoever of where she lived or with whom she stayed during those missing years. "Do you know the book of Michael Ende, *Die Unendliche Geschichte*?" Dr. Reiche asked. "That's what this might be. A never ending story." A mystery that never gets solved.

I had one last stop in Fulda—No. 3 Angel Street. The house where my grandmother was born is a three-story structure built in the early 19th century on a street behind the cathedral, fronted by a small garden with a picket fence. I sat on a wooden bench out front, thinking about my grandmother and her mysterious journey. She spent her first 14 years living within a literal stone's throw of where I was sitting. Then, without an explanation that has passed into modern times, she had just upped and left.

Had she run away from home, fled without her parent's permission? Had she fallen in love with one of the boys she was traveling with? A dozen other scenarios came to mind, as I sat there, none of them provable with anything I had come across during my family search.

But like the masons

Joe Yogerst in front of the house in Fulda where his grandmother was born

Juliana Dorschel's prayer book

of Önsbach, my grandmother left her legacy, if not in stone, then certainly in the DNA that she passed to me and my children. A creative legacy that continues to flow in my oldest daughter's musical talent (she's an award-winning songwriter) and, I suppose, in my own affinity with the written word. In that way, family lives on forever.

JOE YOGERST has worked as a writer, editor, and photographer on four continents including in South Africa, London, Hong Kong, and California. His articles on travel, business, culture, and sports have appeared in National Geographic travel books, the *Washington Post,* and the *Los Angeles Times.*

GET TO KNOW GERMANY

° CELEBRATE

The best time to visit Germany in search of your past is **Fasnacht,** the colorful carnival season that falls just before Lent. Frankfurt's carnival parade is one of the best: hundreds of marching bands, military groups decked out in Napoleonic-era uniforms, meticulously decorated floats, and giant papiermâché figures designed to poke fun at Germany celebrities and politicians.

° COOK

Sauerbraten and wiener schnitzel are tourist favorites but, perhaps, no dish evokes the warmth and comfort of a German family home like *käsespätzle,* the Bavarian version of mac 'n' cheese. Prepare this simple German classic (and 84 others) the way *oma* (grandma) used to make it by following the traditional recipes in **Grandma's German Cookbook** (DK Adult, 2012).

° TOUR

The permanent collections in Germany's largest museum of cultural history, **Germanisches Nationalmuseum** (German National Museum, *gnm.de*) in Nuremberg, document Germanic culture throughout the world from the Middle Ages to the 20th century. Passageways connect the complex's multiple buildings, which would take a week or more to thoroughly explore.

An Indian Summer

From revolution to revelation

BY PICO IYER

The crowning symbol of a vast nation:
India's Taj Mahal

I was 17, with hair down to my shoulders, and I fancied myself a product of the youth revolution that was exploding across the streets of California, where my parents lived in Santa Barbara. To anyone looking at me in 1974, I was also, very clearly, a product of the English boarding school 5,400 miles away, where I studied, in a classroom built in 1441, wearing full tails to class every morning and singing the Lord's Prayer in Latin on Sundays.

The one place I seemed to have no connection with was my parents' India, where they had been born and raised until they came to study in England and made a new life for themselves there and then in California.

I'd been to India just once—when I was two years old—and my mother assures me now that I learned to walk there. She also tells me that every morning of our five-month stay, I'd waddled out onto the balcony, overlooking the sweeping corniche of Marine Drive in Bombay, as the city was called then, and the Arabian Sea and exclaimed, "Mummy, it's sunny!" I'd barely seen the sun in the town of my birth and childhood, Oxford, and was greeting the subcontinental skies as many a man of Empire might, in his pith helmet, blinking in the blinding sunlight. I couldn't speak a word of any Indian language, I'd not often eaten Indian food, I hadn't even, consciously, heard Indian spoken (since my parents' only common language was English; as good products of Christian schools in British India, they seemed to

A beach on Mumbai's Marine Drive, where the author, Pico Iyer, visits his grandparents as a young child

The sights and sounds of India's busiest city, Mumbai, largely escaped the two-year-old author on his first trip to India.

know more about Shakespeare and Tennyson than about the ancestry that was officially theirs).

India was mostly interesting to me then insofar as it was said to be the spiritual home of sex and drugs and rock-and-roll (or at least the Kama Sutra, naked holy men smoking strange-looking cigarettes, and the guy who taught the Beatles how to meditate)—a fantasy, in other words, for those of us incarcerated in British boarding schools.

Yet the fact that I felt so slight a connection with India was precisely the reason my parents felt I should go back there and see it with them, for my last summer before graduating from high school and being set loose on the world. And I, being 17, didn't have much say in the matter. So I gathered my precious worn cassette tape of *Songs of Leonard Cohen;* stuffed my suitcase with

> 66
> The fact that I felt so slight a connection with India was precisely **the reason my parents felt I should go back.**
> 99

books by Jung (to prepare for a talk on the collective unconscious when I got back to school); and, most important, gathered my prize possession, my new acoustic guitar, to prove to anyone watching (no one was) that I was my own man. My parents might think they were introducing me to my—and their—past, but I would secretly hijack the project by turning into a dark-skinned Leonard Cohen, irresistible to poets and beauties alike, on the back roads of Tamil Nadu!

I MET UP WITH MY FATHER IN BOMBAY, and I can still remember him greeting me in the clamor of the airport one hot June day; 22 inches of monsoonal rain had fallen in the previous 24 hours. One day earlier I'd been in my tiny cubicle in New Buildings in Eton, Berkshire, sharing a roof with a Gutenberg Bible

The icon of India, the Taj Mahal

and the ghosts of 11 viceroys, numerous red-faced governors-general of India, and the names, scratched into walls, of 18 prime ministers. Now my old man was pointing to a tall, friendly gentleman, leaning down to shake my hand, and proclaiming, "This nut is my youngest brother!"

In all my 70 seasons on earth, I'd barely met an uncle before, though my summer in India would disclose six of them, and a whole cluster of "cousin-uncles," father's cousins (who count in India as honorary uncles), and young, bright-eyed actual cousins. My uncle's house in Bombay was a quiet sanctuary of food made delectably mild for my Anglicized tastes, tea (and a newspaper) kindly brought to my room every morning at six, and highly civilized evenings among relatives who seemed to have imbibed the whole of Victorian poetry along with the Bible (none of my English schools had ever deigned to teach us those, of course).

Our family was scattered all across the country, so my father—it seems impossible to me now—took me on a series of long train journeys (26, 36, 42 hours) to Secunderabad, and Bangalore, and Madras, and Agra. I winced as a guide led my parents and me, after my

mother joined us, around the erotic temples of Khajuraho, explaining that the sculpted carnal gymnastics we were witnessing were mostly to be found in "Madagascar and the polar regions." I set foot in my ancestral region of Tamil Nadu for exactly 24 hours

Connections

Hacking my way unmelodiously through Neil Young's "Heart of Gold"—my parents had given me a guitar when I was 16— I could hardly manage even an A or a C chord. On my magical summer in India, a few months later, I met a long-haired vagabond—the country was full of them then— who was thrilled to see the guitar case by my side. "Just never stop moving, man," he counseled. "Always stay in motion." He was talking about the fret board, but at some deeper level I listened to his advice long after I'd given up the guitar. —Pico Iyer

The young and embarrassed: Pico Iyer tours
India's erotic Khajuraho temples with his parents.

The Buddhist Ellora Caves, another stop on the author's visit to India as a teenager

("Iyer," as any Indian will tell you, is a quintessentially Tamil Nadu name), and so far that's been the only day of my life I've spent in the land of the Iyers. I walked around the Buddhist caves at Ajanta and Ellora with a kind uncle and aunt, and decided that exercising my power over fond and admiring younger cousins was much more fun than sightseeing.

I did the things, in short, that many a visitor longs to do in India, but I was the rare visitor determined to see as little as possible—or to like it if I did. I might have been inspired by the man softly strumming a guitar in front of the Taj by moonlight, but I was certainly not going to confess that to a soul. In Bombay I tried to show how unaffected I was by my surroundings by following the last days of President Nixon in the newspaper every morning, before wandering across a large, open space to a dusty, imperial library in Elphinstone College with birds in the rafters to read through a one-volume *Collected Shakespeare*.

In Bangalore, then a quiet, green city of slow-moving bicycles and parks, I even got to know a cousin quite close in age—the closest I'd gotten to a sister!—and succeeded in walking around the romantic gardens and palaces of Mysore with her, writing songs about doves and loves that Leonard Cohen would have renounced within seconds.

It was a trip full of wonders—human, if not cultural—if only I'd been in a mood to admit it. I spent three weeks in a home in New Delhi, where more family embraced me. My aunt—famous for her renditions of "Spanish Eyes" and "Guantanamera"—told me not to feel discomfited by anything or obliged to honor any Indian custom; she knew I was a bit of a stranger and didn't expect me to know all the rules. I got my first taste of Bollywood movies—never dreaming they'd soon become the stuff of Hollywood fantasy—and heard about warfare from an uncle who was a lieutenant colonel in the Indian Army. Three of my grandparents were still alive then, and suddenly I got 15 years' worth of affection and presents showered upon me, along with tales of long-ago journeys to Nikko, Japan, and Cambridge, Massachusetts.

One morning an overnight train trip—the enduring landscape of India flashing past, glasses of tea passed to us through windows of our compartment, to accompany Indian tiffin boxes full of curries packed for us by an aunt, and no shortage of inquisitive Indians eager to talk about life and eternity and whether we knew Mr. Singh in Fresno—deposited my father and me in a tiny town called Pathankot at dawn. From there, we took a four-hour, lurching drive around switch-backs, through heavy August fog, to a modest cottage, where we were welcomed into the living room of the Dalai Lama, whom my philosopher father had come to know as soon as the Tibetan leader came into India, 14 years before. I sat on a couch and enjoyed the first of 40 years of talks with the openhearted Buddhist as he offered rigorous, lucid explanations of emptiness and compassion while mist gathered above the Kangra Valley through his picture windows.

> **66**
> ## We were welcomed into the living room of the Dalai Lama, whom my philosopher father had come to know.
> **99**

WHEN I RETURNED TO SCHOOL, for my final three-month term, I barely talked about India, though I'd taken pains, after earlier summers, to go on and on about my wild adventures in Berkeley, Big Sur, and the other hippie meccas of California. I think I was embarrassed to have spent my vacation in a country associated mostly with shady gurus and pictures of the blue Krishna (and on an extended family vacation, besides). I gave the talk on Jung I'd prepared in my uncle's quiet bungalow in Panchshila Park in New Delhi, I whispered importantly about the songs I'd composed on my guitar, and I wrote long essays about how Watergate might relate to the poems of Philip Larkin. India had left no mark on me, I thought.

Nor, in truth, would it seem to have done so for decades. My parentally inspired trip was effaced, nine months later, by a three-month jaunt across South America by bus with a friend from school,

A special friend: Pico Iyer meets the Dalai Lama with his father.

Pilgrims and tourists crowd a market in New Delhi.

and soon I was on my way to Morocco and Cuba and Burma. The minute I was free from the clutches of parents and teachers, I made it my mission to travel as far as possible from anywhere connected with England or India. I needed to make myself, my destiny, far from the realm of any relative, I thought, blessed as I was with a teenager's shortsightedness.

But at some point, after I hit 50, perhaps, I began to realize how much that formative trip had taken root in me. It was, for one thing, the first time since I was a toddler that I'd set foot in Asia, which ultimately became my home and my preoccupation for decades, after I moved to Japan. It was my first exposure to a wild, chaotic, often underdeveloped place that could not have seemed farther from the comfortable England and America I knew, and lived by laws very different from theirs. I thought back to wild faces in the dark outside the airport terminals at 2 a.m., fires along the road as we drove into town, the millions I'd seen sleeping and eating and dying on the streets.

And yet, amazingly, it didn't seem feverish or wild at all when I was 17. Once I started going back to India alone, I'd find myself at the mercy of crazy taxi drivers, uncertain hoteliers, men who wanted to show me their uncles' jewelry stores, and others who alighted on my clearly untrained ways (I couldn't speak a word of Hindi!). When I took my Japanese wife on honeymoon to India—partly to meet the same relatives I'd met at 17—I schooled her in not listening to the petitions of the street, not being seduced by the beggars banging on our taxi windows, not being tricked into anything by the country's 1.1 billion sweet-talking strangers.

Only then did I realize how blissfully peaceful and calm and easy India had been when I was sheltered by lovely homes and aunts (and even small cousins) to protect me. Every meal was delicious—I never had to worry about germs—and if you'd asked me what India was like after I returned from my teenage trip, I'd have said, "Pretty much like

England. Safe and a bit antiseptic. Friendly and warm, but really a little boring."

Only when I was more than old enough to have 17-year-olds myself did I see what a gift my parents had shared with me by opening the door to my homeland, and introducing me to much more than my family and an ancient, rich land, and the spiritual and temporal leader of the Tibetans.

NOW I OFTEN THINK BACK to that mind-expanding trip, and realize that it helped to shape me, to make me feel at home in the world, to show me that India might not be exotic—but something close to home, albeit a home I hadn't recognized: everything that I, as an all-knowing teenager, could never allow myself to see. The very fact I wasn't a native meant that I stepped into a wildly exotic Arabian Nights tale out of a Salman Rushdie novel every time I visited my grandmother's apartment. Someone was talking about a curse placed on an eloping couple by a black magician, and a pair of charming ne'er-do-wells was chattering on about a racehorse that was, they assured everyone, their future.

Almost 40 years later, vacationing on Maui, my wife glimpsed a teenager and his father strolling past us on the beach.

"It makes me think of you," she said. "When you were growing up."

"Hardly!" I shot back. "I never took vacations with my father!"

Older and more appreciative, Pico Iyer, at left, on another Mumbai family visit

But then I recalled that, in truth, I had: my Indian summer at the age of 17. The trip had gained meaning and depth as the years had gone on. And when my father abruptly died, in his mid-60s, it came to mean even more, as the one big adventure I'd shared with him. My trip to a home I couldn't quite call home had given me uncles and grandmothers and cousins and aunts. But it had also, quite unexpectedly, given me parents and a sense of how much their homes, on both sides of the world, would always be mine.

PICO IYER is the author of many books of travel, including *Video Night in Kathmandu, The Lady and the Monk,* and *The Global Soul.* A Distinguished Presidential Fellow at Chapman University, he has been based in rural Japan for the past 27 years.

GET TO KNOW INDIA

• CELEBRATE
Hindus across India joyously celebrate the end of winter with the often wet and typically wild **Holi,** or **Festival of Colors.** Neon-bright red, pink, green, and orange *gulal* (dry powder) is thrown about, transforming celebrants into a human kaleidoscope. In March, look for a Holi festival in your area, and dress prepared to play. To find a festival near you, check out *festival ofcolorsusa.com.*

• DRINK
Although regional influences produce a culinary potpourri across India, the ubiquitous *chai* (tea)—preferably served hot and ceremoniously—is universally beloved. Sip a steaming cup of spicy masala chai while learning about the history and traditions of India's tea culture in ***Chai: The Experience of Indian Tea*** by Rekha Sarin and Rajan Kapoor (Niyogi Books, 2014).

• TOUR
Make the colonial-style **Chhatrapati Shivaji Maharaj Vastu Sangrahalaya Museum** (*csmvs .in*), set in a lush botanical garden, your first stop on a walking tour of the bohemian Kala Ghoda Art Precinct, Mumbai's cultural hub. Preserved in the museum and throughout the neighborhood are art, artifacts, and architectural designs reflecting India's various empires and colonial influences.

Japan's ancient Koyasan
Buddhist temple

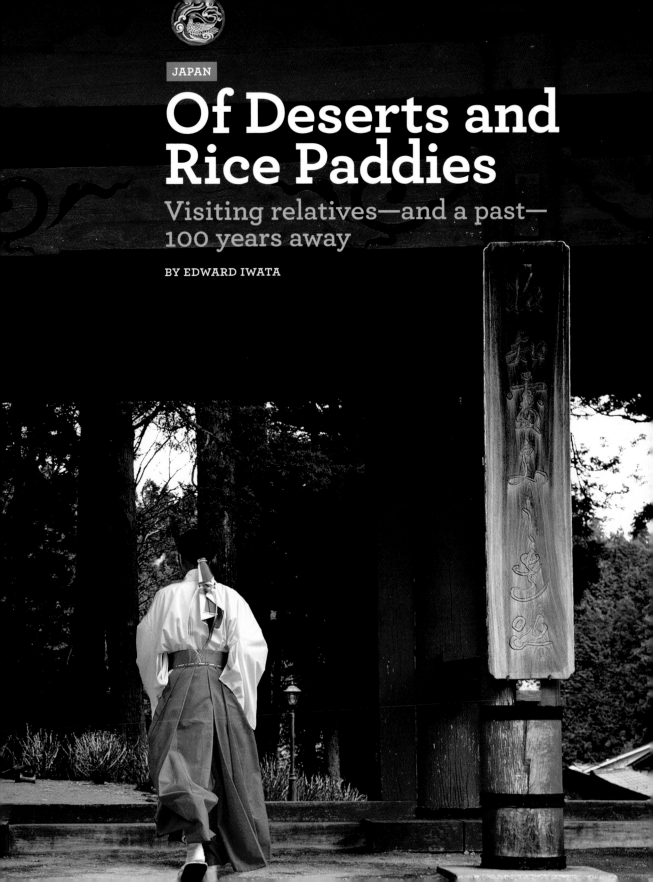

Of Deserts and Rice Paddies

Visiting relatives—and a past— 100 years away

BY EDWARD IWATA

O ur train clanks past suburbs, deeper into the green countryside. At each stop, the crowd of Japanese businessmen thins, while housewives and school-children clamber aboard. Rice fields and eel ponds glisten in the morning sun.

It is spring 1989 in Wakayama, Japan. For the first time, my parents and I are meeting blood relatives whose families have lived on their rice farms for two to three centuries. Remarkably, they have preserved the tradition of handing down the family homestead, or *honke*, from generation to generation.

My mother and father smile. "Look at all these bud-dhaheads!" my Dad says, using Hawaiian slang for Japanese Americans. "Never saw so many in my life!"

Farmers stoop in the fields, planting spring crops. A sweet tropical scent fills the air. Pine, cedar, and bamboo trees drape the hills. We rumble past a century-old train station at Koyaguchi ("entrance of Koya Mountain"), and then stop at another old station, where we get off.

"Over there!" my mother says. A small group of people wave at us from across the railroad tracks. They smile and stand close together, as if posing for a picture. We walk timidly toward them.

AS A YOUNG JOURNALIST, my quest for a family legacy quickens as my grandmothers near death.

Author Edward Iwata's relatives are among those who have farmed Japan's neon rice fields for generations.

The author encounters a country of shrines and temples—this one in Koyasan.

My parents and 18 relatives—nearly all U.S. citizens—spent World War II behind barbed wire in Manzanar, the U.S. military internment camp in a remote desert patch of northern California. While uncles served in the U.S. Army, my folks stayed at Manzanar for three years. When I was a kid, my mother told cheery tales about the war era to shield me from the past. In truth, the internment was a civil rights disaster that shattered lives and dreams.

Then a political movement ends nearly 50 years of silence. In 1988, Japanese-American lawmakers and community advocates persuade Congress to pass legislation directing the U.S. government to apologize and pay $1.6 billion to camp survivors ($20,000 to each, including my late parents) for their financial losses. For many, redress leads to a searching of the soul.

MY 1989 JOURNEY BACK TO JAPAN takes my parents and me on this spring pilgrimage to Manzanar, joining thousands who gather each year in remembrance. As I walk amid the camp ruins, the ghosts are powerful. But I find no easy answers.

I delve more deeply into my ancestral culture. In my embrace of the past, I begin a search for new meaning.

At the train station in Wakayama, everyone bows. A short, gray-haired man grins and offers his calloused hand to me. He is Masao Iwata, head of the Iwata family, my grandfather's nephew and a well-known local rice farmer.

"Hello, Masao," he says, greeting me by my Japanese name, which means "righteous boy." We laugh at our shared names.

Our relatives drive us into the hills to Masao's large home and Japanese-style guesthouse with curved gabled roofs. This is the Iwata honke—the main household where our family began. A century ago, my paternal grandfather, Yasujiro Iwata, and his ancestors were born here.

Iwata means "mountainous rice field." Today, the 200-acre farm is muddy from rain. Tired from travel, we go inside and soak for a long time in a hot Japanese bath.

Masao and his gracious wife, Akiko-san, serve us a country-style meal. We gobble down sukiyaki (meat

The hills of Okayama, Japan, contain a burial plot of the author's family.

and vegetables in broth), *gobo* (burdock root), and *o-kayu* (rice cooked in tea). The rice is the lightest I've ever tasted.

My father stares at Masao. With their dark skin, bushy eyebrows, and jaunty grins, the two easily could be brothers.

After dinner, we talk about the family history. Portraits of ancestors hang over our heads. Masao's brother, Mitsuo, a pilot in the Japanese Imperial Army, died during World War II. Ironically, one of my uncles, Jack Kunitomi, was based in postwar Japan as a U.S. Army translator.

GRANDFATHER IWATA WAS A WELL-EDUCATED young man, studying English daily with Buddhist monks. Tall and gaunt, he trudged through the rice fields from dawn to dusk.

When poverty hit Japan in the late 19th century, the Iwata family raised silkworms and sold raw silk to make a living. In 1899, Grandfather Iwata took a steamship to Seattle, vowing to return after striking it rich.

He soon moved to Los Angeles and mastered the dry soil there. Businesses hired him to start orange orchards, and he leased land for his own fruit-and-vegetable farm.

After Japan attacked Pearl Harbor in 1941, the U.S. military evacuation of Japanese Americans forced Grandfather Iwata and his family to abandon their small farm. He never returned to Japan.

Before we leave Wakayama, our relatives take us to honor our ancestors at the family gravestone at a local cemetery, behind an old Buddhist temple.

Guarding the entrance are little statues in red aprons that symbolize the gods of dead children. We pour water over the large gray headstone to purify it, then clap twice and pray.

"Your grandpa is resting here," I tell my father. Eyes moistening, he touches the gravestone and nods.

That week, we also visit the family of my grandmother Tatsue Iwata. In the warm home of the Noguchi family, we sit at a low table, sipping green tea and eating sushi and dried squid from stone platters. All of us are eager to speak, but we're too polite to talk first.

Finally, Takashi, an in-law, lifts his beer. "To your coming from the United States," he says. "For health and good fortune—*kanpai!*"

One relative was a 19th-century lumber merchant. Another was a newspaperman. And an in-law was married to a geisha. Grandma Iwata was an 18-year-old "picture bride" who traveled by ship to Seattle to wed my grandfather in 1909.

While Grandfather worked the farm, Grandma raised three children, wrote haiku and tanka poetry and worshipped at a Methodist church. Grandma

Connections

Buddhist beliefs practiced by Komika Kunitomi, my late maternal grandmother, have been a cultural lodestar for me in seeking my family history in America and Japan.

During spring pilgrimages to the historic site of the Manzanar internment camp in California's Mojave Desert, Grandma placed bowls of water in the cemetery. As the wind and dust lashed her face, she set the water in front of a soaring, white stone obelisk etched with black Japanese characters that read "soul consoling tower."

"The spirits are hot and thirsty in the desert," she would say. —Edward Iwata

wrote often to her relatives. One of her poems, "Shiro Shobi" ("White Roses"), reflected the emotional pain of her mother in Wakayama:

Sadly, Mother clung to me:
As my only daughter,
I cannot offer you to an alien land.

Grandma Iwata feared that her children in America would lose their Japanese values. I tell my relatives that a missionary introduced Grandma to Christianity in Los Angeles. One day, the missionary, quoting Exodus ("Thou shalt have no other gods . . ."), grabbed Grandma's small Buddhist altar from her bedroom and burned it in a field.

"Did grandma write why she no longer believed in Buddhism?" I ask.

Michiko, a close relative of grandma, shakes her head no. We fall silent.

Our afternoon ends in a flurry of photographs and exchange of gifts. I give Michiko a book of poetry that Grandma Iwata wrote 50 years ago.

She bows and thanks us, cradling the book as if it were a baby.

A TRAIN RIDE AWAY IN OKAYAMA, we pray for my mother's ancestors at an old countryside shrine. The names of Kunitomi family members are engraved on the temple's cracked walls. At a nearby cemetery, the ashes, hair, and fingernails of Grandma Kunitomi and others have been blessed and placed in the family plot.

One of our relatives, Kiyoshi, a retired high school principal, spent a decade tracing the family lineage in government archives and temple records.

"Our family tree is not forged like many other genealogies," says Kiyoshi, as we relax at the rice farm of Kinichi Kunitomi, the head of the family.

Kiyoshi believes that several ancestors fought for Lord Ikeda, who ruled feudal Okayama in the 18th century. Two were low-ranking officers: One helped command soldiers armed with guns, another led a horse brigade.

For their loyalty, the Kunitomis were rewarded with large rice payments and plots of land. They also

Okayama is a quiet hub of temples and rice farmers.

Edward Iwata's widowed grandmother raised nine children in Los Angeles's Little Tokyo.

received a surname, a rare honor. "Kunitomi" means "land of wealth."

"You and your parents are Japanese inside," Kiyoshi says. "It takes time for Japanese who leave Japan to become real Americans. Maybe more than 100 years."

Does Kiyoshi really believe I am Japanese in my heart and spirit? Throughout our journey, the strong-minded American inside me fought to crack through the Japanese shell of conformity I learned from my parents.

Later one night in Okayama, we visit the rice farm of my mother's cousin Kusuyuki. A short, impish man, Kusuyuki loves to drink sake and tell tales. He shows us pictures of Grandma's pilgrimages to Mount Koya, a sacred mountain to Buddhists. He brings out the family crest, framed and gold-plated.

The . . . American inside me fought to **crack through the Japanese shell of conformity I learned from my parents.**

Kusuyuki worries about the fate of his land. He's getting old and the younger generation shows little interest in farming.

"Your parents' era is ending," he tells me. "You must come back to Japan to maintain the tradition."

Grandma Kunitomi sought to preserve traditional values after she settled in Little Tokyo, a thriving enclave in downtown Los Angeles for Japanese immigrants seeking better lives in America.

Before World War II, she raised nine children and ran a general-goods store after Grandfather Kunitomi died in a truck accident. She taught her kids hard work, respect for one's elders, and pride in the family name. Her daughters, my mother, and Aunt Sueko, wore kimonos and performed Japanese folk dances at street festivals. (Forty years later, Aunt Sue, an educator, would lead the charge to get Manzanar recognized as a historical site.)

Our relatives serve us tea, then bring out old letters written by Grandma and my aunt Choko. I ask our translator to read them. Grandma wrote of her hardships in California, and she grew nostalgic about her childhood on the rice farm, catching fish, and crayfish in the creek behind the family house.

"The mountains in America are bare, not green," Grandma wrote. "I miss Okayama very much."

One letter came from Choko shortly after Grandma died of illness in 1983 at a nursing home in Boyle Heights near East Los Angeles.

"I'm clearing Baachan's things and keeping busy," she wrote. "But when things are quiet, I get very sad."

My mother listens, her lips trembling.

"Your aunt says the Kunitomi family was once very prosperous," the translator says. "And now, years later, it is all fading away."

IN THE DARKENED AIRLINER, my mother and father sleep like children to the drone of the jet engine. I drape blankets over them to fend off the chill for the long flight home.

Gifts from relatives fill the overhead bin. Silk fans. Rice crackers. Good-luck amulets. A large *furoshiki*, a green cotton cloth bearing the Iwata family crest, called "four diamonds within a circle."

Throughout our trip, my mother's face glowed as she spoke Japanese, feeling the grace and power of a language that drew stares of hatred in her youth. My father, bored by retirement, strode like a young man and joined conversations with a new vigor.

I also feel proud, more complete. My family history has not been silenced by the injustice of the internment camps. Our tales stretch back centuries. In small ways, I'm still kin to the Japanese.

My hands cup a faded wedding photograph of my ancestors, clad in kimonos and *hakama* (male skirts). Their gazes cross generations to reach an American descendant in the new Heisei Era, Year One.

The jet shudders. I rub my eyes and breathe deeply, but I cannot fight off the feeling of sadness and loss.

The backbreaking work of centuries: a rice field worker in Wakayama, Japan

A temple in Wakayama, where the author's family still owns a rice farm

REVISITING THE FAMILY HISTORY always unleashes a wave of memories from my relatives back home. My sister Nancy recalls the elderly Kusuyuki, our closest Japanese relative, dancing madly at her wedding to the delight of everyone.

"He was always so happy to see us," says Nancy, who flew to the rice farm to see Kusuyuki before he died a few years ago.

On the Iwata side, Masao and Akiko have passed away. Their daughter, Tomoko, now 60, has kept the rice farm in Wakayama to honor her father and tradition. When she was younger, her parents showed her how to farm and how to act in public as the future head of the honke.

"I am proud of my father," Tomoko writes. "He lived by his words, 'to be a helpful man to others.' "

Much of the Kunitomi rice land was sold years ago to developers, who built offices and apartments over the rich soil. Kusuyuki's college-educated granddaughter, Urara, who grew up working the fields, is sad that much of the old rice-farming culture in Okayama has waned. Urara, who lives in Tokyo with her husband and baby daughter, writes that some young Japanese today are interested in agriculture.

"As the child of a farming family," she writes, "I can tell them that farming is not a job to be taken lightly!"

In a last twist to the family tale, I'm surprised to learn from an American cousin that Grandma Kunitomi owned much of the land for the Kunitomi rice

Edward Iwata (left) and his late parents visit relatives in Wakayama.

farm after World War II. But well before her death, she quietly handed over ownership to Kusuyuki's family in Okayama, according to my cousin, Phyllis, who was very close to Baachan (Grandma).

Why didn't she keep the property for herself? I ask my cousin.

"Because Baachan knew that she would die here and never go back," she says. "She always knew that she would never return to Japan."

EDWARD IWATA is an award-winning business journalist, fiction writer, and editor/ghostwriter in the San Francisco Bay Area. Research and translation by Akira Ueno in Tokyo.

GET TO KNOW JAPAN

• TOUR
Before traveling to Japan, immerse yourself in Japanese culture closer to home by visiting the **California Japantowns** (*californiajapantowns.org*) in San Francisco, San Jose, and Los Angeles (Little Tokyo). Throughout the year, each neighborhood hosts heritage programs, such as Little Tokyo's mid-August **Nisei Week Japanese Festival** (*niseiweek.org*), the nation's largest and oldest Japanese-American event.

• CELEBRATE
In addition to the spectacular blooms, the three-week **National Cherry Blossom Festival** (*nationalcherryblossomfestival .org*) commemorating the 1912 gift of 3,000 cherry trees from Tokyo to the city of Washington, D.C., includes the annual **Sakura Matsuri Japanese Street Festival** (*sakuramatsuri.org*). The six-block event ending at the White House celebrates all things Japanese, with sake tastings, sushi snacks, and dance performances.

• EXPERIENCE
Few sights are as patently Japanese as a flamboyantly costumed Kabuki actor adorned with exotic makeup. Tokyo's **Kabuki-za Theatre** (*kabuki-bito .jp/eng/top.html*), designed exclusively for the all-male Kabuki dance and theater art form, offers an English Earphone Guide service offering dialogue, lyrics, and helpful explanations during performances to enhance the experience for non-Japanese visitors.

Vietnam's Ba Valley rice field, the watery site
of daily toil and an engineering triumph

The Birthday Present

Filling in the blanks of a beloved father's short life

BY THOMAS FULLER

A friend of mine says her favorite color is "rice paddy green." This came to mind as I stopped by the side of the road in the valley of the Ba River in southern Vietnam. The rice fields were seas of brilliant, vibrant emerald stalks. Farmers in conical hats walked past the vast and lush paddies, their bicycles parked nearby.

As a reporter covering Southeast Asia, I had traveled a number of times to Vietnam. But this was my first trip to the Ba River Valley, a relatively obscure but picturesque series of villages about 300 miles north of Ho Chi Minh City.

My curiosity on this trip was more than purely journalistic. My great-grandfather, Antoine Fayard, had been a French colonial engineer in what is now Laos and Vietnam in the first decade of the 1900s, and he had spent more than a year in a village called Phu Sen.

My family knew he had drawn up blueprints for a dam in the Ba Valley. But what I quickly learned—and what we didn't know until my visit—was that his project was much more than just a dam. He had designed a vast irrigation system that helped lift a destitute part of Vietnam out of poverty.

Fayard's daughter, my grandmother, is now 95 years old, and my trip was a birthday present to her, to report back on the faraway projects that her father had carried out before she was born.

During my weeklong expedition I interviewed villagers and engineers. I carried with me photographs that Fayard had taken of people, of the landscapes, of his humble dwelling in Phu Sen, and of his forays into the jungle. I tried to locate some of the same places seen in the photographs.

And I traveled along the Ba River to the end of a bumpy dirt road until I found the Dong Cam Dam. It was constructed just high enough for the river to flow over while diverting some water into the manmade canals on either side of the valley. I was the first member of our family to see the dam.

I HAVE ALWAYS BEEN CLOSE TO MY GRANDMOTHER, and knew she would appreciate the research into her father, who died when she was only 23. She was born a decade after he left Indochina and has never been to Vietnam. But she remembered her father's stories, and soon after his death in 1942 wrote up a short report she titled, "The First Missions of My Father in Indochina."

Armed with her account, as well as Fayard's photographs, letters, and copies of silk maps that he had drawn of the region, I decided to construct a picture of Fayard's legacy in Indochina.

So much of what he described in his letters were the travails of

The Ba Valley dam, designed by author Thomas Fuller's great-grandfather

A rice farmer surveys the fertile land of Phu Sen, in part the handiwork of Thomas Fuller's great-grandfather.

clearing paths through untamed wilderness. It was a measure of how far Indochina has come—despite the wars and deprivation—that my journey retracing his steps a century later was mostly over well-paved roads.

Fayard's life and the pictures we have of it are emblems of another era. He traveled on horseback or sometimes by men-toting palanquin. He had a retinue of 25 laborers, who carried tents, cooking utensils, and surveying equipment. I was surprised to learn from his letters that his entourage carried bottles of rum, ham, condensed milk, salted butter, and red wine, which sounded like a moveable feast. Family legend has it that he drank wine because the water was often dangerously dirty. One of the photos shows him at

Fayard's life and the pictures we have of it are **emblems of another era.**

lunch in the jungle, surrounded by towering trees and creeping vines but sitting before what appears to be a banquet set with tablecloth and bottles of wine. He was inseparable from a wicker armchair that the coolies carried for him.

My journey was more modern and in many ways more ordinary. Along with Eric Melzer, a photographer and old friend, I traveled by car, never ending bus rides, and rented motorcycles. Our meals often consisted of pho, Vietnamese beef noodle soup. Only in the smallest villages was the arrival of two Westerners met with curiosity.

Eric and I began our trip in Bangkok, where I am based, and drove ten hours to Thailand's border with Laos. I left my car at a hotel that doubled

A farmer powered by an old tradition in Ba Valley

FAYARD, WHO WAS IN HIS MID-20S when he arrived in Indochina, worked and traveled during perilous times. One of his friends died of *la peste*, the plague, by Fayard's account. Another perished from infection after stepping on an animal trap. An interpreter met an agonizing death after being bitten by a venomous animal, possibly a scorpion.

In 1904, just days after a 25-day steamboat journey from France that passed through the Suez Canal, past Sri Lanka (then called Ceylon) and Singapore, Fayard arrived in Saigon, now called Ho Chi Minh City. He immediately was laid low with dysentery.

During one of his expeditions into the hinterland, Fayard met a French priest, Father Jean, who warned of leeches and the risks of bad water in otherwise remote, pristine patches of jungle. But most of the priest's admonitions centered on a forest-dwelling group he called the "Mois"—a term now considered derogatory that meant "savages"—who lived on the plateau and who he said had not yet been "pacified." The tribesmen were not systematically hostile toward Westerners, he advised, but they were very superstitious—and could be ferocious. Never refuse the rice wine offered at ceremonies, the priest advised, and if you decline an offer of fresh chicken blood, you will be accused of attracting bad spirits to the village and will be "assassinated."

Fayard's encounters with the tribe members went much more smoothly than Father Jean had warned. The daughter of a tribal chief had a fever that Fayard successfully treated with unspecified Western medicine. To show his appreciation, the chief assigned a "slave" to guide Fayard and protect him.

Using the blunt terminology of the time, Fayard also wrote that the tribesmen "do not have any civilization, do not use any form of money."

"We pay them with salt and copper bracelets," he told his mother in a letter dated July 1904. He noted that watches fascinated the tribesmen. "They ask us to put our watches up to their ears," he said, "the tic-toc makes them laugh."

as a brothel, and we crossed the border into Laos on foot. By taxi we made it to Pakse, a small Laotian city with some flashes of French colonial charm, and had dinner on the banks of the Mekong River.

Pakse is on the outer edge of one of Fayard's silk maps, and I began to wonder whether I was walking down the same streets as my great-grandfather—104 years later.

We explored the charming Laotian town of Champasak, also on Fayard's map (although he spelled it Bassac), where I met an Italian archaeologist, Patricia Zolese, who was helping restore the nearby ruins of Wat Phu—part of the same empire as Angkor Wat, the famed Cambodian ruins.

Over lunch in an ancient, two-story teak house, I unrolled Fayard's map and we discussed the French colonial legacy and the precariousness of life in the remote wilderness a century ago.

"At the time, people died very quickly and very young," Patricia said.

> We discussed the French colonial legacy and **the precariousness of life in the remote wilderness a century ago.**

IN READING FAYARD'S LETTERS, I had a hard time believing that they were only a century old. The contrast with the Vietnam that I was traveling through was stark. Mobile phones and motor scooters are ubiquitous in Vietnam today, and although there is poverty, there is also a growing middle class, not to mention cosmopolitan pockets of extreme wealth and modernity in the bigger cities.

To get a sense of the arc of history and pace of change, I met with the oldest people I could find. I found Nguyen Dinh Sum, 85, in a small village next to the irrigation canals that Fayard had designed.

"We used to be very poor," he said. "We had to go into the mountains to find something to eat."

Villagers ate roots they harvested from the forests "and a little rice," he said.

I met Tran Chu, 91, who as a boy had been at the opening ceremony of the dam and canals in 1930.

"Before the canals we only had water from heaven," Chu said.

Another farmer, Nguyen Phuc, 86, calculated the benefits of the dam.

"Before the canals we only had one harvest a year and the yield was very low," he said. Now, with year-round access to water, farmers can plant twice a year and each crop is much more plentiful. "The yield increased by four times," he said.

Connection

The cursive is exquisite, a symbol of the discipline of the times. And the return address is surprisingly simple: "Antoine Fayard, Qui-Nhon (Annam), please forward." I have the good  fortune that my grandmother still has her father's century-old letters from southern Vietnam, known as Annam. Without them, tracing his footsteps would have been nearly impossible. I soak up the handwriting as much as the content. "I am already half Annamite," he wrote his mother in June 1904. "I eat rice, walk barefoot in the house, and dress like them."
—Thomas Fuller

The ruins of an ancient Khmer temple in Laos, Champasak

All-too-modern transport in the rural Vietnam of the author's travels

Sum, the 85-year-old, told me: "To be honest, many people didn't feel comfortable being under the authority of the French but they admired them for what they did."

"The French built this," Sum said, referring to the canal, "and it brought us prosperity."

It would be enchanting, but helplessly naive, to think that these approving sentiments encapsulated the story of French colonialism in Vietnam. The French presence was very much a master-servant relationship. Around the time the dam was being completed, the French authorities were putting down uprisings in the northern provinces partly brought on by famine. French rule was self-serving and at times brutal.

Yet the Ba River Valley was an illustration of the benefits Vietnam realized under years of French influence and rule that also included the creation of the Vietnamese Roman alphabet by a French Jesuit in the 17th century, railways and roads, grand government buildings in Hanoi, and sweeping boulevards of Ho Chi Minh City.

FAYARD ARRIVED AT THE BA RIVER in March 1904 and settled into a house in Phu Sen. He had few instructions as to how he should proceed.

"I'm in charge of finding a place to build a dam on the Ba River," he informed his mother. "The engineer didn't give me any further explanations, but I'll figure it out."

He spent several months calculating the flow of the river and plumbing its depths to find the right spot for the dam.

"There's not a single square meter that I haven't dipped my feet into," he said.

He was busy but alone, able to speak only a few words of Vietnamese. Local "notables" came to his house to offer gifts—bananas, chickens, among them—and they prostrated themselves. He seemed to disapprove of the obsequiousness, but he did not show it, he said. "I made sure not to grimace," he wrote his mother.

His living quarters, a traditional house in Phu Sen, were rudimentary.

"The walls are made of dirt and the roof is straw," he wrote. He was not given a desk, he said, so he fashioned one out of his suitcases, where he would do his technical drawings.

Toward the end of his work in the Ba Valley, Fayard wrote that he was skeptical that the project would ever be

Traditional Vietnamese pho

completed. The project, he said, was "too huge for the country, even though it would provide great wealth."

He was partly right. The project was ambitious and during its construction, after Fayard had returned to France, 52 workers died from malaria, drowning, and an explosion that appears to have been related to the use of dynamite.

When I arrived at the site of the dam, I spotted a small shrine on a hill overlooking the river.

"This is a temple to commemorate the pioneers who built the Dong Cam Dam," said a sign in Vietnamese. "Visitors should preserve the area and be respectful."

By coincidence I arrived on the eve of a celebration to mark the construction of the dam. Workers were burning gold-colored paper at the shrine as an offering for those who died. There were photos of the dam under construction and brochures that boasted that the dam provides water to 19,000 hectares, or 73 square miles, of rice fields.

I met Tran Tien Anh, the head of the company managing the dam and irrigation system, and showed him pictures of Fayard. It was dusk and he invited me back the next day.

When I returned in the morning, a table had been set in the office with bowls of chicken and cans of beer. Workers gathered and listened to Anh offer a toast.

"This is a special day to commemorate the people who built the dam and who now work to maintain it," he said.

For that moment, nationality and politics melted away. This was a tribute to a man who more than a century earlier had set in motion the transformation of an underfed and impoverished valley. Anh filled my bowl with steaming white rice.

"This rice is thanks to the water from the Dong Cam Dam," he said.

I lamented that my grandmother was absent from the toast. Instead, I went out to the dam and, using my mobile phone, called her in France. I stretched out my arm so it would pick up the sound of the rushing waters.

"Do you hear that?" I said. "I am standing on your father's dam."

Based in Bangkok, **THOMAS FULLER** is the Southeast Asia correspondent for the *New York Times*.

Thomas Fuller in the Ba Valley land his great-grandfather helped cultivate

GET TO KNOW VIETNAM

• TASTE

Vietnamese cuisine is infused with French elements including crepes, pâté, and baguettes. Best embodying this French connection is the ubiquitous Vietnamese street food, **bánh mì**—a hollowed-out, crispy baguette smeared with liver pâté and then packed with sliced chili pepper, pickled carrot, cucumber slices, cilantro leaves, shredded *daikon* (white radish), and chicken, grilled pork, pork skin, or tofu.

• TOUR

Vietnam's cultural tapestry is woven by 54 ethnic groups classified according to five ethnic language families: Austro-Asiatic, Austronesian, Hmong-Yao, Tai-Kadai, and Sino-Tibetan. Hear their voices, learn their histories, and see traditional tile-and-thatch-roof homes at Hanoi's **Vietnam Museum of Ethnology** (*vme.org .vn*). The collection is housed in a building patterned after a traditional Vietnamese bronze drum.

• DINE

Vestiges of colonial architecture and café society imbue modern Hanoi with an exotic, French-Vietnamese vibe. Experience a similar ambience stateside at an upscale **Le Colonial** (*lecolonial chicago.com*) restaurant. Each location (Chicago, New York, and San Francisco) is designed to evoke the romance of a steamy, 1920s expat bistro: bamboo shutters, pressed-tin ceilings, potted palms, and, of course, as the French say, *Vietnamien* dishes.

Equestrians at Rancho Santa Emilia,
outside San Miguel de Allende, Mexico

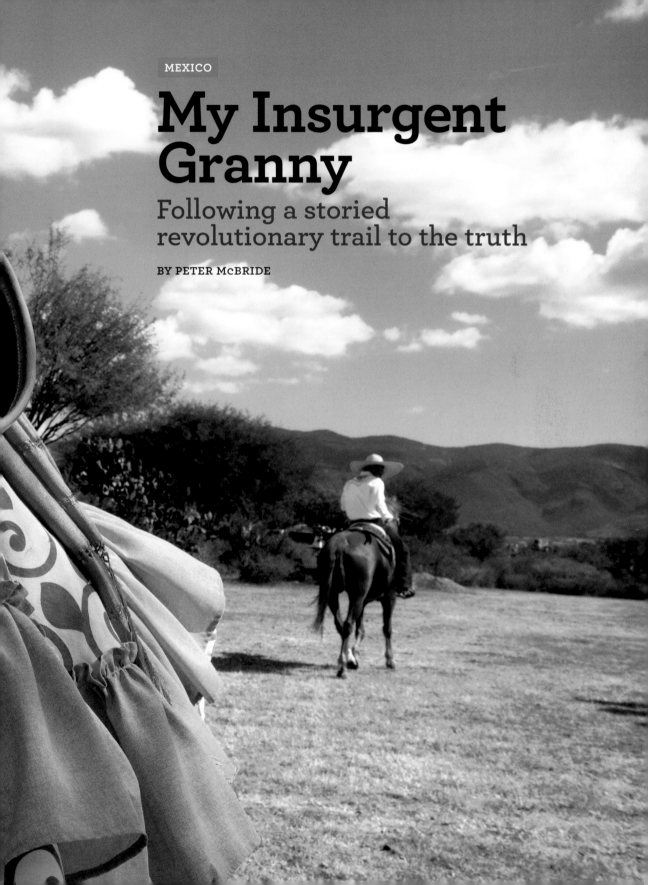

My Insurgent Granny

Following a storied revolutionary trail to the truth

BY PETER McBRIDE

This could be it. A treasure trove of a library in what was a 16th-century Franciscan monastery might be where my great-great-great-great-great-grandmother and I finally . . . meet. Marimba music lilts outside. In the sun-splashed library room, shelves crammed with bound parchment paper, religious leather journals, and government

letters sit below walls hung with statues of Catholic saints and cracked oil paintings. I'm told there are roughly 14,000 historical documents in the archive. What I don't see are temperature and humidity control devices. I better not cough; centuries of Mexico's written record could be reduced to dust.

It's two weeks into my ancestral scavenger hunt through Mexico's central highlands. My quarry, Josefa Ortiz Dominguez, known as "La Corregidora," has thus far been eluding her distant grandson. Too many muddy patches obscuring my craggy roots. But now, perhaps, pay dirt?

David Vega, the librarian here for 30 years, greets me. I explain my mission. Of course he's heard of Josefa: She was and remains the heroine of Mexico's 19th-century War of Independence against Spain. She was also the mother of 14 children. David smiles and suggests he might be able to help.

Within minutes, he brings me a pile of handwritten letters dated 1806. The *G*'s and *Q*'s have flamboyant, playful swirls. I imagine they shadow the arc of the feathers that penned them. Stamped on the letters signed by "Miguel Dominguez, Corregidor"—Josefa's magistrate husband—are Spanish government seals. Moments later, David returns to my table and hands me a thick book. It is an account of "Los Corregidores'" offspring. Pay dirt. Finally something. Querétaro's oldest building (now a UNESCO World Heritage site) is going to unveil my family's genealogy story.

For generations my family has boasted about our connection to Mexico's great revolutionary. Without her courageous involvement, the story goes, Mexico's liberty would have been delayed—at the very least. (In the end, after 11 years of war, the colonial government had no choice but to hand the reins to the local loyalists.) Heroism aside, though, it is Josefa whom I credit for my bleeding passion for Latin culture, food, and rumba beats. I want to know her better.

I open the book David gave to me and think of my grandfather, who introduced me to our family's famed heroine. Years ago, he gave me a rare, devalued 20-peso Mexican bill with Josefa's faded portrait. I carry it with me now.

MY SEARCH STARTS AND ENDS on La Ruta de Independencia, a series of winding mountain roads that connects the colonial hot spots of San Miguel de Allende, Hidalgo, Guanajuato, and Querétaro—all key to Mexico's revolutionary history.

Guanajuato's many colors shine in the late afternoon sun.

Spectators take to the dance floor after a rodeo.

Some two hours north of Mexico City, I drive down a cactus-covered hill as the radio crackles to life with the accordion strains of *norteño* music. Candy-colored buses and tired-looking trucks flank me. On the road's shoulder ahead, three *charros* (cowboys) move a herd of loose-skinned Brahman cattle, swirls of dust chasing the men's sashaying horses. Over the next hill, on the outskirts of the prosperous city of Querétaro, I head north onto a mighty historic stretch of road. On September 13, 1810, a rider galloped some 40 miles from Querétaro to the cobblestone streets of San Miguel. He carried an urgent message from an activist named Josefa—Maria Josefa Crescencia de la Natividad Ortiz Tellez Girón Domínguez—to be precise. Yes, the leading lady of my bloodline.

No one knows the exact words of that note, but history got the message: Begin the revolution *NOW*. In 1810, fed up with the second-class treatment of Mexico's people, Josefa and her revolutionary colleagues spawned a plan from her Querétaro home to break from Spanish rule and liberate Mexico. Josefa's husband, Miguel, aware of his wife's activities, locked her up in their home. Somehow she managed to slip her historic notice through the keyhole

Connections

When I pulled the dark green, oily bill from the envelope, it was clearly from another country, another time. Heavily creased in half, I opened the 20-peso note and stared at the profile portrait of the woman on the left side. Stern. Proud. Stubborn. Elegant. Clearly, this woman earned her place on Mexican currency, and in history.

As the accompanying shaky handwritten message from my grandfather explained, this was the rare, now devalued Mexican 20-peso bill, and the woman pictured was Josefa Ortiz Dominguez, the great Mexican revolutionary heroine and my alleged insurgent granny. The minute I saw it, I wanted to know her. It would take me some 20 years, however, to fully understand my connection to her.
—Peter McBride

to a rider. That simple act toppled the first domino in what would come to be known as Mexico's War of Independence.

My plan is far less ambitious: Follow in Josefa's footsteps and the trail of her insurgent message. Artsy San Miguel (picture colonial Mexico meets Santa Fe) is my first stop. I expect to find revolutionary trivia and lore scattered in inviting secret alleys and magnetic music-soaked plazas.

Although I discover a culturally rich town with sweeping views, I uncover nothing about my ancestor. So I attend a rodeo at a local ranch to balm my frustration. An old friend has invited me to Rancho Santa Emilia, an elegant throwback to the 1800s, where the horse stalls are crafted with hand-hewn timbers. When the rodeo starts, I watch another century swirl before me. Sombrero-clad charros gallop through explosions of red earth as *escaramuzas* (cowgirls) ride sidesaddle in swishing Spanish dresses. Bulls are ridden and mariachis trumpet.

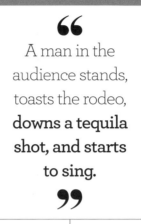

> **66**
> A man in the audience stands, toasts the rodeo, **downs a tequila shot, and starts to sing.**
> **99**

A man in the audience stands, toasts the rodeo, downs a tequila shot, and starts to sing. His deep baritone carries the haunting nostalgia of a broken-heart ballad. The 12-piece mariachi band immediately jumps in. Violins pierce the air. The crowd is captivated. Dust clings to the sweat on my face. I am right where I want to be—back two centuries and ready to add to the music.

By car it takes me 30 minutes (half a day by horse in 1810) to reach the plaza of the blue-collar pueblo of Father Miguel Hidalgo, Josefa's co-conspirator. On September 15, 1810, Hidalgo received her secret missive. The following morning, September 16, celebrated as Mexico's Independence Day, Hidalgo rang his church bell and delivered a historic sermon that would serve as a rallying cry.

It was time to pick up arms, march north, and send the Spanish home.

I visit the cathedral where Hidalgo inspired his flock, mostly peasants, to become an army. Outside, a jovial scene: people singing and two-stepping to

The author, Peter McBride, combs for family news through the crumbling books of Querétaro's Museo Regional.

A bust of La Corregidora, the heroine of Mexico and the author, keeps vigil in Dolores Hidalgo.

the polka beat of folksy *ranchera* music. A young woman belts out a heartfelt solo, her eyes clenched shut and her brow furrowed. I ask her what the song means. "It is a song of love and freedom," she says, adding, "I love to sing—music carries my blood."

I PUSH ON TOWARD GUANAJUATO, down the Revolution Highway, for more Josefa scouting and for Day of the Dead festivities. The road is just about empty, with spectacular curves and sweeping views of La Sierra Gorda. The few vehicles I encounter, mostly weathered trucks, wave me on. Within an hour, eye-popping views of Guanajuato's kaleidoscope-colored architecture flash past as I descend into the city's tunnels that transport me, mentally, back in time.

In late September 1810, Hidalgo hurried his rag-tag wagon train of insurgents along the route I now drive. When they reached Guanajuato, they solidified the revolution by surprisingly overtaking the Spanish barracks. Hidalgo's army then moved north. A few months later, he and his cohorts were captured by the Spanish and executed. The Spanish displayed the heads of Hidalgo and his three top men on the corners of a granary—for ten years. Contrary to plan,

the gory symbols served to strengthen revolutionary resolve. I walk through the granary, now an open-air museum. A giant mural of Hidalgo's caged head covers the stone floor. His eyes seem to follow me.

The next day, I visit a cemetery blanketed with people and fresh flowers celebrating the Day of the Dead. The holiday is all about recalling the departed. I spend the afternoon wandering the walled Pantheon that overlooks hilly Guanajuato and its gravity-defying architecture. Murals of skeletons made from colored sawdust magically appear on the pedestrian streets. One looks to be a rendition of Hidalgo with Josefa profiled in the background. But I've seen enough statues and murals. I want the real Corregidora. It's time to visit her home in Querétaro.

This is not my first visit to the colonial city. Call it a simple twist of fate. Twenty years ago, in an attempt to work on my Spanish, I'd applied for a college semester abroad in Spain. I was turned down—and offered an option to study in a city I'd never heard of, Querétaro. I said yes. En route by train from Mexico City, I opened a package my grandfather had given to me before I headed off. In it were a 20-peso bill emblazoned with a picture of a woman, a bundle of letters, a

Peter McBride fills his impromptu dance card during his Mexican visit.

hand-scribbled family tree, and a typed note: "Peto—I am delighted to know you are going to Querétaro. You are headed to the center of your family's history."

Querétaro appears about twice the size I remember it. To my delight, I quickly find Calle La Corregidora and turn toward the *centro historico*, weaving through vaguely familiar blocks until I reach Hotel La Casa de la Marquesa. Located a few cobblestones from the central plazas, it is the perfect base for my familial explorations. My room's name: Doña Josefa. No kidding.

I walk the streets. Déjà vu greets me on every corner. The statue of Josefa looming over the Plaza Independencia looks better than I recall. I climb to the city's aqueduct overlook. Just above sits Josefa's tomb. Once the site of heated revolutionary fighting, Querétaro's Pantheon is now a memorial for Josefa, her husband, Miguel, and other historical dignitaries. Inside, I listen as two Mexican women discuss the revolution. I ask them about Josefa. The shorter of the two looks at me, cups her right hand low by her waist, moves it up and down, and smiles. I understand the gesture of male bravado perfectly. The taller of the two women shakes her head. "I

don't agree," she says. "Josefa was just doing her duty. Little do they know that the woman in question is my *huevos grandes* (ballsy, that is) granny, five generations back.

The next day, I tour Josefa's home, now the town's main government building. Two guides kindly lead me to the stateroom. It is the very room where Josefa's history-changing "Start the revolution" message slipped through the keyhole—and went viral. As her distant relative and, I like to believe, kindred spirit, I cannot help but wonder: Could I start a revolution? Do I, or my inner Latino, have the guts?

THE NEXT MORNING, on the suggestion of a friend, I visit Querétaro's regional museum, considered the epicenter of revolutionary history. Within those museum walls is a library . . .

When David the librarian hands me the exact text I've been searching for, I know I have reached the dragon's lair of my quest. From my pocket I pull out the handwritten family tree my grandfather handed me two decades ago, swallow my hesitancy, and open the book. Immediately I find a family tree and zealously search for familiar names.

I trace the chart of names detailed in my grandfather's letter—backward. I cross-reference with the book—going forward. Dominguez–Dominguez. They start to match.

But then they don't.

Something isn't right. I check both again—three, four, five times. The two lists don't line up. Our family names don't match any offspring of Josefa's grandchildren. *No bueno.* Then I notice a blurb about Josefa's fifth son, named Miguel (our alleged link). He moved to southern Mexico (our Dominguez relatives lived there too), but I find little documentation of his life beyond that. He married but had no marriage license or children. Then I read in Spanish: "One family claims to be related, but have been proven to be imposters."

The marimba music outside stops. A shadow sweeps across the room. I realize I am not who I think I am. I have not descended from a famous revolutionary. The *sangre* (blood) of Mexico's great heroine does not dance in mine. My nonrevolutionary blood starts to rise.

I leave the museum in denial. Must be a mistake. My grandfather liked stories, but how could this tale carry on for seven generations? Is this the power of mythology—a story too good to be disrupted by the facts?

Imposters. Within 24 hours, it starts to sink in. My family's proverbial connection to historical fame is, well, fiction. Or is it? Many revolutions have led people to change identities. And there is always the question of illegitimate children. After Hidalgo was executed, Josefa was captured and sent to Mexico City by a Spanish battalion (she allegedly spat in the face of every soldier). Her life was spared but she was imprisoned for eight years.

Was there a secret 15th child during imprisonment? Did her son Miguel have undocumented offspring? Does it really matter?

My last night in Querétaro, I stumble on a little Oaxacan-style restaurant. Two musicians play aching *campesino* tunes.

My lurking inner Latino may not come from Josefa's DNA, but it still jumps when a mariachi wails. People merrily share tables, jokes, and tequila. Such simple joy, such decadent molé, and such rich, decent humanity. Isn't that enough to fight for? I would fight for this. Maybe this is not the Mexico Josefa dreamed of, but it seems better than the one she revolted against.

Perhaps fate's humor is that my grandfather died before discovering our family's genealogy twist. I'm not sure he would have cared whether it was truth or myth he carried onward. Why not do the same? It is fun having a force in one's past—real or imagined. So I decide to adopt Josefa Ortiz de Dominguez, La Corregidora, as my favorite and only insurgent granny, just like my grandfather did.

Colorado-based **PETER MCBRIDE** is an award-winning photographer, filmmaker, and writer. His work has appeared in *National Geographic* magazine, *Outside,* and the *New York Times,* among other national and international publications. He loves salsa dancing and spicy food.

GET TO KNOW MEXICO

• CELEBRATE

For Mexicans, death is more of a celebration of a person's life, rather than a day of mourning. Every November 1–2, cities around the world celebrate **Dia de los Muertos,** the Mexican Day of the Dead, which symbolizes keeping the spirits of loved ones alive. Check your local listings for the festival, and be prepared for sugar skulls, parades, and crowds.

• COOK

Nothing brings the memory of home closer to mind and heart than food. Tacos, the authentic Mexican staple, can be found almost anywhere throughout the world, but chef **Roberto Santibañez's** cookbook *Truly Mexican* (Houghton Mifflin Harcourt, 2011) teaches you how to bring the authentic taste straight into your kitchen.

• TOUR

Sprawling on almost 20 acres within Chapultepec Park in Mexico City, the **Museo Nacional de Antropología** (National Museum of Anthropology; visitmexico .com) is the definitive place to go for a comprehensive look at the history and culture of Mexico, starting from the Maya civilization and continuing on to the present day.

Following the Son

A child's curiosity propels a family to embrace its inner Norwegian.

BY DAVE HAGE

A glacier-sculpted fjord of
Norway's Flåm Valley

When our family gathered for holidays in the small prairie towns of western Minnesota in the middle of the last century, my uncle Carl invariably began the meal with a Norwegian grace. His own parents, though born in the United States, spoke Norwegian at home, and Carl kept the language alive with a certain solemn pride.

"*I Jesu navn,*" he would say, "*går vi til bords. Å spise drikke, på ditt ord.*"

I learned a few words of Norwegian from my father and his siblings, but I never understood the full prayer until many years later, when our own son Sam, then ten, announced his intention to learn the language. A local Lutheran church, Mindekirken, offered classes on Saturday mornings, and every week Sam would set off, happy and earnest, for the church basement, mostly in the company of elderly blue-haired ladies whose own inflections were acquired in the home, not in a classroom. "In Jesus' name," he said, translating Uncle Carl's prayer, "we go to the table. To eat and drink, by your word."

When Sam completed the course a few years later, my wife was so proud that she declared she would take us on a family trip to Norway. In Minnesota, if you announce such a trip, people assume you are going in search of your ethnic roots. Minnesota has nearly a million residents of Norwegian descent, more than any other state—and a fifth the current population of Norway. The state has produced no end of Scandinavian giants, from novelist Ole Rolvaag and journalist Eric Sevareid to politicians including Hubert Humphrey and Walter Mondale. Minnesota is a place where, to this day, people unconsciously mutter "*uffda*" (yikes) when they drop their keys in the snow and argue vigorously over the best way to serve the lutefisk at Christmas dinner.

But I had no interest in visiting the ancestral graveyard or meeting my long-lost Lillehammer cousins. I wanted to see the modern Norway, the nation my people had built—a 21st-century society of high incomes and low poverty. Minnesota is occasionally called "the little Norway"—not for the accents or the winters, but for its high taxes and egalitarian ethic. I wondered if some socialist gene had crossed the Atlantic in the 19th century along with dried cod and linen chests with rosemaling.

SIX MONTHS LATER, WE FOUND OURSELVES trekking through the mountain range that runs like a spine down the center of Norway, and I had my chance to find out. It didn't take long to discover that today's Norway is quite different from the impoverished country our farming ancestors left in the 1860s.

Preparing the lutefisk of author Dave Hage's traditional Norwegian holiday family meals

A fairyland settlement along the Nærøyfjord

We had spent a cool, rainy day hiking the Flåm Valley, a spectacular vale of pine-clad cliffs and foaming waterfalls, and by evening, we were very hungry. At dinner, in a beautiful small hotel in the village of Flåm, we naively expected to find the ethnic foods we celebrated at all those Christmas gatherings in the 1950s and 1960s—the potato wrap called *lefse* and the lye- and salt-soaked whitefish, lutefisk, staples of hardscrabble 19th-century peasants. But the cosmopolitan restaurant menu included smoked salmon, reindeer tenderloin, and chocolate mousse. Ask Norwegians today why you cannot find lutefisk on the menu and they will give you a puzzled look. It was comforting, in a way, to stroll through villages where everyone looked like us—tall, broad-shouldered, and fair. But it turns out that today's Norwegians favor French cooking and Italian slacks.

The adults in our group were dismayed at this discovery, but Sam took it with customary aplomb. At a posh Bergen restaurant one evening, we sat down to find whale fillet on the menu. Several of us recoiled at the prospect of eating this spectacular animal, but Sam ordered it and pronounced it delicious. It was

Connections

When I was growing up, the trimmings for Christmas dinner were always Norwegian. My father and his sister would make a pilgrimage to a Scandinavian specialty store in Minneapolis, Ingebretsen's, and return laden with delicacies: the lye-treated cod known as lutefisk and pungent sausages made from lamb trimmings or cow's blood. The children would sample them dutifully but always saved their appetites for the buttery Norwegian cookies—crunchy *krumkake, sandbakkel* shortbread, and melt-in-your-mouth *spritz*. A generation later, in the kitchen of their great-aunt Betty, my three children learned to make the cone-shaped krumkake cookies with an iron like this one. —Dave Hage

At the foot of Norway's Bøyabreen Glacier

harvested from a small species plentiful in Scandinavian waters, he said. "And besides," Sam added, "it's a mammal. It tastes like steak."

Despite Norway's breathtaking evolution, our visit still provided ancestral touchstones. One bright, brisk morning we found ourselves motoring down the Sognefjord, the longest and most famous of Norway's fjords. It's a landscape that rivals the Swiss Alps for jaw-dropping beauty, where towering granite mountainsides plunge into steel gray water and wisps of clouds play tag across the sharp peaks. As we cruised down the channel, we could pick out tiny farmsteads clinging to the sheer hillsides—a red barn here, a bright blue chicken coop there—linked by narrow lanes with hairpin turns. The village of Undredal, the goat-cheese capital of the world, lies up an arm of the Sognefjord so remote that it was not accessible by paved road until the 1980s. On that morning, I understood why the farming people of my great-grandparents' generation emigrated: The soil was rocky, the farms were small—especially when divided again and again with each generation—and an aloof royal family had no interest in the penury of their rural subjects.

But that day also explained the aching homesickness felt by many of my immigrant ancestors, a pang articulated by Liv Ullman's character, Kristina, in the great 1972 film *The New Land*. Emigrants like my great-grandparents arrived in America to find that their new paradise consisted of an endless expanse of lonely, windswept prairie, scorched by drought in the summer and buried under blizzards during the six-month winters. Stuck in an isolated sod house during the marathon winter, she missed her mother, her church, and the lovely village where she had grown up—the lovely villages that were now giving us goat cheese, brown bread, and strawberry jam. It's no wonder that as many as a third of all Scandinavian immigrants to the United States gave up and returned home within a decade or two of emigrating.

Two days later we took a second look into our history, this time turning the pages back several centuries. Norway's most celebrated museums lie along the great harbor at Oslo, on a long peninsula called Bygdøy, which in summer you can reach by a polished wooden ferry. Here, the Viking Ship Museum contains the world's finest collection of Norse artifacts, including two spectacular, ninth-century-or-so Viking longships excavated from the country's most important archaeological sites and reconstructed in painstaking detail. Under the museum's low, white plaster ceilings, the boats seem enormous, sweeping lengths of black oak planking and towering masts. But compared to the oceangoing frigates and clippers of later empires, they are tiny, scarcely rowboats with dragons' heads. To understand that these small boats crossed the Atlantic, mastered the brutal North Sea, and dominated the Mediterranean for decades is to appreciate that Vikings were not simply bearded marauders, but brilliant navigators, diplomats, and strategists. They were not nice people; they really did pillage monasteries, burn villages, and take slaves. But they also dominated international trade in northern and central Europe for two centuries and founded the cities that would later become York (Jorvik) in northern England and Barneville-sur-Seine in Normandy. You've heard of the Norman Conquest? "Norman" is an Anglicized version of Norseman: The red-bearded people who civilized northern France and conquered England in 1066 were my ancestors.

IT WAS IN OSLO THAT I FOUND THE NORWAY I had come to discover. Measured by one definition of per capita gross domestic product (GDP), Norway is richer than Switzerland or Japan. But it also relentlessly plows its wealth back into its people and public services. It ranks first on the United Nations Human

Development Index, a composite measure of income, health, and literacy. Some years ago, an economist friend, Richard Freeman of Harvard, returned from a conference in one of the Scandinavian countries and gave me a call. Setting aside my envy that the Ivy League scholar got to Norway before I did, I asked him what he thought of my homeland. "The good news is there are no poor people. The bad news, a glass of beer costs $15."

As we discovered. One day in Bergen, a lovely old trading city wrapped around a harbor that dates back to the 11th century, we stopped for lunch in a little café. We might have been in Greenwich Village or Berkeley: The chalkboard menu offered vegetarian sandwiches, café latte, and carrot cake. A modest lunch for four came to $165. Later, at the little supermarket near our hotel, I decided to price a four-pack of beer.

> **"**
> It was in Oslo that **I found the Norway I had come to discover.**
> **"**

Imagine my relief when I calculated the sum as just $6, before I realized that was the price per bottle.

Our guide for part of the trip, a science teacher named Martha (pronounced "Marta"), gave some insight into this expensive but still comfortable society. She lives in an affluent neighborhood of Bergen with her husband, a university professor. And though they both work full-time and Bergen is a city of 258,000, they get by without a car. He rides his bike to work; she generally takes a bus or tram. They own a second home in the country but seldom drive; they simply pack up their cross-country skis, and a frequent train takes them out of the city to within walking distance of the cottage. Martha worries that Norway became affluent too fast and that the generous social safety net could undermine the nation's work ethic. She is proud, nevertheless, of the social

The author finds the fjord-threaded Norway "a country of pine-clad cliffs and foaming waterfalls."

Oslo's Opera House exemplifies modern, sophisticated Norway.

compact that has emerged. "Norway is an expensive place to live," she said. "But we have what we need, and everything works."

High taxes are one explanation for Norway's stratospheric cost of living. Some years ago, the public health authorities deduced that alcohol accounts for a disproportionate share of the country's modern diseases, social pathologies, and traffic accidents, and imposed a hefty excise tax on beer, wine, and liquor. These days, a big night out in Bergen is two glasses of wine.

Of course, the other driver of high prices is Norway's fabulous oil wealth. When petroleum was discovered beneath the North Sea in the late 1960s, offshore drilling made Norway one of the world's leading exporters of crude oil and natural gas and pushed its per capita GDP into the world's top five. But riches on that scale can have a distorting effect on a nation's economy, especially in a country whose labor force is smaller than that of Minnesota or Connecticut. One evening at our hotel in the mountain

village of Geilo, we retired to the book-lined library for an introduction to the country by the hotel manager, who had trained at Cornell and worked in American hotels long enough to acquire almost unaccented English. "You are wondering why Norway is so expensive," he began. "And I have a simple answer. The chief cook in our kitchen is from Poland. I pay him $80,000 a year, plus holidays, fringe benefits, and family leave. Why? Because he could leave for the oil fields tomorrow and earn twice that amount."

A few days later, strolling through the Norwegian Folk Museum in Oslo, we came upon a model farm from the 14th century, where a young woman was stoking a wood-fire oven and baking lefse. She looked like my sister and, though she was speaking Norwegian, sounded like my rural Minnesota cousins. Listening as she described the farm to a group of tourists in front of us, I thought I could detect an accent I hadn't heard in our travels through the southern part of Norway. I asked if she was from the north. "No," she replied with a hint of a blush. "Sweden. There are more jobs here."

What can you buy with wealth like that and a commitment to public investment? We found out the next day, on a walking tour of Oslo. The city has been described as the least charming capital in Europe, and it certainly lacks the elegance of Paris or the genial bustle of Dublin. What it offers is an eminently friendly urban environment: green, walkable, clean, and safe, full of educated and courteous people. The streetcars are punctual, the streets spotless, the parks manicured.

ON THE EVE OF OUR DEPARTURE, a guide told us to line up the next morning outside the hotel to catch an airport bus at 11 a.m. The hotel was immense, and I reckoned that Sunday morning would be a madhouse of tourists departing for the airport. We arrived outside the hotel 15 minutes early—to find the sidewalk all but empty and a fleet of glistening motor coaches lined up at the curb. A courteous driver with perfect English sold us tickets, and the buses departed punctually.

As our bus approached the airport, I wondered what Uncle Carl would have thought about the modern Norway we had visited. Carl was a conservative man, a gruff fellow who wore woolen pants and heavy boots whether supervising employees at the little family lumberyard or chairing a meeting of the county historical society. He spent much of his

life cursing lawyers and politicians, and I'm sure he would have taken a dim view of Norwegian socialism. But, like me, he took pride in his resolute and, the Vikings' more brutal habits aside, decent ancestors. Had he come upon those spotless streetscapes and punctual buses, the courteous and educated store clerks, I think Carl would have been proud.

And Sam, the reason behind our Norwegian outing? Not long after we came home, he confessed that he and his sister had made a pact to move to the land of their ancestors some day. After all, he already spoke the language.

DAVE HAGE is a Minnesota native of Danish and Norwegian descent. An author and an editor at the *Star Tribune* of Minneapolis, he is working on a book about bison.

Dave Hage with his wife and son, Sam, who inspired their trip, in Norway

GET TO KNOW NORWAY

• CELEBRATE

Dance, eat, and get Nordic for **Syttende Mai** (17th of May), also called Constitution or National Day, commemorating the 1814 signing of Norway's constitution and independence from Sweden. Norwegians around the world celebrate. In the United States, check out Seattle's **17th of May Festival** (*17thofmay.org*)—its community parade winds through the Ballard neighborhood.

• TASTE

Lutefisk is Norway's most infamous traditional food; however, the most beloved dish just may be the unassuming *fårikål,* a simple, slow-cooked stew made with mutton, cabbage, and, often, potatoes. Typically a fall favorite, fårikål is particularly celebrated—and consumed—the last Thursday of September, designated as **Fårikålens Festdag** (Fårikål Feast Day). Find a recipe at Nordic Nibbler (*nordicnibbler.com*).

• TOUR

The single best place to learn about Norwegian daily life from 1500 to the present is Oslo's **Norsk Folkemuseum** (*norskfolkemuseum.no/en),* the country's largest museum of cultural history. The open-air site, founded in 1894 and open 360 days a year, contains 160 buildings including Gol Stave Church, built in 1200, as well as four other medieval-era structures.

A treasured ancient burial site of northern
Peru's early Moche inhabitants

My Years of Magical Thinking

Reality collides with an idyllic childhood.

BY MARIE ARANA

Twenty years ago, when Peru was emerging from a civil war that ravaged the countryside, left more than 70,000 dead, and swept Shining Path terrorists into the very heart of Lima, I set out to tell the story of my idyllic Peruvian childhood. The trip was partly a fool's errand, partly a dream deferred. I had in mind a notion put forth by the poet

César Vallejo: Lonely is the home that knows no noise, no news, no green, no children. I went back, seeking the noise of memory.

And yet the place to which I returned seemed the very picture of loneliness—silent, secretive, gray—strung with barbed wire and filled with a generation of skittish young who had never known the freewheeling joys of infancy. All the same, I was convinced that my Peru was there somewhere, under the rue and dread.

I was born in Lima, a clamorous city during its mid-century heyday, when postwar optimism had quickened Peru and galvanized a hemisphere. By the time I was three months old, my family had moved to Cartavio, a sleepy sugar hacienda just north of Trujillo. My father's job was to make those vast fields of cane yield not only sugar, but rum, sorghum, paper, cardboard, even shoes made of the plastic residue. He was young, brilliant, ambitious, and our

Workers wield machetes to cut sugarcane, the economic backbone of central Peru.

A valley in Ayacucho, Peru, set among the Andes Mountains, a backdrop of author Marie Arana's childhood

little family was a movable tribe. With a fearless American mother, who had grown up in Depression Kansas, and a Peruvian father, who had high aspirations for his country's future, we set out for that desert coast like pioneers for a wild frontier.

Cartavio turned out to be a stretch of windswept sand, surrounded by fields of sugarcane, fringed by a raging Pacific. Two centuries before, it had belonged to Doña María del Carmen Cortés Cartavio, whose ancestor Hernan Cortés had conquered the Aztecs for the Spanish crown. Although I didn't know it, life there would be an eerie mirror of South America's conquistador past. On one side of the hacienda, cinnamon-skinned indigenous were crammed into a warren of improvised shacks. On the other, in houses whose size corresponded to rank, were Peruvians of a whiter hue. The 1950s were boom days for sugar, the world was hungry for it, and my father's employer, the United States industrial giant W. R. Grace, was making the most of it in this remote coastal hamlet of Peru.

My father made sure that the fledgling town had a church, a school, a clinic—and a welcoming, oval plaza. He reserved the best, most beautifully

gardened house for us. He built a country club, a Swiss-style guesthouse, a movie house, and then roads lined with marigolds to lead to them.

But in the middle, with smokestacks thrusting so high there could be no doubt as to why we were there, were the factories. Out in the fields were the laborers who fed them: sinewy men with bronze faces and steel machetes, moving purposely through the green. In the mill, there were others, forcing cane onto threshers, through iron jaws, into steaming cauldrons. The pulp exited the other side in wide, warm sheets of paper, or glittering sugar, or redolent rum; and trucks, rumbling tirelessly down the coast, hauled away the new incarnations.

My father was not the first to wrest such treasures from that sand. The arid strip that lay between the Pacific and Andes had been cultivated for centuries. The Moche, who had inhabited the northern coast before the Inca, had evolved a sophisticated system of irrigation, transforming a dreary landscape into vibrant fields of green.

It wasn't until the Spanish arrived, however, that sugar sent its roots into the New World and its cane became a staple in the Americas. Columbus had brought it with him on his second voyage. When Francisco Pizarro clambered ashore Peru 40 years later, in 1532, he brought something else: a ravening appetite for gold, and the aim to sack every indigenous temple—every *huaca* (burial mound)—until he found it.

FOUR CENTURIES LATER, when I was a little girl, riding horseback through those sugar fields and scampering through the abandoned, overgrown huacas of the Moche and the Chimú, Peru was still surrendering buried treasures to anyone willing to dig for them. We knew from gossip that enterprising grave robbers—*huaqueros*—had unearthed human skeletons bedecked in precious metals. They had found capes fashioned from hummingbird feathers, ceramic erotica, death masks of fine mesh, richly woven textiles, stones carved with gods—all of them lying deep beneath us, buried by centuries of drifting sand.

My *ama* (nursemaid) would tell me of phantoms and witches who rode the Cartavio wind: souls of slaves beside those of queens, and conquistadores alongside the betrayed Inca. I would need to be careful, she said, and very, very good, or one would fly through the window, grab me by the throat, and suck out my soul. She ran a finger up my arm, and a whole host of creatures seemed to travel my skin, crawling their serpentine way toward my elbow.

The smokestacks of industrial Cartavio, Peru, contrast with the quiet town of the author's childhood.

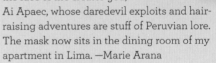

Connections

My father gave me this "death doll" after our trip to my childhood home, Cartavio, Peru, in 1996. It is made of ancient gauze from the Chimú period (circa 1200) that was tossed aside as *huaqueros* (grave robbers) looted burial sites for more precious objects. It has always struck me as a benevolent rendering of the face of the creator god, Ai Apaec, whose daredevil exploits and hair-raising adventures are stuff of Peruvian lore. The mask now sits in the dining room of my apartment in Lima. —Marie Arana

She was not the only one telling stories. My father would regale guests with tales of rich Trujillo families living along that coast—influential bankers who sent employees into the moonless night to dig out the ancient graves. They would bribe my father's truckers to ferry them through the black, and he would hear about it long after the looting was over.

Today, Lima's museums are fairly bursting with precious pottery, accumulated in just such ways. Many of the most valuable were smuggled out and sold to the rich of Europe and North America.

My brother and I, lit by those tales of piracy, would set out for high ground, ready to dig for booty. We would find skulls tucked behind rocks, easily pulled from sand. We plucked out their teeth and screeched with joy as we stuffed our pockets, trying to outdo one another. We scrambled over Cartavio's dunes, hungry for more, our trophies rattling in our pockets. It didn't occur to us that skulls were what huaqueros left behind, and teeth were not what the rich of Europe and North America were after.

Marie Arana's search for family history encompasses Peru's northern Amazon rain forest.

SO IT WAS THAT I RETURNED to Cartavio in the 1990s, more than 30 years after my rowdy girlhood. Our family had spent eight years in that idyll before we had followed my father's work to Lima and on to New York. It made perfect sense that I should bring my father on the return voyage; this time, he would follow me. We made the eight-hour drive up the coast from Lima, eager to see Cartavio again, eager to have him see it with me.

We were both taken aback by what we found.

A wall circled the factory. More circled the houses. Shards of glass warding off intruders jutted from their ledges. The years of terror had taken a toll on our former paradise.

Day after day, it seemed, my father would ask for word about this worker or that, and day after day he was given the grim reckoning: One had lost his life in a raid on the town, another had been abducted along with his entire family, a third had been recruited into the ranks of the marauding terror-ists—the *terrucos*—a fourth had disappeared into the sierra. It was a litany of human loss. Still, physical evidence of our lives remained: the old house with its capacious stoop, the towering factory, the school, the church, the insanely green oval plaza.

That was the year I had traveled all four corners of the Tihuantisuyu, as the Inca called their empire, tracing our family history. I had gone to the mountain aerie of Ayacucho to sort through cathedral records, hoping to confirm a great-grandfather's birth. I had gone to the rain forest city of Iquitos in order to trace the scattering of Aranas south, from valley to jungle to mountain. I had pursued every point of the compass, chased every rumor, pursued every phantom.

YEARS LATER, I DECIDED to return to Cartavio for no other reason than to stand in the shadow of that

Once a coastal colonial enclave of the rich, Trujillo is now a vibrant metropolis and one of Peru's cultural centers.

old house. I wanted to mount that welcoming stoop and sit under the shade of our banana tree. I wanted to be in that noisy green and allow the fragrance of childhood to invade my senses.

In the spring of 2014, I flew to Trujillo, ready to take that last trip home, prepared to witness another transfiguration. What I didn't expect: to find the house gone, the gardens paved over. In less than a generation, the evidence of my childhood had disappeared.

Even nearby Trujillo had changed. Pizarro's jewel, which prided itself in stately mansions, elegant *tertulias* (salons), and afternoon tea, was another work in progress now: a sprawling metropolis.

The Hotel Libertador, where my mother often took refuge in the atrium, sipping her *máte de muña* tea, was still there, but the population of the city

> 66
>
> I flew to Trujillo, ready to take that last trip home, **prepared to witness another transfiguration.**
>
> 99

surrounding it was now 16 times bigger. The rich clung to Trujillo's historic heart, the poor, to its tattered fringes. The city Pizarro had named after his birthplace bristled with fast food joints. Simon Bolívar's residence had become a bank. Family manses were now jeans merchants. The near million that had flocked to Trujillo lived in improvised buildings that furled all the way to the sea. And there, among them: the Pussycat Bar, Le Moulin Rouge, gargantuan casinos throbbing with strobe lights.

Trujillo's newspapers told of street gangs, extortionists, and gunmen who demanded fees from those just wanting to walk a neighborhood. A man could hire a killer to exterminate a foe; a woman could buy a bodyguard if she was being stalked. Tour guides pointed to shantytowns on the hills, where the hit men trained.

Traditional reed fishing boats commingle with beachgoers along a Trujillo beach.

Cartavio's market goods could once be bought from vendors ambling the town's streets.

I knew tiny Cartavio would be spared those urban perils. And indeed, as I turned off the highway toward the town, a field of sugar sprang to welcome me, waving tall banners of green. For a fleeting moment, at least, home was exactly as I remembered it: the vault of sky, the angry sea, the wind-combed sand, the random humps of Moche huacas that punctuated the desert landscape. The oval plaza was still there, as was my father's school and church. The factories still pumped thick, white columns of smoke into the cloudless sky.

But it was obvious that much had changed. The houses so vivid in memory had been replaced by rows of cinder block. Ours with its capacious stoop had disappeared. When I asked where the engineers lived, the people shrugged. The place belonged to the corporation of Casa Grande, which was owned in turn by a dairy conglomerate. No one knew where the bosses lived or what they looked like. "They're in Lima," the residents told me. "They never come."

AND SO IT WAS THAT I LEARNED that my home had passed through iron jaws of a different kind. The first threshing had begun with the 1968 coup that had made Gen. Juan Velasco Alvarado president and nationalized the country's businesses.

The author (far right) and her family on the front stoop of their old Cartavio home

W. R. Grace had been the first to go and, in a broad agrarian reform, the management of the hacienda had passed into the hands of the factory workers. The house where I had grown up had been taken over by a number of families, much as the home of the mythical Dr. Zhivago had been appropriated during the Russian Revolution. Socialism was followed by a decade of terror and, ultimately, my father's factories fell into sad disrepair. Eventually, in 2006, they were bought up at bargain prices. Every huaca I had crawled over, every field of cane, every sandlot was emblazoned with the name of its new master, Casa Grande.

I walked through the market, hung with fly-bitten carcasses of chickens, goats, and pigs. Life was no longer as I knew it. There were no merchants ambling Cartavio's streets, hawking their wares with song.

Out on the highway, tour buses sped past my lapsed paradise to the archaeological marvels of Chan Chan, the Huacas of Moon and Sun, the Temple of Arco Iris. The world had bypassed my arid stretch of Peru.

When I went up the road, I saw why. My memories of childhood could not compare with the history that had lain beneath me all the while. A few miles from

A burial statue from Peru's ancient El Brujo Archaeological Complex

where I'd lived was the newly excavated El Brujo, a spectacular huaca, which held the remains of a young Mochica queen who had lived 1,700 years before. It was clear she had been powerful. The walls of her funerary temple were lined with frescoes of dancing shamans, naked prisoners, and spiders wielding surgical knives. When they finally found the remains of the Lady of Cao, she was festooned with extravagant jewelry. Her skin, perfectly preserved, was adorned with a tattooed lacework of creatures meant to protect her in the afterlife: Snakes, crocodiles, leopards, and monkeys crawled their serpentine way up her arms, toward her elbows.

My ama had been right. The air we breathed had been full of witches and queens, slaves and conquistadores. They'd been there all along, outside my window, proof that the past was alive, even if the present no longer resembled it.

The green, the noise, the news had always lived on this desert patch of Peru. It was the least lonely place on Earth. It was abuzz with history.

MARIE ARANA is the author of *American Chica* and *Bolívar: American Liberator*. A writer at large for the *Washington Post* and senior adviser to the U.S. Librarian of Congress, she was books editor of the *Washington Post* for more than a decade.

GET TO KNOW PERU

• TASTE
The Inca are credited with establishing Peru's raw fish culinary tradition. It was the Spaniards, however, who supplied the essential citrus fruits—and tangy citric juices—used to "cook" the fish and create **ceviche.** Typically served at lunch, Peruvian ceviche is slightly chewy, usually spiced with red onion, and often accompanied by *choclo* (a white Andean corn).

• TOUR
Immerse yourself in Peru's rich history at Lima's **Museo Larco** (*museolarco.org/en*). The restored, 18th-century mansion showcases rarely seen pre-Columbian masterpieces, such as Chimú gold attire, erotic Moche pottery, and Nasca drums.

• EXPERIENCE
Don some purple for Peru's *mes morado* (purple month) and visit Lima on the **Lord of Miracles feast day** (October 28) to witness South America's largest religious procession. The 24-hour walk is a moving tribute to the Señor de los Milagros (Lord of Miracles), a mural of a Christ painted by an Angolan slave in 1651. Enshrined in Lima's Church of the Nazarene, the image is attributed miraculous powers after surviving multiple earthquakes.

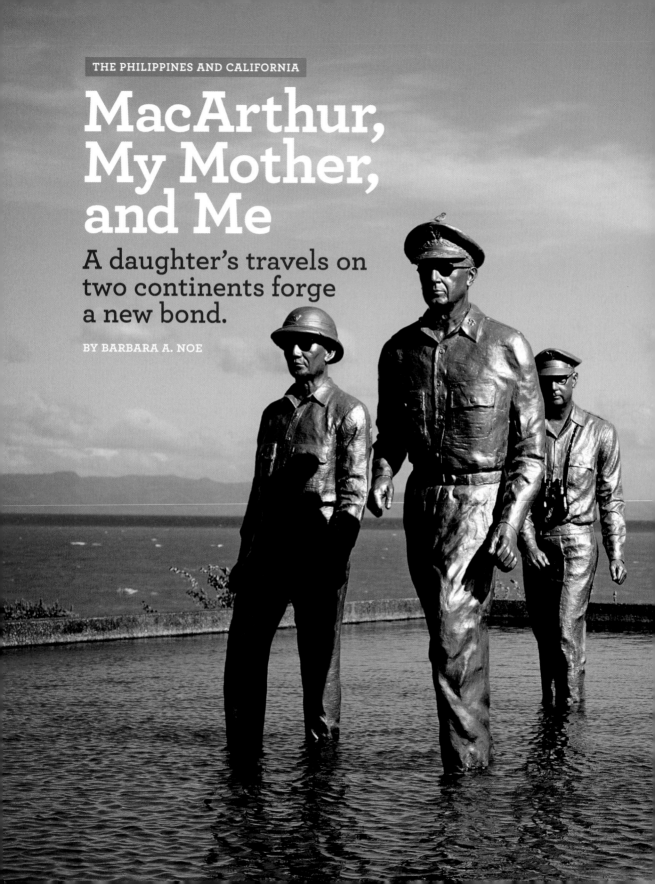

MacArthur, My Mother, and Me

A daughter's travels on two continents forge a new bond.

BY BARBARA A. NOE

The Leyte Island memorial marks Gen. Douglas MacArthur's Palo Beach landing in October 1944 to liberate the Philippines from Japanese rule.

"**W**e're looking for the Dewey Mine," I say nervously. My fiancé, David Kennedy, and I have trespassed on private land deep in Siskiyou County, in northern California, and I'm convinced that the owner may pull out a gun. But I'm determined to stay strong because I'm here in a last-ditch attempt to learn everything I can about my

mother's intriguing childhood (and, dare I say, obtain some insight into our sometimes wobbly, typical mother-daughter relationship during my own childhood).

It all started a few years back, when I accompanied my mother on a trip to the Philippines.

Wait. Let me back up.

Leanne Blinzler Noe, my mother, spent the first three years of her life in Siskiyou County, where her father worked at Dewey gold mine and her mother, who had eschewed a cosmopolitan San Francisco lifestyle, kept house in a two-bedroom shack.

After the mine was closed in the mid-1930s, my grandfather, Lee Blinzler, sought work in the Philippines, where a mining boom was in full swing. My grandmother, Kay, joined him a few months later, in

It all started a few years back, when I **accompanied my mother on a trip to the Philippines.**

October 1936, with their two little girls, my mother and my aunt Ginny.

They lived on the small island of Marinduque in a bamboo Nipa hut, and it looked like their life was on an uptick. In January 1937, my grandmother wrote to her sister back in the States: "It is a very nice sensation to know we are climbing out of debt. Four years of poverty operations and babies isn't easy but we do feel that 1937 will be good for a change."

Alas, out of the blue, with no nearby medical facilities, my grandmother died three months later at the age of 27 from an indeterminate disease. My grandfather placed my mother and her sister in a German convent, first in Manila, then at the nuns' summer place in Baguio, in northern Luzon, near the mine where he worked.

The nuns were strict, of course. But my mother and aunt enjoyed forest hikes, eating the world's best mangoes, and seeing their dad on the weekends, when they would ride ponies at Burnham Park or go to the coast at Miramonte, stopping at barrios along the way to see a cockfight or to pose in front of a carabao.

THEN, IN DECEMBER 1941, eight hours after Pearl Harbor was attacked, the Japanese bombed the Philippines. They invaded the country and imprisoned all Allies, including my grandfather. My mother and her sister remained at the convent until they too were interned in 1944.

The mother of author Barbara Noe (right) and two friends return to the site of their wartime imprisonment.

A desolate remnant of Dewey Mine, in northern California, where Barbara Noe's grandparents lived and worked

When I was growing up, my mother would toss out random stories about her experiences in the prison camp: bedbugs, one-ladle food rations (and her father's sharp command to never eat anything that spilled onto the cement floor while being served), the Japanese death warrant that had been issued on the prisoners as American soldiers neared Manila, and the impressive rescue spearheaded by Gen. Douglas MacArthur.

On top of that was the still present scar in her cheek, and the fact that she cannot to this day open her mouth more than two fingers wide—the result of shrapnel that lodged itself into her jaw during the Battle of Manila. She still keeps the piece of shrapnel in her jewelry box. I used to finger it as a child, imagining the pain and terror she must have felt (though she insists that she didn't feel anything, probably due to shock).

I think my mom's lack of traditional family life as a child created her commitment to building a tight-knit one with my father and my two sisters and me. But sometimes, my mother was distant, lost in her thoughts. I never had the words to delve any deeper into what was bothering her. She's a very strong woman and was devoted to making the best of things and moving forward with her life.

A FEW YEARS AGO, I JUMPED at the chance to join her on a trip back to the Philippines with a group of about 50 former civilian and military POWs, as well as some of the soldiers who had rescued them, to celebrate Liberation Day. It was during this trip that I slowly began to understand the chronology of everything that had happened to her, the details, the significance.

We toured Corregidor, MacArthur's last stronghold before he fled to Australia, vowing, "I shall return." We walked the last half a mile of the Bataan Death March, when more than 70,000

The author and her mother join the Liberation Day anniversary celebration at University of Santo Tomas in Manila.

American and Filipino soldiers were forced on a 55-mile trek beneath the searing sun and thousands perished.

But perhaps the most poignant moment of the trip came at University of Santo Tomas in Manila. The venerable university had been converted to an internment camp for Allied civilians, where my mother—11 years old at the time—and her little sister were imprisoned in March 1944. Her two camp friends Dorothy Mullaney Brooks and Connie Ford were on our trip as well, and we all wanted to visit the classroom that they had called home.

We climbed the grand mahogany stairs to the third floor. The three friends were silent as we strolled down the window-lined hallway and found what had been Room 55-A. As they surveyed the desk-filled room, I tried to imagine 25-odd beds crammed wall to wall, with everyone's meager belongings tucked away in their tiny allocated space.

"Our cots were over there," my mother said, pointing to a spot on the floor.

The friends reminisced about the 6 a.m. and 6 p.m. roll calls and the subsistence meals of *lugao*, or watery rice, and how they had to bow to Japanese sentries. My mother's main job was to stand in the food line to get meals for herself and her father (her younger sister stood in a different line).

My mother shared a story about a rubber doll she

Connections

When I was little, my mother often talked about her hero, Gen. Douglas MacArthur. Of course, the notion of "hero" contradicted so much of what I'd go on to learn about the arrogant, difficult World War II commander. That said, it was due solely to his quick-witted determination that the Santo Tomas POWs—my mother, aunt, and grandfather included—were liberated.

Years later, when my mother was in her 20s, she wrote MacArthur in admiration. He wrote back, rather humbly: "It was thoughtful ... to write me as you have and I appreciate it more than I can say." —Barbara A. Noe

found one day in the outside trash. "Its one arm was a little softened, sticky," she said, "but I don't know why someone threw it away. I took it and nurtured it, sewed clothes for it out of scraps."

My heart went out to that little girl—my mother. She had lost her own mother at such an early age. She nearly starved to death. Obviously, any of my struggles in the urban jungle were incomparable. Maybe that's not fair to me (I say), but I was slowly beginning to understand.

DURING OUR VISIT TO SANTO TOMAS, we commemorated their Liberation Day with an outdoor celebration in front of the Main Building. As I sat listening to a mix of Filipino and American music, enjoying wonderful chicken and pork adobo, it struck me that on exactly the same spot, a different scene unfolded on that day, February 3, 1945. Rumor had it that the Japanese planned to kill the internees of Santo Tomas; MacArthur was adamant that the First Cavalry move to Manila as quickly as possible and rescue them. My mother, who was not aware of an imminent threat, shared her story with me.

"After dinner that evening," my mother told me, "while dishes were being washed, planes flew overhead and a pilot dropped a pair of goggles with a note: 'Roll out the barrel,' referring to the song whose last line is 'the gang's all here.' The planes left and everyone returned to their chores. There was a six o'clock roll call and early bedtime. I could see the light from tracer bullets streaking across the sky through the windows. I heard the rumblings, gunfire in the distance, and the dark sky lit up.

"Around nine o'clock, without warning, the plaza in front of the Main Building illuminated with pink and white flares. Ginny and I rushed down from our room to

> **" Japanese gunfire exploded all around them. The American soldier standing next to my mother was killed—killed! "**

the front hall and watched from the crowded stairs.

"Soon a tank came into view. Everyone was running around and shouting, 'They're here! They're here!' The vehicle came to a halt and several unusually tall and healthy-looking men emerged, looking like big, good-natured giants. Gen. William C. Chase stood up on a table in the lobby: 'I'm so glad to see you,' he said. 'Better to give life than take life.' "

But their ordeal wasn't over yet. A few days later, against all precautionary regulations, my mother and her sister snuck out of the Main Building to the plaza just in front to get some Hershey bars offered by a couple of soldiers they had met. Although they had been liberated, the Battle of Manila was in full swing and as the Americans fought to free the rest of the city, Japanese gunfire exploded all around them. The American soldier standing next to my mother was killed—killed!

My mother speaks so matter-of-factly about the incident; how a chunk of shrapnel became embedded in her jaw; how her sister's arm received a

World War II topside barracks on Corregidor Island, Philippines, housed U.S. soldiers.

The author's mother was among those liberated in November 1944.

couldn't figure out, in this rugged, remote corner, exactly which little road was *the* road.

It was David's idea to simply drive onto the property of the first open gate we found. So imagine my surprise when the man on whose property we trespassed said, "You're on Dewey Mine Road." We were thankful he didn't have a gun.

"It's a pretty bad road," he continued, mentally assessing our rented four-wheel drive. "Wait a minute. I'll lead you there."

We followed his truck for a bit, and just like that, we were grinding along the same forested road that had been the main connection between my grandparents, mother, and aunt, and the outside world nearly 80 years before.

I have letters that my grandmother wrote from there that bring alive her self-effacement and sense of humor, complete with her misspellings. She talks about wanting a Scotty dog instead of a diamond ring: "Up in the mountains a dog would be company for me while Lee is at the mine; a ring would only be a nuisance."

We make it across six creek crossings, bouncing along the rutted route, avoiding holes, boulders, and tree limbs. I recall a story that my mother told me about my great uncles—my grandmother's brothers—coming once to visit. My grandfather advised them against driving at night, but of course they did. And the car turned over. Horses had to be brought the next day to right the car.

After 3.2 miles, we spot a dilapidated building—the stamp mill. We park the car and walk from there. A little creek meanders alongside us in the epitome of a sylvan scene. The air smells of pine and dirt—clean and fresh. Thunder groans overhead, and I wonder if my grandfather is watching us from above.

And then we spot two cabins. Was this where my mother lived? One's smashed to the ground, but the other one remains standing. Corrugated metal covers the front, and two wooden doors lie flat against

wound that would require 90 stitches; how she and her sister were rushed to an evacuation hospital, where they saw others more wounded than themselves; how her father later visited the dead soldier's family in New Jersey.

As we flew out of Manila a few days after the Liberation Day celebration, my mother sat next to me, staring out the window into the darkness of the night, no doubt contemplating all the memories that had been stirred up during the trip. I touched her arm, feeling a closeness that I had yearned for during my childhood.

BACK IN CALIFORNIA, she and I later searched for the tiny mining community near Yreka, where she spent her first three years, but failed.

Now, David and I are trying to track it down. I had targeted in on a map, on one small area. But I

them. We walk to it and I peek inside, a sense of reverence overcoming me as I seemingly peer into the past. I have my grandmother's words:

> The place was all dull grey and
> I have been making the living room
> ivory. Finished our room in cream and
> green. Then Leanne's room is perfect.
> The walls are turquoise blue and the
> woodwork pink. I made a stencil fuzzy
> little white lamb, to go around the wall,
> with a pink ribbon at a rakish angle . . .
> Lee was laughing the other day, thinking what some tough miner will say
> one day if such ever has to occupy
> that room.

But where's the mine?

We continue up the road and, after a fruitless hike up what we finally deem to be the wrong way, we return to the stream, deducing that the mine must have been nearby because it relied on a water source. We see tailings (waste rock) that certainly belonged to a mine. We follow a trail along a hillside. Then, peering into the foliage below, I spot what appears to be a collapsed tree house. I look more closely, and amid the squashed timber I see a wheel. No doubt about it, we found the mine!

The wind whispers through the trees and swaying pines. Everything surrounding us remains exactly the same as when my grandparents lived here as a young couple newly in love. I sense them around me, nodding their heads at my victorious quest. All of the puzzle pieces have fallen into place, and I feel at peace.

I cannot wait to tell my mother.

BARBARA A. NOE is the senior editor of National Geographic Travel Books. She helped her mother write her story in the book *MacArthur Came Back: A Little Girl's Encounter With War in the Philippines.*

Barbara Noe finds the rubble of Dewey Mine.

LEARN MORE ABOUT THE PHILIPPINES AND WORLD WAR II

• WATCH
Nothing brings the internment camp experience into focus like the firsthand accounts of Allied civilian prisoners. In **Victims of Circumstance,** a documentary by Lou Gopal and Michelle Bunn, Santo Tomas Internment Camp survivors (including writer Barbara Noe's mother) share their gripping personal stories.

• VISIT
World War II history books, handwritten letters from internment camp survivors, and pre–World War II memorabilia (such as invitations, hotel brochures, and phone books) are included in the James J. Halsema Collection of Philippine History housed at the **MacArthur Memorial** *(macarthurmemorial.org)* in Norfolk, Virginia. The U.S.-born Halsema was incarcerated and tortured during the Japanese occupation.

• READ
Reading books set in wartime Philippines can help flesh out your own ancestor's story. Two must-reads: **When the Elephants Dance** by Tess Uriza Holthe (Crown, 2002), a lyrically written novel set in the final days of World War II about several Filipino families in Manila, and **Ghost Soldiers: The Epic Account of World War II's Greatest Rescue** by Hampton Sides (Anchor, 2002), the minute-by-minute re-creation of the dramatic rescue of Allied soldiers at Cabanatuan.

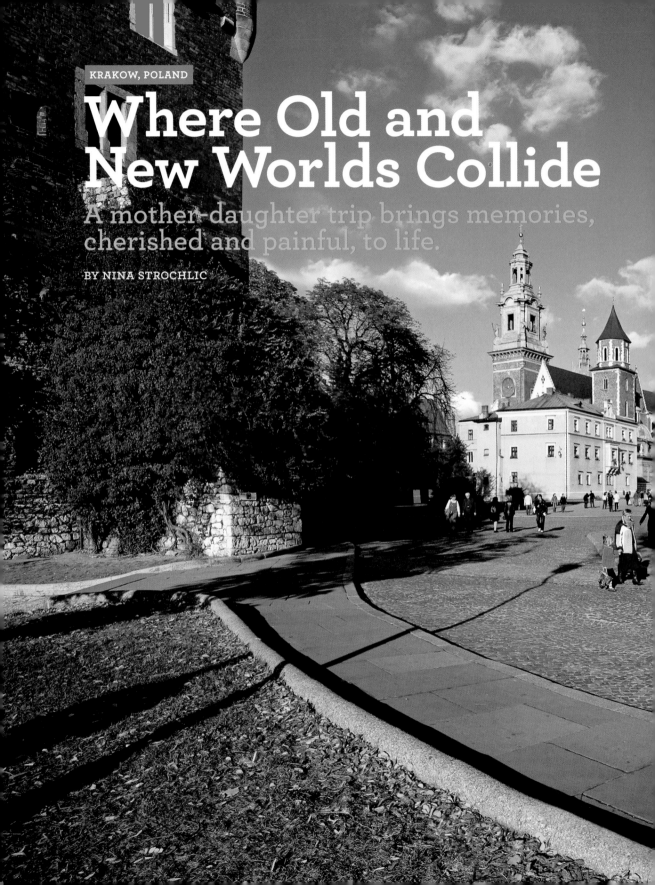

Where Old and New Worlds Collide

A mother-daughter trip brings memories, cherished and painful, to life.

BY NINA STROCHLIC

The quaint and cobbled streets of Krakow, Poland, where millions flock to remember those who perished at the hands of the Nazis

A few times a year throughout my childhood, my mother and I hauled a tan suitcase from the spare room. She would pop open the single working hinge and fish out stacks of sepia-toned photographs and frayed papers—curfew extensions, identity cards, immigration forms. We'd sort through the haphazard piles and decaying photo albums.

The suitcase held the remaining tangible links to my grandparents' prewar lives and a slightly more robust postwar collection. We tried to decipher the old-fashioned, loopy scrawl that explained each picture. In them, she, a chic, blond-bobbed woman with a square face and wide smile, and he, a dapper and slightly older man, stared up at us. Holding these tangible relics, the past felt closer.

At the outbreak of World War II, my grandparents were forced from their homes in Poland and into labor and concentration camps. On nights the suitcase came out, we'd watch videos of my jovial grandpa remembering the miles of frozen marches and how he won my grandmother's affection in the displaced persons camp after the war by scraping together ingredients to bake her a cake. Soon after, they married, got visas for Cuba, and jumped ship in New York City while en route.

Sabina, my grandmother, died long before I was born, and Carl, my grandfather, passed away when I was five, but I knew their stories by heart. Like the one when my grandmother's parents and brother survived the war only to return to the rural village where they'd stored their belongings and be murdered by its postwar inhabitants.

"Never forget" wasn't just a phrase for my family; it was a mantra.

But it was also a challenge: How could we remember what we never experienced? After years of dragging out the old suitcase, the pictures became two-dimensional, the stories took on a folkloric quality, and the pages of correspondence we'd exchanged with surviving relatives failed to satiate our curiosity.

MY MOM AND I DECIDED to set out for our ancestral land. Though my grandfather swore he'd never return to Poland, we felt drawn to fill in the backdrop for our family history. I thought of it as time travel—I imagined Poland was a country of ghosts, a crowd of bearded men walking down cobblestoned streets and hastily evacuated shtetls. A country stuck in the loop of 1939.

But the Krakow we encountered, with its soaring castle- and café-lined medieval squares, was nothing like that. Virtually unscathed by the invading Germans, it had the charm of a young, modern city set amid the mystique of an ancient one. On a warm July day, my mom and I landed armed with a jumble of addresses pulled from the sharp

One way to get around in Krakow

Krakow's hub of activity for 1,000 years, its Main Square

memory of an elderly cousin of my grandmother's, and began a scavenger hunt in search of my grandparents' past. Bursting with Jewish tours, museums, and shops, the city catered to tourists like us—pilgrims unearthing their heritage.

Krakow was a treasure trove of Jewish history and ephemera. Antique shops were stuffed with war-era newspapers, magazines, and boxes of unclaimed family photographs. A sprawling suburban flea market peddled oxidized menorahs and ashtrays decorated with Hitler's face. The Jewish quarter, Kazimierz, had hosted the city's Jewish population for nearly half a millennium, but fallen into disrepair after World War II, when its inhabitants were moved into the outlying ghetto before being shipped to concentration camps.

In the 1990s, after an onslaught of attention following the release of *Schindler's List,* which was filmed in the district, the Kazimierz underwent a face-lift, with a focus on Jewish heritage. Now,

thousands stream in for the annual Jewish Cultural Festival each summer; school groups and brigades of Israeli soldiers tour the historic synagogues; tourists dine at traditional Jewish eateries; and patrons browse Judaica Krakow's bookstores and museum exhibits.

On a corner in the center of the city's Old Town, we found the storefront site of the seasonally rotating ice cream parlor cum fur shop my great-grandparents, Fela and Moses, owned. Crossing a bridge into what once was the ghetto, we photographed a music school that now occupied the building my grandmother, her parents, aunt, and cousins were moved to in March 1941. As Jews were sent into ghettos, my blond-haired and blue-eyed grandmother was hidden for a time outside the city by a brave Christian Pole of noble descent, but she eventually returned to Krakow. He was later caught and badly beaten for this attempt to save a Jew. Two years later, Sabina and her aunt were taken to Plaszow, the camp

On a warm July day, my mom and I . . . began **a scavenger hunt in search of my grandparents' past.**

outside Krakow. They'd spend two months after that in Auschwitz, where, upon arrival, Sabina's aunt was given an orange ball gown to wear and Sabina was dressed in the fabric from an umbrella. They found this so hysterically grotesque, my grandmother later told a cousin, that they laughed until they cried. Their last wartime stop was Bergen-Belsen, where my grandmother and her aunt were when Allied forces arrived in 1945 to liberate the camp.

It was in the displaced persons camp of Bergen-Belsen where she and my grandfather met and were married, in a group wedding of 48 couples on the Jewish holiday of Lag BaOmer. More than a year after being freed, the new couple and her relatives set out for Cuba, hopping off in New York under the care of a distant cousin and promise of a "less-than-two-month" stay, according to her nonimmigrant visa. Her nationality at the time is listed as "without." In the interim, they'd started collecting the photos that now fill our fraying suitcase: David Ben-Gurion speaking to a large rally at Bergen-Belsen, a wedding day pose with my grandmother's family, a blurry shot of the Statue of Liberty as their ship passed by.

KRAKOW WAS A BEAUTIFUL CITY to wander through, but our aim was to see my grandmother's family's prewar apartment, the childhood home of a woman I knew only through photographs and who remained a faint memory to my mother, who was only 10 when Sabina died at the age of 37. Rising from the middle of Krakow, Wawel Royal Castle, a Polish renaissance complex, keeps a watchful eye on

its city, and it was in the high-class streets surrounding it that we knew my grandmother grew up.

Our quest was shorted by a false start: a tour of 28 Podzamcze, a gift shop on a corner across from the castle. My mother let loose an uncontrollable stream of tears while the flabbergasted salesgirl tried in vain to find signs that the small space had once been an apartment. Unsuccessful, my mom plucked a small babushka magnet off a wall as a souvenir. Next to the row of colorful doll mementos was a selection of small magnetic Jews with black hats, curled payot and massive coins clutched in their hands.

We walked out disappointed in a lack of connection and wondering if we had the wrong address. But before we could right it, we were off for a day to Auschwitz, a bleak tour of the war's most notorious death factory. From there, we hopped a train west to Bedzin, my grandfather's hometown.

We found ourselves in a train compartment with no English speakers and little clue to where we were headed. A sign language conversation

A Jewish cemetery in Kazimierz, a Krakow location for the film *Schindler's List*

Today's Kazimierz is abuzz with shops.

with a roving conductor signaled we should disembark at what was, we realized too late, a graffiti-covered old train station miles from Bedzin's city lights we saw glittering against the sunset on the horizon. So, we set off on foot, walking for an hour past decrepit Soviet-style row houses without a sign of life.

We arrived late in Bedzin, a small city of about 60,000, and checked into our hotel. As my mom gave our name at reception, a cry of recognition came from a cluster of chairs in the lobby. An amiable elderly man jumped up with surprising dexterity and introduced himself as a former Bedzin resident and a friend of the family's before and after the war. By coincidence we were staying at the same hotel as a tour group for the Bedzin Holocaust survivors and that next day was a commemoration of the anniversary of the 1942 ghetto liquidation.

We accompanied his group on a tour of the town, watching rows of Israeli and Polish soldiers line up at attention to face the ghetto memorial, their buttons gleaming under the 95-degree sun as survivors took the podium. We traveled to a church that, after the

Nazis burned down the town's synagogue, had taken in escaping Jews, and heard a terrifying account from one of the few who had been saved. Nearby, as the group started climbing up the steps of Bedzin's ancient castle, my mom and I slipped away, counting the address numbers down the main street until we stood facing my grandfather's apartment building.

Carl had left town early in the war, off a tip that volunteering for labor camps was preferable to sticking around until the death camp deportations. He pushed his birthdate to three years later (a change he would only admit at his 80th birthday party) and filtered through 12 to 15 work camps before being liberated and brought to Bergen-Belsen. That tip proved unimaginably fortuitous: Much of Bedzin's Jewish population was later sent to Auschwitz.

We stared from across the street at the second floor of the boxy yellow building that had housed my grandfather, his parents, and seven siblings, some 70 years earlier. A burly man in a black T-shirt stood on the balcony off the floor we thought to be my grandfather's, his thick arms folded against the railing and

The Vistula River winds its way through picturesque Krakow.

a puff of smoke rising from his lips. Maybe it was the increasingly noticeable language barrier, but we decided asking for a peek into his residence would be unwise. We turned and walked back down the street. The glimpse was satisfying—my grandfather had shared his stories with us already. We both knew that the real hope was to see my grandmother's apartment—a tangible piece of the life of a woman who remained a mystery to me and a hazy figure to my mother. We had one last shot.

THAT NIGHT, WE TOOK A TRAIN back to Krakow. It was our final day in Poland and we were armed with another address to try—20 Podzamcze—from a cousin of my grandmother's. She instructed us it was on the first floor, "the windows on the left of the entry when looking at the house from the street." A 1941 German census of Krakow Jews classified the property as a "two bedroom, one living room, one kitchen" apartment.

We found what we believed to be my grandmother's building, a classic limestone structure, on a street

encircling the Wawel Castle, and just a half block up from the corner souvenir shop. Without an apartment number, we buzzed futilely, and had nearly given up when a nattily dressed businessman produced keys to the front door and we slipped in behind him.

Standing inside the dim hallway, we lingered, dragging the video camera over ceramic tiles that

The author with her mother during their Krakow visit

surely predated our family's residency. My mother, holding a note in Polish that explained our quest, rapped on the wooden door of No. 2, which seemed to possess the building's exterior left windows. A middle-aged woman with short brown hair cracked it open and greeted us hesitantly. Her eyes flitted over the handwritten note, and confusion melted into warmth. In choppy English, she introduced herself as Marta and ushered us in.

The apartment was beautiful, with ornate inlaid wood floors, and almost entirely original fixtures. "It hasn't been remodeled, except for the bathroom, since my mother bought it in 1949," said Marta. Her mother, bedridden and sleeping in the living room, had purchased it from a woman who occupied the apartment during the war after my grandparents were forced out. My mom's expression mirrored my own disbelief. I could almost imagine my great-grandparents stoking a fire in the green ceramic-tiled heater that stretched to the ceiling in a corner of the kitchen. The harrowing circumstances that transferred the apartment from our family's hands to Marta's were overshadowed by our incredible luck. We talked to her for an hour, lingering in the apartment that, save a world war, could have been our home.

That evening, over dinner of traditional Polish pierogies surrounded by fire dancers and roving polka bands on the city's medieval square, my mom and I checked off a list of trip goals. We had dug up a trail of our family history through Krakow and Bedzin, filling a 55-year-long void for my mom—and

constructed a stage for the stories of some of her parents' lives. My grandfather may not have approved of our visit had he been around, but we'd found a bittersweet relationship between his Poland and the 21st-century nation struggling to balance a bloody past with a cosmopolitan present. The country no longer conjured only fleeing Jews and ghetto walls. Along with them were pierogi festivals, imposing castles, and welcoming Poles like Marta.

Sabina Strochlic's American nonimmigrant visa application

A few months later, we received an email from Marta. Her mom had passed away and she'd moved into a different apartment in the building. "I'm very happy when you still contact with me," Marta wrote. "I also don't want to lose touch with you, so we see you one day!" My mother and I joked about checking if the apartment was on the market and moving back to Poland, but instead stashed our mementos, the babushka magnet from the souvenir shop, and our photos in the tan suitcase where the old and new worlds could finally merge.

NINA STROCHLIC is a reporter at the *Daily Beast* in New York City. She has an insatiable fascination with genealogy and exploring foreign lands.

GET TO KNOW POLAND

TASTE
One communist-era Krakow relic worth visiting is a *bar mleczny* (bahrr MLETCH-nih), or milk bar, so named because the no-frills cafeterias served plenty of dairy and just about anything but then scarce meat. Associated with cheap Polish food ladled out cheerlessly, the once ubiquitous milk bars have dwindled to a handful. For a somewhat gentrified version of the original concept, try **Milkbar Tomasza,**

where, for about $6, you can fill up on soup and an entrée, such as pierogi or potato pancakes.

TOUR
The new **Museum of the History of Polish Jews** (*jewishmuseum .org.pl/en*) in the heart of World War II's Warsaw Ghetto tells the 1,000-year history of Poland's Jewish population through artifacts, personal stories, and interactive exhibits in eight distinct galleries.

READ
The compelling memoir-travelogue **The Pages in Between** (Touchstone, 2008), by *New York Daily News* reporter Erin Einhorn, underscores the frustrations and complexities of researching family history in a foreign country—specifically in Bedzin, Poland. Einhorn searched for—and found—the Catholic family who hid her mother there during the Holocaust.

The coiffed and colored tops of St. Basil's Cathedral
paint Moscow's night sky.

But now that I was married and had a travel mate, the thought of going for a short visit was much more attractive. I started to explore the possibilities. Baku was very far-flung, and we knew that it would be difficult to get there. We would need an invitation and there was no way that Leonid and Rimma could offer us accommodation in their small apartment.

In the end we chose an eight-day package trip that would take us to Moscow, Kiev, and Tbilisi. We reckoned that Tbilisi wasn't that far from Baku and that the Loshakovs might be able to travel there. As it turned out, Leonid, Rimma, Dima, and Vova all came to meet us in Moscow.

NEEDLESS TO SAY, THE WEATHER THERE in January 1976 was freezing. I had borrowed a shabby fur coat and at the last minute had grabbed an old pair of boots from the back of my closet. It was only when I first stepped out on Moscow's snow-covered streets and felt icy water seeping in through the seams that I remembered why I'd treated the boots with such disdain.

Moscow was a revelation. We were staying in a huge Stalinist hotel. "Bleak" wasn't the word. There was a babushka sitting at the end of each corridor to keep an eye on everyone's comings and goings. The decor was, well . . . Stalinist. One day we went out but returned within minutes because we had forgotten something. As we walked back along the corridor, we saw the chambermaids at work. Bedroom doors were standing open and listening devices were dangling, unashamed, from the ceiling lights.

We saw the family every day. At that time, Russian citizens were not supposed to go farther than the foyer of the hotels reserved for foreigners. But Leonid had chutzpah. He and the rest of the family brazenly walked past the receptionists and made their way up to our room. They were, I am sure, amazed at what they saw as the luxury of our hotel room. But they were savvy, too. When it came to talking about anything remotely political, Leonid would indicate that we couldn't stay in the room but had to head back out to the street.

Our heated discussions about the politics of the day kept us warm as we walked to Red Square, Lenin's tomb, St. Basil's Cathedral, the Kremlin, past the KGB headquarters, in temperatures around minus 20°F.

We also soon learned about more restrictions imposed on Soviet citizens. One day we went for a horse-drawn troika carriage ride in the snow of Izmailovsky Park. That was followed by lunch in a picturesque restaurant in the park. I remember walking into the elegant room. A buffet table was laid with all sorts of delicacies—smoked sturgeon, blinis, pirozhki. There was no shortage of anything, unlike other restaurants we had visited where requests for an item on the menu were mostly greeted with a surly *"Nyet"* (No), Here, smiling women wearing traditional (read "touristic") peasant costumes met

Connections

When I was growing up, the only link I had to my Jewish-Russian roots was my mother's cooking. I savored the borscht, *zharkoye* (stew), and kasha she learned from her Russian mother. Best of all was my mother's creamy cheesecake. She died suddenly just a year after I married, and now I make it in her memory—and because it's delicious!

- 1½ pounds (700 g) curd cheese
- ¾ cup (150 ml) sour cream
- 1 teaspoon corn flour
- 3 eggs
- ¼ pound (approximately 115 g) caster sugar (or to taste)
- 1 teaspoon lemon juice (or to taste)
- 7 ounces (200 g) crushed biscuit crumbs

- Preheat oven to 325°F.
- Grease cake tin (preferably 8½-inch, loose-bottomed), and line bottom with crushed biscuit crumbs.
- Separate egg whites from yolks and beat until stiff.
- Beat egg yolks, cheese, sugar, and soured cream until smooth.
- Stir in lemon juice and fold in corn flour and beaten egg whites.
- Bake in center of oven for about 1½ hours. When a toothpick comes out clean from the center of the cake, it is ready.
- Turn off oven and cool for about 20 minutes before removing from oven. (The cake will rise, and then sink.)
—Hilary Mandleberg

Hilary Mandleberg visits Moscow's Izmailovsky Park with her relatives during her Russian trip.

us and an even more welcoming man was playing "Kalinka" on a balalaika.

The welcome quickly froze, however, when Leonid, Rimma, Vova, and Dima tried to enter the restaurant with us. Immediately our way was barred and it was made clear, in no uncertain terms, that it was for tourists only.

There was nothing to do but walk across the hall to the truly authentic dining room where Russians were allowed to eat. The food may not have been quite so spectacular but there was no way that we would have eaten without the very people for whom we had made the journey in the first place.

Not everything in Moscow was bleak though. We spent a memorable evening at the Palace of Congresses in the Kremlin along with 6,000 others who had ventured out into the January freeze for a concert.

It was sad to say goodbye to the family in Moscow without knowing when or if we would ever

It was sad to say goodbye to the family in Moscow **without knowing when or if we would ever see them again.**

see them again, but the rest of the trip had its noteworthy moments. These included an 18-hour delay at Kiev airport on our way to Tbilisi, after which we all shuffled onto the tarmac at 2 a.m. The plane had finally arrived. My first shock was the state it was in: Was it held together with elastic bands and duct tape? My second shock was when the foreign tourists were ushered on the plane first, while Soviet citizens were left to wait for 20 minutes by the runway in temperatures that must have been minus 30°F.

Another highlight was the moment we entered the foyer of our Tbilisi hotel. No sooner had we walked in, bleary-eyed from our Kiev airport experience, than a man came up to me. I think I heard him say something about dollars, but I cannot be sure. Within seconds, a plain-clothes policeman appeared from nowhere, grabbed him, and frog-marched him to a van

Г. Александрія. Земская управа.

Aleksandria, Ukraine, in the early 19th century, when the author's grandparents left for London

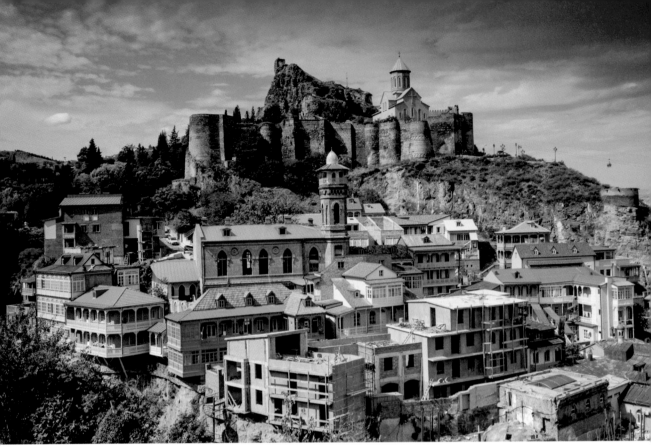

The author's travels take her to the historic Georgian capital, Tbilisi.

waiting outside. It was a far cry from my experience of British bobbies.

But I digress. We had met the family, but what next? I don't know whose strings Leonid pulled, but the following year, in the summer of 1977, we met him and Rimma at Victoria Station in London. Dima was not allowed to travel with them—he was the hostage, to ensure their return. Nor was Vova, who wasn't married yet and might have tried to defect.

Leonid and Rimma stayed with us for several weeks, meeting all the family, doing all the things that tourists in London do, and always looking nervously over their shoulders. Our mid-19th-century house had a number of old fireplaces. I'll always remember how Leonid jumped up from the dining table during one of our first meals at home together and went to look up the chimney for "bugs." ("You can never be too sure!")

Nor will I forget how he and Rimma read banned works by dissident Russian novelist Aleksandr Solzhenitsyn as they hid under the sheets.

THOSE SCARY TIMES are now, one hopes, a thing of the past, and all my family is happily settled in the United States. There were struggles to get there,

Hilary Mandleberg and her husband, Stephen, brave a Russian winter.

though. The Ginzburgs—Zoya, Misha, Vova, Rita, and their son, Daniel—were the first to leave. (Rosa, the lady whose address on a postcard started the whole chain of events, wanted to leave too, but died before permission was granted.)

As Soviet Jews, they all became refuseniks and were not allowed to emigrate. Their application to emigrate to Israel was refused in 1981 on the grounds that their "invitation" wasn't from a close enough relative. Misha lost his job but was eventually reinstated at less than half his salary. Rita was obliged to quit her violin studies at the conservatoire but subsequently returned, though she was fearful that because of the atmosphere there she might not be able to complete her course.

Eventually, in 1987, the Ginzburgs were able to leave and move to the United States. They were allowed to take just one suitcase each, and Rita had to leave her violin at the border. She hasn't played since.

Meanwhile the Loshakovs—Leonid, Rimma, Dima, and now also Dima's wife Irina—sat tight. They were fearful that because the Ginzburgs were trying to emigrate, it would make life difficult for them. Leonid and Rimma were also worried that, as teachers of Russian language and literature, they would be unable to find work in a new country. Plus they worried that if they applied for an exit visa, Dima would be expelled from medical school.

In 1989, of course, Gorbachev initiated perestroika and many of the old-style apparatchiks in government were replaced. Reform came slowly, but the

London's Victoria Station was the site of a second, Cold War family reunion, in 1977.

Loshakovs, who probably feared they would never see the Ginzburgs again, seized their chance. They emigrated from Baku and arrived in the United States in May 1991.

Here, they and the Ginzburgs have carved out a new American life, with four generations scattered between Brooklyn and elsewhere in the Northeast. There has been happiness and sadness—births, marriages, and deaths. Life goes on. I cannot say how pleased I am to have found everyone and to perhaps have played a small part in their lives.

HILARY MANDLEBERG is a London-based freelance writer, editor, and translator. Weather permitting, she earns her living from an office created from an old construction site hut at the end of her garden.

GET TO KNOW RUSSIA

• COOK
Russian émigré and award-winning food writer Anya Von Bremzen and her mother, Larisa, cook their way through Russian history in *Mastering the Art of Russian Cooking: A Memoir of Food and Longing* (Crown, 2013). Reminiscences about daily life in the Soviet Union make the recipes—such as *chanakhi,* Stalin's favorite Georgian lamb stew—even more appealing.

• VISIT
Known as Little Odessa, **Brooklyn's Brighton Beach neighborhood**—home mainly to Russian, Ukrainian, and Uzbek immigrants—is a microcosm of the former Soviet Union: Cyrillic signs; ubiquitous *ushankas* (fur earflap hats) in winter; street vendors hawking heated piroshki (sweet- or savory-filled turnovers); and Russian spoken—and understood—everywhere.

• TOUR
Even the extravagant, imperial Winter Palace in St. Petersburg's historic center is only big enough to display a sampling of the **State Hermitage Museum's** (*hermitagemuseum.org/html_En*) staggering three-million-piece collection. Among the Russian cultural artifacts are more than 1,000 folk costumes and women's headdresses and accessories, including earrings and necklaces.

Finding William

Hitchhiking through history

BY ANDREW EVANS

Beneath Scottish skies, the pinnacles of iconic Storr "Sanctuary" on the Isle of Skye guard the Sound of Raasay.

The best journeys happen when you have no money to travel, but somehow, you still get where you need to go. The bank called to say my account was in overdraft. I was penniless and procrastinating my thesis, plotting my escape from the library.

The next morning I moved out of my room and got a refund on my housing deposit. What the bank didn't keep, I cashed, folding the colored handful of British pounds into my pocket and filling a black canvas knapsack. I was homeless now, but I had options.

Hitchhiking was the cheapest way to go, so I stuck out my thumb and skipped north to Glasgow. Those were my people up there—the Glaswegians, or "Weegies," as they're known.

My last name—Evans—is most certainly Welsh, and I had already traveled to the little hamlet in South Wales from whence my father's family originated. My first name, Andrew, points back to the patron saint of Scotland and my mother's Scottish roots. I had never been, though I had dreamed of Scotland for as long as I could remember.

I had memorized that page in my world atlas and, as a child, I would trace over the impossible islands and busy coastline with my fingers, reading out the strange names of towns and cities. This is where we came from—this is the country we had left and forgotten.

MY FIRST DAY BACK IN THE MOTHERLAND was unglamorous. Glasgow was gray and dismal with steeples and spires that poked through the fog and church bells that rang out at odd times. It rained and rained for hours, and my shoes squished on the cobblestones as I trudged from one landmark to another.

I wandered the Gothic churchyards looking for any surnames that matched the three branches of my Scottish family tree—McAllister, Campbell, and McGregor. I found plenty of graves under each name, but the dates failed to match any of my own records. Was this my kin, lying six feet below the soggy ground near a city bus stop?

The mystery weighed on me, so that after an afternoon perusing museums and tourist gift shops, I began to color in the blanks of my family's past with folksy imagery—the misty backdrop of stained-glass cathedrals, the rebellious Rob Roy, and a friendly band of Brigadoon-like villagers wrapped in cheery tartan prancing to the bright echo of soul-stirring bagpipes.

My Disney illusion kept me searching for actual clues, and

The headstones of Glasgow's old churchyards bear surnames of author Andrew Evans's ancestors.

century of

I enlisted the help of a librarian, who found nothing on Scotland's national registry but failed to give up on me, sifting through all the church records prior to 1855. Together, we guessed at ages and came up with several false leads before switching to the 1841 census. Suddenly I was transported into the digitized spread of longhand-written sheets—a national profile of every individual in Scotland from more than 150 years ago.

Scrolling through the pages, I read through each of the carefully scripted ink names, until I saw it:

William, 7

I was staring at the handwritten name of my own great-great-great-grandfather, William Campbell McGregor. My heart soared, and I imagined the scene in my head—that early summer evening back in 1841, when the census takers knocked on a door of a stone house in Glasgow. Somewhere in that house stood a seven-year-old boy, perhaps clinging to his mother's skirt—and he was counted. I wondered if I look like him. To this day, my mother insists my dark, curly hair comes from the McGregors.

Like stage curtains flung apart, the past was opening up to me. From the census, I was able to confirm William's father's name, Alexander McGregor, and with more searching, I was able to track down a death record for him in 1872, along with his last home address in the nearby port of Greenock.

I rode the train to Greenock the next day, a detective with a lead. From Glasgow, the railroad followed the broad wash of the Clyde River that shone purple as it flowed westward toward the sea. The sun was shy, dissolving into clouds that dumped more and more rain on the stone city around me.

IF GLASGOW WAS GRAY AND MELANCHOLY, then Greenock was even grayer and sadder. The buildings were square and plain, and the streets were empty except for a few schoolboys who looked bored and angry.

I already knew a lot about my ancestors. Family members had written whole books documenting their histories. My great-great-great-grandfather William had come to Greenock as a boy and worked at the local rope factory to save money for his passage to America. He was only 20 when he sailed to New Orleans, then rode a Mississippi riverboat north to St. Louis before driving a team

The shores of Greenock mark the place where the American chapter of the author's family story begins.

of oxen across the Great Plains to join up with the Mormons in Utah.

In the town's museum I found a thick length of jute rope from William's period—a time when Greenock supplied the British Empire with fast new ships and when sugar flowed back across the Atlantic. William's family had lived on Greenock's Tobago Street, named after the sugar colony in the Caribbean. I found the address, though the red sandstone building was surely not the same one from more than a century ago—or was it?

Wandering through Greenock, I felt like a ghost, waltzing backward through time, imagining away the telephone wires and replacing the cars in the street with rolling carriages. My own ancestors had walked these same streets—and now I was here, floating upward to the cemetery.

The hill was steep and the rain fell hard, but I stomped through the black puddles and into the cemetery office with my wrinkled list of names from the library. Every plot was mapped and numbered,

and the kind lady behind the desk circled the spot where my family was buried.

It took me a while to find it—the light was falling, and this particular corner of the cemetery was touched by time and overgrown with thorns, thick oaks, and flowering fuchsia bushes. Crumbling headstones leaned this way and that, so that the statues slept standing up. Some graves had collapsed altogether—fallen memorials that melted into the vivid grass. But every stone marked a person's life, as did the unmarked plots in between.

I stopped at the numbered rectangle that was the final resting place of William's father, Alexander—my great-great-great-great-grandfather. The headstone was long gone, worn away by too many years and too much rain. I knelt down in the wet grass and felt the continuous drizzle on my head. This patch of ground was all that was left of my family—our final estate in Scotland. Generations and centuries of ancestors had thrived in the city and surrounding Highlands, but this grave was where it

The bonnie cliffs of the Isle of Skye

all came to an end—the last period in the last sentence of a long book.

I stayed at the grave a long while, soaked to the bone and weepy from the bittersweet moment of finding and losing family. Then I walked back down the hill and followed the empty road to the docks at the place where the Clyde meets the sea.

Back in 1854, the year William sailed, the port of Greenock was overflowing with tall-masted ships from around the world. Now the river was cold and bare, a sheet of steel beneath the soft mist. I stepped to the edge of the dock and stared at the rippling waves. Here, too, was my family's story— our bridge to the past. This was the spot where William had left Scotland, boarding a ship for the other side of the world. I wondered what he thought as the ship sailed away from his homeland. Was Alexander waving from the dock? Was it foggy back then, too?

> **"**
> I belonged to this land. I felt it intensely and **wanted to travel deeper into the mists of the unknown.**
> **"**

The mist had taken over, erasing the city, the sky, and the land, stranding me at the river's edge, and at the edge of time and place. I had come full circle, returned from America to this spot from which William left so long ago. I had connected the dots and seen my ancestors' lives and felt the heart swell of my own Scottish pride.

ALL GOOD TRAVEL IS A PATH to self-discovery, and to go somewhere new is to invite serious self-reflection and curiosity, leading to a stronger sense of who you are. Going to Scotland showed me that I belonged to this land. I felt it intensely and wanted to travel deeper into the mists of the unknown.

There was more to this country than an unmarked grave and an empty dock. Over the next few weeks, I traveled back to Glasgow and beyond, thumbing

The valley of Glencoe is the site of the infamous 1692 massacre of Clan Donald.

The author finds a "haunting and heavy beauty" in the bloody history–steeped Glencoe mountains.

rides in cars and trucks and, eventually, fishing boats, from one island to the next.

Hitchhiking up the west coast, I saw more sheep than people. There were times when I got stranded—in some lonely glen, or deep in the woods. One time, after hours walking alone on the road, I was rescued by the local school bus, where I listened to the children chatting in Gaelic about Harry Potter. Another time I hopped into the back of truck, atop a pile of fresh-cut lumber, and for a good 50 miles, I watched the ever changing sky of the Highlands.

With no money and no agenda, I simply followed my luck, finally arriving at the Isle of Skye. For endless days, I hiked in the mountains, 23 and carefree, sleeping in barns and sheds and spare beds. If ever I needed a bath, I braved the ice-cold waters of the nearest loch, happy for the sun if it was there.

I went back to school when my money ran out, but I was content. Gone was the cartoon version of my family history. After weeks of roaming Scotland,

I had a bagful of real memories and an unshakable love for this spot on the map.

It took me more than ten years to get back to Scotland, and this time, things were different. For starters, my bank wasn't calling me with bad news. Even better, I

Roaming the Isle of Skye: a Highland cow

had reservations at a hotel that served breakfast in bed. I had a rental car too, and I drove freely through some of the most staggering landscapes in Europe, remembering with each mile how very much I loved Scotland.

It was January and the tourists were few. Snow spotted the Highlands, and the mountains looked more brown than green, but the barren beauty of Scotland never let up, made even more resplendent by the shy sunbeams poking through the winter sky.

Long before Greenock, and long before Glasgow, the Campbells and McGregors lived here, in the western Highlands of Scotland. History is filled with their stories and not all of them are nice. In 1692, an army regiment lead by one Robert Campbell massacred 38 members of Clan Donald at Glencoe. Though centuries have passed, the adage "Never trust a Campbell" has survived, so that even now, at the pub in Glencoe, a brass sign states, "No Hawkers or Campbells."

Regardless of my family ties with the Campbells, I ate dinner at the pub, and the next day I drove through the impressive valley of Glencoe. The scenery was magnificent, with waterfalls pouring down from every mountain and a single whitewashed cottage punctuating the boundless landscape.

The Highlands offer a haunting and heavy beauty that wows me again and again. No traveler can ever escape the ghosts of the past and I felt it in Glencoe—a vast hole in the land where history echoes in the cry of the ravens overhead and in the tears of the flowing mountain streams.

Donning the family McGregor tartan kilt, Andrew Evans hikes Ben Nevis in the Scottish Highlands.

This was my Scotland, too. Once upon a time, my ancestors walked these same mountains. They lived and died in this glen and in the mountains beyond. These hills carried their memories long after they left, and to this day, I feel a sacred connection to this lovely, little, rainy country that gave me a name— and a story.

ANDREW EVANS is National Geographic's former "Digital Nomad." He is the author of four books, including guides to Ukraine and Iceland, and a contributor to several others including *100 Great Cities of the World*, *1,000 Places to See Before You Die*, and National Geographic's *Four Seasons of Travel*.

GET TO KNOW SCOTLAND

• EXPERIENCE
Traditional Highland games tick all the iconic Scottish boxes: bagpipes, tartan, kilts, clans, and feats of strength including tugs-of-war, caber tosses, and wrestling. Scotland's official games season is late May to mid-September, highlighted by the **Braemar Gathering** (*braemar gathering.org*) in Aberdeenshire, the royal family's favorite (they've missed only two in the past 35 years).

• TOUR
Six Scottish-focused galleries at Edinburgh's **National Museum of Scotland** (*nms .ac.uk/our_museums/national_ museum_of_scotland.aspx*) feature art and artifacts from the Paleolithic era to the present. Of particular interest to family genealogists: "Leaving Scotland," which examines why an estimated two million Scots emigrated during the 20th century.

• COOK
Few Scottish experiences test your mettle like preparing **haggis,** the national dish whose ingredients read like a Dickensian daily special: minced sheep, pig, or cow innards and stomach; hard fat; and oatmeal. If you're up to the challenge, chef Jennifer McLagan's *Odd Bits: How to Cook the Rest of the Animal* (Ten Speed Press, 2011) includes an easy-to-follow haggis recipe.

The sacred Greek Valley of the Temples in Agrigento,
the pride of Sicily, dates back to the sixth century B.C.

A Hunger for Family

Finding roots at the table

BY RENÉE RESTIVO

I have heard my grandfather's stories about the family farm by the small village of Castrofilippo all my life. "It's right down the block from the Valley of the Temples in Agrigento," he bragged, as if he had been there himself.

Over a decade ago, I made my first trip to that town in southern Sicily to meet my Italian relatives and see Agrigento's ancient Greek temples. My grandfather wasn't that far off. Castrofilippo is ten miles from Agrigento's ancient shrines. Fruit orchards and groves kissed by the sun surround our ancestral village of Castrofilippo, known as *il paese della cipolla,* the town of the onion. On Sicily's southern coast, the countryside is ripe with fig and almond trees. Today, my cousins still grow succulent *uva da tavola,* table grapes, and are known for the quality and variety of their sweet onions and garlics.

A sweet Sicilian smile

Before my journey, images of an island, both raucous and pastoral, fascinate me, and this mystery at the heart of the Mediterranean beckons as a waking daydream replays in my mind: Dusty sirocco winds blow in from North Africa, moving strings of mandarin orange–colored beads that hang from my aunt, *zia,* Maria's doorway. Family stories about this faraway land have always intrigued me and now feed my deep desire to unravel family mysteries.

Our family was separated in the beginning of the 20th century when my great-grandfather Calogero left his Sicilian farm for America. Throughout his life of 92 years, he sent his savings to Sicily to save the farm, but he never returned. The last years of Calogero's life were the first of mine; I cherish the photo of me sitting on his lap when I was two. I remember his calm presence, and I was in awe of him. He loved to have his wine by his side all the time. After his passing, his daughter, my great-aunt Sadie in Queens, kept in touch with the family in Castrofilippo, starting a tradition of letter writing between the Italian and American side of the family that has lasted well over a century.

When I told my grandfather, Salvatore, that I planned to go to Sicily, he typed three sentences in Italian on a page and sent them to our family in Castrofilippo: *"Dear aunt I am the granddaughter of Salvatore, I am here in Sicily, wanting to know about my family. My grandfather Salvatore, son of Calogero, asked me to come and see you. He says always that he would like to come and visit but it didn't happen yet and doesn't know when, but wishes you the best and sends his regards."* We sent the note a month before I departed.

It seemed impossible. Just three sentences mailed to a foreign address would lead to one of the most important moments in my life: meeting my family in Sicily.

Agrigento's Scala dei Turchi's cliffs line Lido Rossello.

I didn't receive a reply. "They'll never know who I am," I thought. Nervous but undeterred, I went anyway.

WHEN I ARRIVE AT the Grand Hotel Dei Templi in Agrigento, I learn that my cousin Lillo had called for Signora Restivo at least four times before I got there. As I step into my room, the phone rings. A guide at the hotel translates: "They'll be here to pick you up in five minutes!"

I dress in a mad rush and head to the lobby where two tan, handsome, 20-something men in denim jackets are walking in. One smokes a cigarette, gazing at me with curious eyes that ask if I am the one they're looking for.

Surely *that* cannot be them . . .

"Renée!" one shouts. He is my cousin Lillo, a farmer. Both brothers raise their eyebrows just the way I do. We hug, kiss, and I blurt, *"Non capisco*

> ❝
> Three sentences mailed to a foreign address would lead to **one of the most important moments in my life.**
> ❞

Italiano! I do not understand Italian!" I hand Lillo a note with Italian words that translate as "Please take me to the town square." "No problem!" Lillo says, escorting me to his sleek Alfa Romeo. I learn that those are the only two words he knows besides "Hello." After five minutes in his car I am sweaty and anxious. Lillo is speeding, smoking, and yelling to his brother and my aunt. Nervous, I look for my seat belt, but there is none. The smoke is getting to me, and my cousins here are louder than my cousins in Queens! Soon, dirt roads and cobblestone merge, and darkness is lifted by ancient streetlamps as we cruise into a village with whitewashed walls and streets so narrow I'm afraid the car will not squeeze through.

This is not a tourist town. Lace tablecloths and dresses hang above wrought-iron balconies; houses are spare, with weathered doors.

"Castrofilippo!" Lillo declares, pointing out the window at windy alleyways. The stone walls of Calogero's village glow in the moonlight. We drive past the town square, and I recognize, from family photographs and my grandfather's stories, the town monument, an obelisk. It's a war monument in the center of town with the name RESTIVO engraved on it. Then I spot the church where my great-great-grandparents married. We pass a statue of the Catholic saint Padre Pio, a bar, and a couple of pizzerias. Homes in the *centro storico* (historic center) were once stables that have now been restored; others are crumbling to the ground, abandoned by those who left Sicily for America.

The Alfa Romeo stops on a narrow street in the middle of town, as cousins emerge from doorways. Lillo leads me inside to meet Zia Maria and she pinches my cheeks, giving me a dozen firm kisses. More relatives trickle in. The men are all dressed in V-neck sweaters and ties with plaid or houndstooth caps.

My aunt tells me that Calogero's mother waited her entire life for her son to return to her. I realize that I am here in my great-grandfather's place, and my father's and grandfather's. They never returned, but now I am here.

My family's Sicilian dinner feast, in honor of my arrival, looks like a set for a Fellini film—only it's real! Dozens of aunts, uncles, cousins—Maria, Concetta, Carmela, Angela, Calogera, Ila, Angelo, Diego, Lillo, Luca, Giuseppe, Andrea, Giaocchino, and others—shepherd me to the family table, which extends through every room of the house, even the bedroom. Behind the table is a dressing room table and mirror, and a crucifix hangs above statues of saints next to vases with gold-painted handles, cameos, and religious scenes. The combination of food, family,

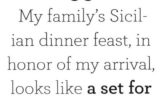

> " My family's Sicilian dinner feast, in honor of my arrival, looks like **a set for a Fellini film.** "

Temple of the Grecian gods, Tempio della Concordia, in Agrigento

The nectar of a nation: Sicilian olives

conversation and gestures. As everyone savors their pasta, they shout, *"Mangia,* Renée!*"* The vino is rustico and *intenso* and tastes the way I imagine my great-grandfather Calogero's homemade wine tasted. My father has fond memories of days watching him stomp grapes in Astoria when he was a child.

NOW I UNDERSTAND WHERE THE TRADITION of all those huge family gatherings in Queens comes from. When I was a child, my grandfather took me to Astoria each month, for the regular Restivo family gatherings. It was the family's tradition to meet, laugh, tell jokes, and share a great feast. At countless dinners in Astoria, my grandfather's sisters and Aunts Sadie and Millie welcomed us with hugs and good food. I remember my aunt's *struffoli* tempting

heirlooms, photos, and religious scenes reminds me of Aunt Sadie's house in Astoria.

Cugina (cousin) Carmela, a petite woman, wears a silk kerchief tied tight around her ears, covering her hair and exposing her gold earrings, its edge just above her alluring, dark eyes and dramatic eyebrows. She carries a bowl, at least two feet in diameter, filled with pasta, toward the table. Sicilian-size portions of ziti with *ragù* are piled on each plate. Hands on her hips, she orchestrates the meal and is the last one to sit down and eat. In her flowered apron she is authoritative, warm, and gentle. "Renée, *pasta Siciliano!*" she smiles, heaping some on my plate.

We say a prayer together, making the sign of the cross. Then Lillo sits next to me and sprinkles cheese onto my pasta. *"Pecorino Siciliano!"* he says. His gestures add emphasis when he speaks, and the entire family is enlivened by this trait.

Carmela is at the fire-burning stove, emptying more pasta into another enormous bowl, which she cradles in her arms. Soon, she comes by to give me a second helping. "Renée, *mangia!*" All the cousins around the table laugh. My aunts are dressed in black dresses, and like Carmela, some wear knotted scarves as head coverings. I point to my full stomach, while searching for the right Italian word in my dictionary. Zia Cetta's sweet, loving gestures, delicate profile, and petite stature remind me of my aunt Millie.

Between bites of sausage and roasted potatoes with rosemary, salad that tastes of the earth, artisan bread, and *vino rustico,* I get lost in a blur of

Connections

My aunt Sadie's handwritten honey ball recipe has been passed down to my cousin Margaret, who shared it with me. We make the sweets every Christmas at our family reunion in Queens.

HONEY BALLS

- 7 eggs
- 1½ to 2 pounds flour
- 1 teaspoon salt
- 1 cup sugar
- 3 teaspoon baking powder
- ½ stick butter
- 2 cups canola oil or Crisco
- 1 cup Italian honey
- 2 tablespoons fresh lemon juice

Combine all ingredients, except oil or Crisco, honey, and lemon juice. Knead well and put in a bowl. Shape into a ball. Roll out and cut into one-inch-wide, foot-long strips. Cut small pieces and roll out into nickel-size balls.

Heat oil or Crisco in heavy-bottomed pan until very hot. Cook pieces of dough and fry until golden brown. Drain on paper towels and place on a serving dish to form a pyramid. Heat honey in a saucepan, add lemon juice, and mix. Drizzle warm honey over the honey balls. You can also sprinkle with nonpareils, then serve!
— Renée Restivo

The bounty of Sicily includes olive tree groves.

me as I entered her home; her nickel-size fried balls of dough, drizzled with honey and sprinkled with nonpareils, were unforgettable.

After dinner, Lillo drives me to the Valley of the Temples to see the Greek ruins by moonlight. We whirl along winding roads and speed past the Temple of Concord, its elegant Doric columns illuminated by a sliver of the moon above the hills. Lillo calls me *amore*. He is irresistible and charming, as Sicilian men are known to be. There's a sense that we've known one another for years, even though we have just met. He teases me, and there is a kind of playfulness and kidding around when we are together.

When it's time to say good night, I say *"Buon giorno!"* to my family in my best Italian accent. Zia Cetta points to the starry sky, "No, Renée! *Buona sera!"* shaking her head. *"Buona sera!"* I repeat. Zia smiles and in a firm,

The author cooks up the Italian-style ziti recipe of her ancestors.

loving tone says, *"È la tua cultura.* It's your culture." She tells me I must learn Italian, and without a dictionary I understand. I hug her, making a promise to myself and to her that I will become fluent in the language of my family someday.

A few years later, I return to the farm, speaking enough Italian to understand Zia Cetta. In beginner's Italian, I ask Zia Cetta if I can cook with her. *"Possiamo cucinare insieme?"* I ask. She invites me into the rustic kitchen, and I learn to use ingredients just picked from the farm. Cooking side by side in her *cucina*, we are enveloped by mingled aromas of capers, olives, tomatoes, and sweet onions. Zia takes me by the hand and leads me to a small room hidden beside the kitchen—her *segreto* (secret). She reveals a room filled with herbs, garlic, and the most beautiful onions ever. *"Della nostra terra,"* she says smiling at me with her deep, dark eyes as she places bouquets of dried wild oregano in my arms, "from our land." We crush the leaves and sprinkle them into a pan of swordfish, and the scent of fresh herbs from the Sicilian farm fills the cucina. We stir sauces and make meatballs that I imagine are flavors my Sicilian grandmother Josephine once cooked.

"Per il nonno. For grandpa," Zia Cetta says, smiling at me as she stuffs oregano, garlic, and white onions in my bag. I leave the farm with a bottle of Lillo's Nero d'Avola wine from the family farm to bring to my grandfather in New Jersey, so that he can taste flavors of our ancestors.

YEAR AFTER YEAR, I RETURNED to Sicily to explore layers of culinary history and intense Mediterranean flavors. Eventually, I began working at a cooking school on the island and discovered a culinary world I never knew existed. In 2006, I left New York and moved to the baroque town of Noto, Sicily, just a few hours from Castrofilippo.

Today, I run a cooking school, Soul of Sicily, inspired by my many visits to the family's (now Lillo's) farm. I speak with ease to Zia Cetta in Italian, and am learning the Sicilian dialect of my cousins. Speaking the language has led to experiences and friendships and a life I could have never imagined. It also allows me to record my family's stories.

Thousands of miles away from where I was born in New Jersey, Italy renews my spirit and nourishes my soul. To me, this place, this land is a blessing. This *terra,* where so many of my ancestors lived

and farmed and have passed with time, remains a magnetic place, a compass for my soul, where I will always return.

When I am far from the farm and longing for it, I recall the words of a Sicilian man I met while traveling. When I told him how I first returned to Sicily—in the place of my great-grandfather Calogero—to see the farm, and began my quest in search of my roots in Sicilian food, he smiled at said: *"Ricordati che questa è sempre la tua terra.* Remember that this is always your land."

RENÉE RESTIVO owns Soul of Sicily in Noto, a town known for baroque architecture and pastries. She is writing a book about Sicily's culinary traditions and landscape.

The author, Renée Restivo, and her uncle Gioacchino with his prized onions from the family farm

GET TO KNOW SICILY

• CELEBRATE
Each May, San Diego's Little Italy neighborhood hosts the largest Sicilian-American festival in the United States. Launched in 1993 by Sicily native and local bakery owner Mario Cefalu, the **Festivale Siciliano** *(sicilianfesta.com)* is a colossal street party including music, dancing, grape stomping, kids' activities, and, of course, Sicilian eats.

• COOK
Discover the richness and diversity of Sicily's heritage through its food by staying and cooking at Case Vecchie, the Sicily home of the famous **Anna Tasca Lanza Sicilian Cooking School** *(anna tascalanza.com).* Or prepare the school's farm-to-table recipes in your own kitchen with **Coming Home to Sicily: Seasonal Harvests and Cooking From Case Vecchie** (Sterling Epicure, 2012).

• WATCH
Sicily's vanishing tradition of **Opera dei Pupi** (Sicilian puppet theater) dates back to the early 19th century and, according to UNESCO, is "the only example of an uninterrupted tradition of this kind of theatre." Learn about the art of puppetry in **Rehearsal for a Sicilian Tragedy,** the 2009 documentary based on actor John Turturro's journey to his maternal homeland.

Sky lanterns illuminate the night in Taipei, Taiwan.

The Eighth Sister

A young American woman is embraced by the Chinese family she never knew.

BY MEI-LING HOPGOOD

It is my second night in Taiwan and my sisters take me to Shilin, one of most famous night markets in Taipei, a place that they have known for much of their lives, a place that could not seem more exotic to me.

I'm suddenly surrounded by thousands of Taiwanese and Chinese, who fill the labyrinth of alleys, stalls, and shops, feasting, spending, and bargaining for the best prices. Oyster omelets sizzle in grease, squid grills on sticks, and catfish boils in herbal broth. The night sky is ablaze with signs scrawling blue, green, and red Chinese characters. Chinese pop music blasts from open storefronts. I'm dizzy from the buzz of Mandarin and Taiwanese, languages I don't understand apart from a few random words: good, eat, want.

It feels strange to be among so many people with hair and eyes as dark as mine. I'm acutely aware that I am *laowei*, a foreigner.

This is my first return to the land where I was born. I left Taiwan when I was eight months old, to be adopted and raised by a family in Michigan. Nothing I knew in the suburbs of Detroit was like this. Taipei, a city of 2.7 million people, is a gleaming metropolis of skyscrapers, temples, and traffic jams. Shilin market, located near the Keelung River in central Taipei, feels like its gritty and pungent heart.

Fortunately, my *jiamei*, my birth sisters, are guiding me through the jungle of people. They know this place, the taste of special spare ribs, the smell of cuttlefish, the songs of An-Mei, as I would know Taco Bell, movie popcorn, and Bon Jovi. My sisters coax me forward, feeding me quail eggs and fruit on ice. They insist on treating me to anything I might want and don't quite want. One of them finds some earrings, small silver dolphins.

"Pretty!" She exclaims.

"*Buyao, xiexie,*" I insist. I don't want it, thank you. I'm flattered, but I don't want them to spend their money on me. In my suddenly fragmented English I stammer, "Too much!"

She ignores my pleas. My other sisters gleefully join in to bargain for the best price, shouting, waving their hands in the air. The deal is struck, and the small package thrust into my hands. My sisters want me to feel at home.

Taipei's Shilin night market abounds with food and goods.

BEFORE THIS FIRST VISIT TO TAIWAN, I didn't have much interest in going back. I was an American kid: class president, pompon girl, fan of french fries and chocolate ice cream. My Caucasian parents hoped that my Korean brothers and I would embrace our "home culture." They tried to enroll us in Korean and Chinese school, took us to diverse restaurants and festivals, and hired Asian-American babysitters. But I wanted little to do with anything Made in Taiwan.

The skyline of a city that dazzles, Taipei

Then, shortly after I graduated from college, I was reunited with the nun who arranged my adoption, and she put me in touch with my birth family. Immediately after we reached out, my mailbox, answering machine, and email filled with pleas to return to Taiwan. I learned I had two living parents, six sisters in Taiwan, another who was adopted by a family in Switzerland, an adopted brother, plus a gaggle of aunts, uncles, brothers-in-law, and nieces and nephews. And the lot of them set out to convincing me to return.

Giving you up devastated us, my family told me in their letters and emails. *Please come back.*

I was cautious at first, unbelieving and unsure of whether I was ready to uncork my past. The pull began sometime when my sisters started to describe the foods they like to eat (beef noodles, stinky tofu, chicken feet) and the interests they had (reading, singing karaoke, cooking). They sent me emails that made me laugh and photographs that made me curious. I found myself studying their faces, in pictures of weddings, of family vacations and high school graduations. I studied the slant of their eyes and the curve of their lips to see who looked most like me.

It became clear that the idea I'd grown up with—that I had been lucky to leave Taiwan and this "poor" family—was more complicated than I had believed. They told me that after my father made money from selling land, the family thrived and moved into the middle class. My sisters went from picking vegetables in the field to attending universities. Some were married and had children. They seemed close.

I was cautious at first, unbelieving and **unsure of whether I was ready to uncork my past.**

I began to realize that I had, indeed, missed something. I was intrigued, and finally accepted their invitation to return.

I tried not to expect—to distance myself, view the trip as a tourist or a journalist. Expecting too much, I reasoned, could lead to heartbreak. At the same time I wanted to prepare. I learned some Chinese words and phrases from a friend. I rehearsed the things I thought I was supposed to say as well as the things I wanted to say. I could manage "I love you" and "I'm full." I could order a drink and say thank you. I bought gifts and read travel guides. In 1997, at age 23, I boarded a flight as ready as I'd ever be.

WE ARRIVE AT THE AIRPORT IN TAIPEI. I'm with the nun who arranged my adoption, standing at the luggage claim, a wreck from the 24-hour journey.

A crowd of Chinese greets arriving passengers with waving signs and emotional shouts. I step forward and spot my name on a sign: "Mei-Ling."

A dozen family members surround me. A lei is thrown around my neck and my sisters practically push my parents forward. Suddenly the arms of my Chinese mother and father are around me. Tears spring to my eyes, and an enormous knot fills in my throat.

"*Nihao.* Hello," I gulp in my infantile Mandarin. My parents quickly turn away, wiping the tears

Fresh fruit bounty at Shilin night market

from their eyes. I am surprised to feel yearning and remorse for these people I never expected or even wanted to meet.

But the hurricane that is my family does not allow time for lingering in emotion. In rapid succession, my relatives introduce themselves. *I am your sister. This is my son. I am your uncle. I am your brother-in-law.* We take dozens of pictures in the airport lobby, pile into cars, and drive into Taipei.

For a week, the family parades me around Taiwan. They feed me elaborate dinners, stuffing food into my rice bowl and correcting the way I hold chopsticks. We examine jade tablets from the late Neolithic age and sip steaming jasmine tea in mountain teahouses. They give me gifts, and constantly take pictures and movies. Most of the time, I like the attention, but sometimes I recoil. I feel a bit of a spectacle: *Look, the daughter we gave up has come back.* The fact that my parents sent me away embarrasses my sisters deeply, I learn later, but the girls put on a happy face for me.

One day, my parents stay in to rest, and my sisters and I set out to lose ourselves in the city. We drink cans of Taiwan Beer, and take the train to Jiantan Station, in central Taiwan.

Along Wenlin and Dadong Roads, my sisters and I dodge the women selling neon T-shirts illegally from a rack in the middle of the street. Boys nose their mopeds through the fray. Young girls with their hair dyed blond and pink try on sunglasses.

Connections

One of the first things my birth father told me when I arrived in Taiwan was that he wanted to buy my wedding jewelry (never mind that I had no plans to be married anytime soon). My sisters loaded me on the back of a moped and drove me to a block full of gold stores.

Most Taiwanese insist on buying only 24K gold because it is the best quality. Because I thought it looked gaudy and didn't want my parents to spend so much money on me, I refused to choose anything. Instead, my sisters picked a delicate bracelet engraved with Chinese zodiac signs, a ring, and a charm with my sign, the Ox. —Mei-Ling Hopgood

Monument to another time: Taipei's Chiang Kai-shek Memorial Hall

I am wide-eyed, overwhelmed. I observe my sisters as they flitter back and forth, buying things. My style feels acutely American: shorts, long polyester skirt, jeans, always color coordinated. Theirs is more feminine and often chaotic: An older sister wears a flowing summer dress, with her husband's oversize warm-up jacket over her shoulders. A younger sister dons a tight orange shirt and short skirt. Two are wearing high-heeled sandals and their toenails are painted. I'd always hated the sight of my feet; I have a split nail on my smallest toes. But my sisters have shown me, with glee, that they all have split nails too. Now I want to wear sandals. I see potential beauty and confidence in myself, in spots that once embarrassed me: my forehead, my legs, and even my feet.

A woman motions to me. "*Xiaojie!* Miss!" I gather she wants me to buy something. I shake my head. *I don't know what you are saying,* I try to tell her.

She keeps pushing. I feel a hand slip into mine. My younger sister leads me away. The sensation of our fingers intertwining jolts my body. Women often hold hands here, my sisters explain. This intimacy feels both strange and comforting, and I let her lead me away.

I succumb to this closeness, to the smell of fried dough, to the screaming singsong of women peddling knockoff clothing. There are many more of these foreign yet familiar moments as the week unfurls. I ride behind my younger sister on her moped, squinting as her long hair flies in my face, wincing as she dodges cars in the gnarled gridlock of Taipei while I cling to her waist. My sisters and I squeeze into a karaoke room and sing "Like a Virgin."

THE FAMILY TAKES ME TO TAITUNG, the city where I was born about 150 miles south of Taipei, to the

The author, Mei-Ling Hopgood, visits still undeveloped Taitung, Taiwan, where she was born.

house where my sisters grew up. Taitung is one of the last rural areas in this hyperdeveloped, heavily populated island. I was born in a Catholic hospital there in 1973. More than anything, my traditional father wanted a boy, to carry on his name and bloodline. So my parents kept having children, despite their poverty. When I was born, my birth parents were already struggling to feed five daughters. At the hospital they met a nun from Metro Detroit who knew my American parents. A match was made. I stayed in the hospital for the several months it took to complete the adoption.

Some years later, my father gradually built a three-story concrete home on the edge of a field in Taitung. I'm amazed at how big it looks. My father and sisters call me upstairs and I climb two flights. There, I stand before the gilded, painted wooden alter, black-and-white photos of my father's parents, and the Buddhist deities that watch over this place. My father and sisters teach me how I'm to honor my ancestors, *baibai*. I hold three incense sticks into the flame of a lighter, stand before the shrine, and wave the incense up and down, three times. I turn to the pictures of my grandparents and do the same. The acrid, sweet smell burns the inside of my nose.

I'd never wanted to visit Taiwan or my biological family before, but here I am, feeling as if I never want to leave, magically assimilating to a place and people I'd never known.

I feel lucky to be given this moment. I also begin to feel for the first time the sense of loss that many

Mei-Ling Hopgood (middle) with two of her sisters on her first visit to Taiwan, in 1997

people always had expected that I should feel as an adoptee. "Don't you want to go back?" they'd ask me. Many people never understood that I was not born with a sense of Taiwan as my homeland. The United States and my midwestern family were my world. Romantics might say you can miss something you never knew existed, but I never did.

Until now. Until I meet my sisters, *wode jiamei*. They infuse me with their memories, and I try to make their history my own. I feel comfort slurping their favorite *niu rou mian,* beef noodle soup. I pray to our ancestors. I let Taiwan absorb me. I'm a sign promising the best price, a carp swimming in a tank, a dumpling sweltering in soup. The neon characters hovering above Shilin leave a brilliant stamp in my mind.

Later, I'll look back and wonder if this intense sense of belonging was a dream, an illusion of desire. I will visit Taiwan several times in the years that follow. I'll find my birth father's desire for a son and my mother's passivity almost intolerable at times, because of the pain and sadness they brought my sisters. The secrets will distort my perception of the culture. I'll stand in alleys of Shilin, on other humid and hopping nights, and think that the smell of dried squid

> Romantics might say you can miss something you never knew existed, but **I never did. Until now.**

is overpowering, the price of jeans too expensive, my family history too complicated. My feelings about the place will become enmeshed with my feelings about my family, a conflicting mixture of grief and anger, admiration and love.

But this first trip back to Taiwan is emotional and not yet complicated. My family and I laugh over my errors in Chinese, and we will cry about saying goodbye. On the day that I depart, my sisters rush me to the airport. The very late hour and promises of return keep us from feeling too sad. I hurry through immigration and toward the gate. I try to keep things light, blowing kisses at them dramatically through the thick glass that separates us. Another flight carries me away from Chiang Kai-shek Airport, Taipei, and Taiwan. My suitcases are heavy with gifts of teapots and pineapple cakes, and my imagination full of questions about the fate and the home that might have been mine.

MEI-LING HOPGOOD is a journalist and author of *Lucky Girl* and *How Eskimos Keep Their Babies Warm.* She is an associate professor at Northwestern University's Medill School of Journalism.

GET TO KNOW TAIWAN

• COOK
Whether spooned over hot rice *(lurou fan),* stuffed inside a steamed bun *(gua bao),* or sucked straight off a sparerib, slightly sweet/slightly salty braised pork is the common ancestor of many Taiwanese street food favorites. Learn the art of braising pork in Amy Wu's cookbook-style memoir **What's for Dinner, Mama?** (CreateSpace Independent Publishing Platform, 2014).

• CELEBRATE
Enjoy a rich cultural and culinary menu at **TaiwanFest** *(taiwanfest .ca),* staged in late summer in both Toronto and Vancouver. The event ranges from top Taiwanese musical acts and dance troupes to culinary demonstrations and contemporary Taiwanese art shows.

• VISIT
Plan a trip to Taiwan around China's biggest holiday, the two-week Chinese New Year, celebrated late January to early February. Taipei City holds its **Pingxi Sky Lantern Festival** *(pingxiskylantern.tw/en),* when thousands of flickering, floating lanterns are released each year, beginning on the evening of the first new moon of the Lunar New Year and ending 15 days later.

The luminous nightglow the Tanzania savannah

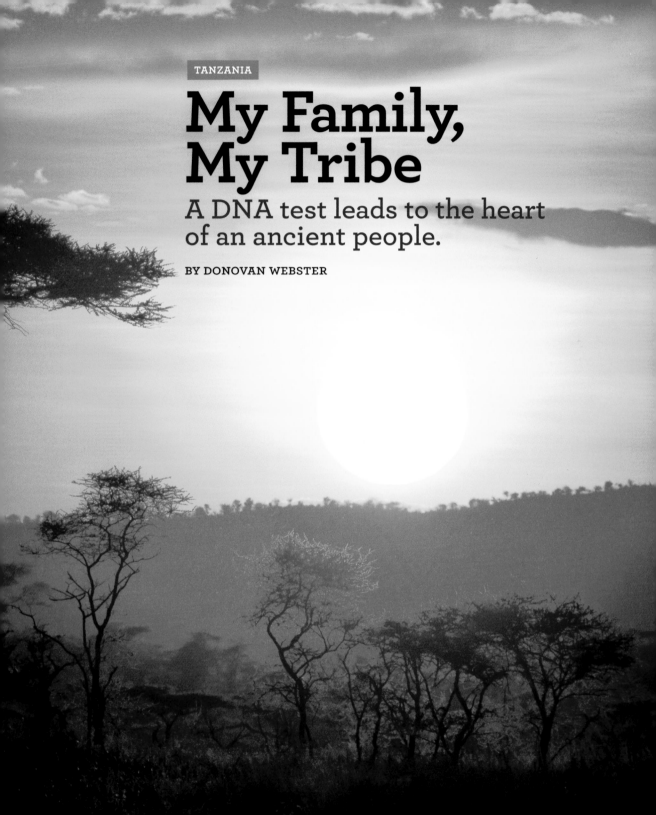

My Family, My Tribe

A DNA test leads to the heart of an ancient people.

BY DONOVAN WEBSTER

Julius Indaay !Hun/!Un/!ume, a long-lost cousin of mine, and I are stalking the savannah of Tanzania's Great Rift Valley. It's a June morning. The blue sky is tufted with puffy white clouds. The earth is powdery gray and sandy brown. A few miles to our north is the hanging cliff of the Ngorongoro Crater, which has walls that look like a broken

brown molar. Closer to us, there are scrubby acacia trees and plants with green leaves silted with ashen dust.

But Julius, chief of the Hadzabe people, and I aren't here to sightsee. We're hunting with bows and arrows. We're not walking linearly. When the wind shifts, we move downwind. It is silent.

A migratory embrace near the Serengeti, Tanzania

"As I understand it, this place became crowded a long time ago, food became scarce, and not everyone could stay," he says, in a language that is all clicks and pops and is interpreted through a friend of ours, Robert. "Many of our original people, many in our original family, moved away. But now you have come back. We are pleased to have you come."

Then from somewhere to our left, Julius's pack of four dogs tears away to a dry riverbed. He pauses to listen. In a few seconds, as he discerns where the dogs are moving, he selects a couple of arrows from his passel and begins running a fast sprint through the bushes and brambles. Despite being a football wide receiver in college, I cannot keep up.

In another few seconds, the pursued runs out. It turns out to be a shaggy, dusty-brown warthog weighing maybe 65 pounds that comes into sight. Its eyes are small and black and bright with terror. In a single, fluid motion that takes about a second, Julius halts his sprint, nocks an arrow, lifts his bow, takes aim, and fires.

With a resigned grunt, the animal takes the arrow on its left side, just behind the front shoulder blade. It falls into the dirt and quickly dies, bleeding out into the sandy soil. Its body flexes and contracts. Death takes less than a minute.

I begin to gut and clean the warthog with the other men in our group, as Julius goes back to retrieve the rest of his armor. Fifteen minutes of butchering passes before it has been quartered and gutted. We keep out one side of the rib cage and

The family of man: The author, Donovan Webster, joins a group of Hadzabe tribespeople on an outing.

the left foreleg for ourselves. The men place the rest of the hog—its ears, snout, legs, back fat, entrails—atop a small travois made of two sticks cobbled together with vines.

Then one man makes a circular concavity in the dust. From his shoulder bag, he extracts a narrow, four-inch-long length of pale softwood with sockets bored into its top. He gathers up some tinder and puts it in one of the wooden length's larger sockets. He pulls a length of straight cane from his collection of arrows and places one end of it into the socket with the tinder. He begins to spin the cane, higher up its length, between the palms of his hands.

The man is making fire.

In less than a minute, the first whiffs of pale smoke lift from the socket. The other men add more tinder as the man with the cane begins blowing lightly on the smoking wooden piece. It looks like he's kissing it. The tinder poofs into flame.

Once we have a good fire going, the tribesmen toss the warthog's left foreleg and the side of ribs directly onto the fire. In about 15 minutes, everyone uses their hands to scrape off and eat the cooked meat with their fingers. It's good, if strong tasting, with hints of ammonia and nuts.

When we're done eating, a few of the men gather up the travois loaded with the rest of the meat and cleaned insides to take back to the elderly and the women and children back at the camp.

Ah, the joys of sharing a meal with family.

I WAS INTRODUCED TO JULIUS through the Geographic Project at National Geographic and its director, Spencer Wells. He's a population geneticist with a Harvard PhD, and a cool guy. What he figured out, along with colleagues, was that samples of DNA—taken by swabs of people's mouths and examined by computational models—can get a pretty true track of your deep history.

As it happens, DNA only wants to make more DNA. Inside of each of us—alongside 85 million brain cells and six miles of nerves—is enough DNA to stretch to the moon and back, at least 30 times. Made of only four different nucleotide bundles—sort of like positive and negative electricity—DNA is the blueprint for our life.

Sometimes, as the DNA is making more of itself, it makes a typographical error. And as people continue to breed, those specific typos stay in the genetic system, creating little regional cores that have the same DNA typos—with starburst lines leading out from the central core—meaning, thereby, the people who own it share a common ancestor. The trick, which the Genographic Project has done, is to get a large enough set of DNA samples to see how DNA has migrated around the globe. The sample size, as well as samples taken from Dr. Wells before he went to work there, is now more than half a million.

> ❝
> I had the same DNA, with the same typos in it, **that left Africa 60 million years ago.**
> ❞

For Julius and me, we have several different and specific typos in our DNA, R1B (m343), actually, about 30 of them in common, meaning we have at least one common ancestor, if not a lot more.

I'D ALWAYS THOUGHT I was an old-line American: my family first arriving here in North America in the 1620s and '30s. One of them was a Scottish slaver who ended up owning the farm that became Yonkers, New York. Another was a pillar of John Winthrop's Massachusetts Bay Colony.

But when Dr. Wells told me I had the same DNA, with the same typos in it, that left Africa 60 million years ago, and were also the same as Lebanese Arabs in the Bekaa Valley, Tajiks in Uzbekistan, and Basque Spaniards, I was flabbergasted. There was only one way to have the specific DNA that I had, and that was to be related to these different varieties of people.

A Hadzabe man hunts the way of his—and the author's—ancient ancestors.

Tanzania's baobab trees are the lifeblood of the Hadzabe diet.

He went on to tell me that, most likely, as ice from the last ice age retreated, the majority of my deep ancestors followed the melting ice north, foraging and ending up in Britain.

I walked out of his office at National Geographic headquarters in Washington, D.C., stunned.

BECAUSE I ARRIVED a few months after the "rainy season," most days with the Hadzabe started with fruits and berries. And also honey, gathered from a hive inside a hollow baobab tree nearby, plus tubers dug up with sharp sticks, not all that different than the potatoes Americans eat when they go to Western Sizzlin'.

Because I'm not part of the 1,200-person tribe, I am not allowed to live among them. But every day, I walk the roughly 300 yards to their camp and I eat with them. I never go hungry. Supplementing the diet of fruits and berries—and limited meat—is a dry paste the Hadzabe make from the fruit of the baobab tree. In hunter-gatherer Africa, baobab fruit hangs

around the daily diet the way high-fructose corn syrup does at an American convenience store, in soft drinks and Twinkies and energy bars.

Connections

Despite all the memories and insights I gained on my trip to Tanzania, my most treasured thing is the necklace that I traded with my distant relative, Julius. It hangs from a knob on the glass-fronted cabinet of our Charlottesville, Virginia, kitchen that holds our dishes and glasses. Hardly a day goes by when I don't think of Julius and his Hadzabe tribe and my time with them, as I'm setting the table for dinner.
—Donovan Webster

Hadzabe women make their
own clothing and jewelry.

Home on the Tanzania range for a lioness and her cub

for meat again. Just after sunrise, we nab an eland, something like a large deer. Meat for a week!

We dress it and go back to camp. After a quick and early lunch, the woman work with hollowed reeds on strings and grains poked through with small, sharpened points. They're making necklaces and bracelets. The men sit around the fire, relaxing and taunting. The children play tag.

Later that afternoon, as the women go out for more tubers and berries and baobab fruits, Julius says, "Come with me."

We get up and begin walking across the savannah, with the hanging Ngorongoro Crater up the mountain in the distance. As we walk, he begins pointing out medicinal plants along the way. He stops and touches the leaves of small shrub. "This one is called *mokei* or *kanni quea*," he explains, translated by Robert. "We crush it up and make tea with it, to treat coughs." A few steps farther along, he stops at another bush. "This is *madazgue*. If a mother is breast-feeding, it helps to create milk for the baby." In another four or five steps Julius grabs a spindly plant. "This is *undepicala*. Also called *congo lok*. This is a very special plant. It gives life in many ways. Its stems make good arrow shafts and pieces for jewelry, as they grow very straight. The roots also provide snakebite treatment. One of the men in my family, the one called Ma Yoyo, was bitten by a puff adder last year. It was the roots of this plant that saved his life." We take a few more steps and Julius points out another shrub. "This is *mugalombea*. If you want to make a daughter with your wife, you cook the leaves of this plant into a soup. You make soup with this, you get a daughter." As we walk, he shows me many more plants for assistance and maladies.

"And all of these work reliably?" I ask.

"Oh, yes," Julius says. "We have hosted Western doctors and researchers. And yes, they were

Baobab fruit goes into everything. Crushed between flat stones and mixed with water and berry juice, it becomes a nutritious paste that's astonishingly rich in antioxidants, potassium, and phosphorous. It is said to contain six times as much vitamin C as a similarly sized orange, and twice the calcium of a standard, eight-ounce glass of milk. A "flavor mimic," not unlike a more liquid version of tofu, baobab paste takes on the taste of whatever it's mixed with. And after you eat it, you don't feel bloated or weighed down. (The U.S. Food and Drug Administration has approved baobab fruit to go into things like candy bars.)

In my notebook I write: "Everyone eats a lot, and when they begin to run out, the women add more crushed baobab fruit and water, until there is plenty again. The amount of food here seems endless."

The Hadzabe are an incredibly long-lived tribe. Genetic testing indicates they go back more than 100,000 years and are one of the primary roots of the human tree. They also have the same—or longer—life expectancy as Americans.

>
> **The Hadzabe . . . go back more than 100,000 years** and are one of the primary roots of the human tree.

Thousand-year-old baobab trees tower over giraffes on the Tanzanian plains.

surprised too. But my ancestors figured this out a long time ago and have passed it along." Ahead of us now is a towering baobab tree. "See the bees up in the top," Julius says, pointing at the air clouded with honeybees and the hive up in the tall branches. The honey oozing out makes the trunk look slick and shiny. "We harvest the honey each month," Julius says. "Usually we get about 80 liters of honey a year." Up the trunk's side, two-inch-diameter sticks have been jammed into the trunk at intervals of about 18 inches each. It's the ladder to the hive.

"But this is what I want to show you," he says. We walk around to the far side of the tree, where a huge,

We walk around to the far side of the tree, where **a huge, cave-like hole has been cut into the hollow trunk.**

cave-like hole has been cut into the hollow trunk. "This is where the babies get born," he says. "When a mother is getting ready to have her baby, she comes here and climbs in and waits. Her mother and sisters come too." The hole and cave inside is large enough to hold several sleeping people. "This is where we have always been born, for thousands of years. Where grandfathers of grandfathers of grandfathers have been born. This is where I was born."

"Am I a descendant of this tree?" I ask.

"Of course," Julius says, a look of consternation on his face. "We all come from this tree."

The tree—and others like it—represents much of mankind's heritage.

ON THE LAST NIGHT with the Hadzabe, I am sitting in a chair in my camp, watching the day become night, when Julius arrives. He sits in a chair opposite me. I am drinking a Kilimanjaro Lager from a now ice-free cooler. Julius asks, "Can I have one? I have been to the towns. I like beer."

"I also have bottled water and Orange Fanta, if you would like," I say.

"No, please, a beer."

I get Julius one from the cooler, opening it with my Swiss Army knife. Robert excuses himself for a minute, saying he can come back if we need translation, while Julius nods a thank you for the beer. Then, as I set the knife down on the table between us, Julius lifts his left eyebrow at me and points at the knife.

"Sure," I tell him by lifting the open palms of my hands into the air. He picks it up and begins playing with it—all of its little tools. He pulls one of his necklaces off of his shoulders, over his head, and makes a sort of swapping motion with his hands. I nod in the affirmative, and he hands me the necklace and takes the knife.

Then we sit in the chairs and watch the night gently arrive as we drink our beer. We don't really need a translator anymore.

Donovan Webster's "long-lost cousin" Julius

DONOVAN WEBSTER writes for *National Geographic, Vanity Fair, Garden & Gun, The New Yorker,* and a host of other publications. He is also editor at large for the *Virginia Quarterly Review (VQR)*, an instructor of media studies at the University of Virginia, a husband, and a father to two teenagers.

LEARN MORE ABOUT TANZANIA AND YOUR ANCIENT ROOTS

• COOK

In Tanzania and other Kiswahili-speaking countries, *ugali* is the staff of life. A dense, cornmeal base with the consistency of putty, ugali is often tightly packed into a ball and used to scoop up stews. Ugali is among the 204 recipes in New York City restaurateur Marcus Samuelsson's cookbook *The Soul of a New Cuisine: A Discovery of the Foods and Flavors of Africa* (Houghton Mifflin Harcourt, 2006).

• LEARN

Regardless of race, nationality, or religion, all family trees are rooted firmly in the cradle of humankind, the East African Rift Valley. *The Human Family Tree* (2009) is a National Geographic Channel documentary narrated by Kevin Bacon and available on DVD that chronicles the Genographic Project and traces the origins and follows the migratory footsteps of our common ancestors *(shop .nationalgeographic.com)*.

• TOUR

More than six million years of human history is contained within the walls of the **Anne and Bernard Spitzer Hall of Human Origins** at New York's **American Museum of Natural History** *(amnh.org)*. Pairing fossils with DNA research, the hall's exhibits—including films, interactive media, and ancient artifacts—present the history of human evolution and the direction our race may be heading.

A precarious and misty perch along Northern Ireland's windswept North Antrim coast

Three Generations, One Distant Family History

A mother takes her family, young and old, to the foreign landscapes of their ancestors.

BY LIZ BEATTY

A

faint, throaty "cuhh" marks each slumbering inhalation, like a slow, breathy metronome. "That's amazing," marvels my son, Mack, in 11-year-old wonder, gazing about ten inches from the open mouth of his grandmother. Despite the crush of passengers settling in for our flight to Dublin, my 85-year-old mom has fallen deeply,

blissfully asleep in the few minutes since we've taken our seats.

"How are we going to do this?" sighs my husband Tim, bag in hand and peering into the already packed overhead bin. I was just thinking that, but not about our luggage.

No sugar coating. Transporting five people with birthdates spanning seven decades across the Atlantic, then squeezing them into a midsize hatchback to drive 400 miles of remote Irish coastline on some ancestry scavenger hunt—well, it's one big, messy ordeal.

Still, if there's such a thing as shared genetic memory, the idea of our three generations summoning it together just seemed important. And with every sip of my unchilled airline Chardonnay, I'm feeling more hopeful that it really is.

WE FIND THE EMERALD PASTURES of great-great-grandfather's farm an hour and a half northwest of Dublin, just "beyond the pale" in medieval Irish terms, near the rural market town of Cootehill in County Cavan, Ulster. Our road trip begins here, back home, in a sense. We are bound for northerly shorelines of this olden province, composed of Northern Ireland plus three counties of the Irish Republic—a region at times riven by religion, but forever fused by deep roots in ancient Ireland.

Standing at the farm gate, I picture William, Sr., and his wife Frances, my great-great-grandparents, setting off with their young family, bound for timber reaches in far-off northern Canada in 1835, ten years before the start of the Irish potato famine. I knew coming here would feel this way, as if we are their emissaries, making the return journey that they knew they never would.

With their 85-year-old grandmother, Mack and his older brother, James, 18, pick small cut stones from the ruins of a well, the last vestige of our Beatty homestead. Mom is humming "Irish Eyes" as the three huddle from a steady drizzle under her red drugstore umbrella. We clutch the stones, warming them in our hands, as if they'll divulge the sense of our ancestors that we've traveled so far to know. What steeled their resolve to leave? What here made them who they were, who we are? The answers, we hope, are on the road ahead.

A night on the Dublin town

Sheep-dotted cliffs of Ireland's Slieve League add to the "primal vibe" of the Beatty family's outing.

"THE BEST STUFF I LEARN here comes from the pub," Mack tells the Mullen's Lounge barkeep between sips of ginger ale. An odd revelation from an 11-year-old, but true. Sitting on the next stool, a wizened regular of this Cootehill pub directs us to two grave diggers in neighboring Scotshouse—our new lead on local Beattys.

Ten miles west, we find the pair at their place of work, and with shovels in hand they direct us to Dermot Beatty, who reportedly sips his first pint every day at about this time, 4:45 p.m., at Connolly's Wines and Spirits just yards down the street. That's where we find him.

"You must be Dermot," my mother says. His ruddy, 40-something face blanches somewhat as a five-foot octogenarian sidles up to his stool at the otherwise empty bar. Emboldened by our mission, Mom soon has Dermot corroborating our research. He confirms that our people arrived in this area in about 1609 via the Scottish Protestant "plantation," the beginning of a raw chapter in Ireland's conflicted Protestant-Catholic, Anglo-Irish history. Dermot adds that precisely 101 Beattys were "planted" here around Cavan to work and live off meager tracts of much larger estates. The forces of King James I of

Connections

I only recently learned the extraordinary story of my grandfather's second cousin, Sir Edward Wentworth Beatty (at right). Among his accomplishments, he led Canadian Pacific Railway, a global transportation empire. He built Toronto Fairmont Royal York Hotel, once the tallest structure in the British Empire. He spearheaded sweeping immigration strategies for Canada's West. He was chancellor of Montreal's McGill University. He directed shipping of Allied troops and supplies in World War II. He started CP Air. He was knighted and befriended by royals, including Edward, the Prince of Wales, at left. Still, most remarkable to me, Edward had the opportunity to do all this because of the courage and industry of my great-great-grandfather, William, once a tenant farmer born in County Cavan, Ulster. —Liz Beatty

England killed off others of our horse-thieving clan along the Scottish borders.

I'm weirdly proud of these underclass roots in an era when native Gael chieftains lost control of their land to Protestant nobles loyal to the British throne. Eventually, both the titled and we lowest of Scottish "planters" became known as Scots Irish or Ulster Scots.

It felt odd too, at first, that these southern Irish counties would still identify so strongly with their archaic northern roots, over 90 years after the partitioning of British-controlled Northern Ireland from the south. But then I think of the centuries of tumult that has galvanized this ancient northern province—warring tribes, Irish kings, British overlords, Scottish colonists, the English persecution of both Irish Catholics and Scot Presbyterians, the famine. Ulsterites' connection to their land, and each other, has always been complicated, but never ever indifferent.

From Cavan, we head west, then north, soaking in the primal vibe of the Donegal coast. At Slieve League, we brace against 55-mile-an-hour wind gusts to glimpse some of Europe's highest ocean cliffs, dropping nearly 2,000 feet to an angry sea. Our route winds through a wild, deserted mountain bog to the top of Glengesh Pass—breathtaking and bleak. The road hairpins out of sight. I've completely misjudged our travel time to the village of Dunfanaghy. As the

skies blacken, the heavens open, and mother hums "Stormy Weather." With 30 miles left, all the road signs turn Gaelic. Clearly, this long day isn't over.

At Dunfanaghy, a rising tide fills the wide shallow harbor just outside Arnold's Hotel. Inside, Mack presses for another family story before bed. He's our lore guy, for years collecting tads of our history the way a robin gathers twigs. Tonight he wants more bits on our local connection to a long-lost relative—Sir Edward Wentworth Beatty.

In 1865, great-great-grandfather William invited his nephew, Sir Edward's father, to join the family shipping and timber business that he'd built with his sons from nothing in northern Canada. Twenty years later, a legal donnybrook razed this family partnership. So deep was great-grandfather's fury and sense of betrayal toward Edward's father, even my late father—born four decades and two generations later—burned old photos and court documents from the conflict. In effect, Sir Edward and his branch of our family tree ceased to exist until I glimpsed a newspaper story mentioning him a few years ago.

Still, he must have been a hard guy for our side of the family to ignore in early 20th-century Toronto. In 1918, Sir Edward became the first Canadian-born president of the Canadian Pacific Railway, a global transportation empire. Shipping and rail titans like

Ireland's Fanad Head Lighthouse keeps watch over perilous shores.

The author's family rides along Northern Ireland's Dunfanaghy tidal flats.

him seemed to be the Zuckerbergs and Jobses of their time, connecting and shrinking the world with new technology.

Mack mentions a photo we found of him—chuffed, stogie in hand, standing next to his friend His Royal Highness, Prince Edward of Wales. In 1930, the heir to the British throne christened Sir Edward's new *Empress of Britain,* the fastest and grandest transatlantic ocean liner of her day. Ten years later, she was struck by German U-boat torpedoes and sunk just miles from here, off Dunfanaghy's shores. With the storm still blustering outside, we vow to find a good lookout tomorrow—see what we can see.

By morning, everything has changed. The sun shines. The breeze is warm and gentle. We hike to Tramore Beach's vast empty expanse. The boys race down its massive dunes, formed in the great storm of 1839. We ride big-boned Irish ponies across the Dunfanaghy tidal flats. And in one brilliant, no-granny-left-behind mission, James insists that he and his dad half-carry my mom up a steep, craggy path to the highest, most westerly lookout of Horn Head peninsula. As they reach the summit, I see in James's eyes a satisfaction born out of wisdom far beyond his 18 years. His grandmother's joy is palpable,

infectious, as together we survey what feels like the northwest corner of the universe—just the Atlantic and blooming heather as far as the eye can see.

To the north and east, dry stone walls climb the hills and cross the broad, treeless valleys of Donegal's Inishowen Peninsula, at once stunning and desolate. Here and at home, stone walls evoke for me a sense of permanence, hard work, and accomplishment. I think of the chunks of dolomite piled along property lines in our rural area northwest of Toronto—slogging, land-clearing labor of pioneer farmers, many of Ulster descent. What I see here near Clonmany, however, is like no wall I've known.

From the window of our B&B, we spot the wobbly gray line across the valley ascending 275 yards straight up Binion Hill, so steep and craggy in spots that a wall there seems to make no sense at all. It divides nothing from nothing.

Indeed, separating properties or herds was not the point. This is a famine wall, a make-work project run by landlords during the Great Potato Famine of the 1840s. Seemingly futile, this wall, a resident tells us, gave a purpose to many here who had lost the will to live, a job in exchange for a scrap of food each day. It is a sad, desperate reminder of horrific times.

Kicking up the tunes at Madden's Bar in Belfast, Northern Ireland

Still, to me the wall offers too a glimpse of our humanity—of the primal instinct for even a shred of self-determination. It seems clear this, perhaps above all, is what steeled the resolve of my great-great-grandparents, and likely many other immigrants before and after them.

THE SMALL CAR FERRY from Greencastle, Inishowen, to Magilligan Point, Northern Ireland, takes less than 15 minutes, but delivers us a world away. In its wake, we leave the forsaken allure of Donegal for the gentrified verdant shores of Northern Ireland. We sip Irish whiskey at the world's oldest distillery, Bushmills. We teeter on the precarious Carrick-a-Rede rope bridge. We scale the curious mounds of hexagonal basalt at Giant's Causeway along Antrim's striking northern coast. Still, our mission—to burrow inside the complicated sensibility of our Ulster ancestors—draws us farther south to peer through the squared windows of an old Belfast black cab.

Our cabby guide Tom drives inland, away from the sparkling waterfront renaissance of Belfast's new Titanic Quarter, and toward the Loyalist, predominantly Protestant, working-class neighborhood around Shankill Road. Brash murals flanking buildings commemorate leaders and other scenes of religious and political strife known as "The Troubles"—here and in the republican, largely Catholic neighborhood nearby. Vibrant graffiti is splattered across a peace line, a massive Berlin-type wall, built as a temporary buffer between the two fractious neighborhoods in the 1960s. It was later fortified with corrugated metal and chain link that still hangs over backyards of adjacent homes.

This is not the war zone it was. Yet, here the wall stands over four decades later. Gates between the two sides still close after dark and on Sundays. Surveillance helicopters still circle overhead, at least on this day. Tom says the wall still helps keep the peace, but also thwarts the grassroots dialogues that underpin deeper reconciliation. We find even in Belfast's largest cemetery, dating back to the 1860s, sunken walls separating Protestants and Catholics above and below ground. To be sure, we Irish know how to carry a grudge.

All this illuminates the fey bits of my own Beatty DNA: a touch of genetic truculence I know well in myself. It is the darker, passionate Irish side that would wall off huge parts of our family history for almost four generations.

THOSE 400 MILES NOW BEHIND US, the five of us pour one last time out of that godforsaken hatchback. Our road trip has come full circle. Now back inside the "pale" of Dublin, we ponder how best to kill seven hours before flying home. Sleep? Pshaw. Like any self-respecting Irish progeny, we go to the pub.

Mack tosses five euros in an open guitar case to seal the deal. The bandleader introduces his grandma Ruth. She's surprised but doesn't hesitate. "I don't know the words that well," she says, squeezing up to the mic through a throng of Gaelic football fans at Dublin's Oliver St. John Gogarty pub. This Temple Bar hub pulsates with blue-and-white-garbed revelers, their beloved "Dubs" having just recaptured the championship after a 16-year drought.

"If you don't know the words, you can't sing the song," yells the banjo player as Ruth taps the mic for a sound check.

"Just say them here," she grins, pointing to her right hearing aid. Eyes roll. A buzzkill seems imminent as the band proffers a few bars of a familiar lead-in. The song: "Danny Boy."

What follows is transcendent. As she leans into her audience, lyrics flowing seamlessly in one ear and out her mouth, her classically trained, freakishly youthful voice sends this Celtic gem soaring. At the end, band members hug her, a large Texan behind us weeps, and locals line up to shake her hand. "Imagine what she could do if she knew the feckin' words!"

shouts the banjo guy over deafening applause. A chant builds, "Ruth, Ruth, Ruth!"

Later, in that quiet descent to slumber, I replay this moment. Yes, her voice, but more her pluck, her fearless embrace of the moment.

It is a most apt denouement to a journey that has been, in many ways, all about pluck. And in questing to know better that of those long gone, I think I'm most grateful to know better the best in us all here and now.

Toronto-based writer **LIZ BEATTY** is a frequent contributor to *National Geographic Traveler* magazine, among others. Whenever possible, she still opts for the big messy ordeal of family travel.

James (left) and Mack Beatty at the Giant's Causeway, Northern Ireland

GET TO KNOW NORTHERN IRELAND

• CELEBRATE
The three-day **Eagle Wing Festival** (*discovernorthernireland .com*), staged each July in the historic Northern Irish town of Groomsport, celebrates the historical connections between Northern Ireland and the United States. Named for the Ulster-Scots ship that set sail for the New World in 1636 in an ill-fated attempt to establish North America's first Presbyterian settlement, the festival includes live music,

storytelling, and lots of living history events.

• TOUR
More than a dozen U.S. presidents have family trees rooted in Northern Ireland. During a trip to Ulster, tour four presidential ancestral homes open to the public: the **Andrew Jackson Cottage** in Boneybefore, the (Ulysses) **Grant Ancestral Home** near Ballygawley, the (Chester) **Arthur Ancestral Home** near Cullybackey, and the (Woodrow) **Wilson Ancestral**

Home near Strabane. For more information go to *discovernorthern ireland.com*.

• EXPERIENCE
Board a full-scale emigrant sailing ship, walk the cobbled lanes of a preindustrial Irish village, and watch reenactor craftsmen at work at the **Ulster American Folk Park** (*nmni.com/uafp*) in Omagh, a National Museums of Northern Ireland living history site dedicated to the 18th- and 19th-century Northern Irish emigrant experience.

A Heartland History

Mining old memories and creating new ones in America's Midwest

BY DIANE JOHNSON

Corn emerges in the morning light among the spring fields and farms of Illinois.

A forgotten grain elevator building outside Chenoa, Illinois, a town of author Diane Johnson's childhood

The trains that rolled though Chenoa were the stuff of romantic childhood lore.

MY ROOTS WERE IN MOLINE, Illinois, and in two little towns in the eastern part of the state, Chenoa and Watseka, where my grandfather and my mother's sisters and brothers lived. The family had arrived there in the 1820s. We spent summers, Christmases, Thanksgivings in Watseka or Chenoa with these aunts and uncles, cousins and neighbors, and I knew every corner of their houses: the mysterious double staircase in Chenoa, the dressing room, the sewing room, the old-fashioned taps and rusty smells of the plumbing, the spotted mirrors, the cookstove and ceiling-mounted drying rack where the laundry was hung in bad weather. Above all, I remember the tantalizing attic full of shrouded trunks and peculiar shapes under Indian bedspreads.

Then, when I was 17, everything connecting me to these loved places vanished. My father was transferred to Oregon and I went off to college, far from Moline, Watseka, and Chenoa. Over the years, my aunts and uncles died, friends from high school moved to other towns. The houses sold. And, with no one I knew there, I had no real wish to go back.

I lived in California, then in France. Before I knew it, 50 years had passed.

Fifty years!

And then, as happens to people, I was seized with a wish to see these treasured places after all. For one thing, I'd been stung by a conversation I'd had with a French friend. She said that in her experience, Americans didn't know much about history, even their own. She thought this really unnatural. People in France are connected to the long pasts of their families, regions, traditions. But I had to admit it was true that Americans, at least in my case, were careless about gathering up the strands of the past, or else had been deprived of them by war and immigration. Who were the great-grandparents who had trekked out to Illinois, and when, and why? Who settled the little towns?

I also had a corollary wish, born of the idea that people aren't much interested in little midwestern places. I wanted to know more about the history of the whole area, with its American Indian and French town names, its landscapes of hill and leafy oak, its starkly beautiful cornfields, silos, and barns.

A migrating white pelican makes a stop in Moline, Illinois.

had ever read them, including—I assume—my mother.

These are the old things that I imagine families like ours stow in attics, the garage, old suitcases—places where people put things they cannot bear to throw out, until they do, to the regret of history.

For me, those letters were the first place to start my investigation.

Once I started reading, I realized I had a treasure: a long memoir written two centuries ago by my great-great-grandmother and a great-great-great-grandmother, two women named Anne Catharine. I also found a religious testimonial written by the young husband of the first one, Mr. Perkins, whom they treated with pork brine and flannel when he began to suffer from a "canser."

There were letters, letters, letters, allowing me to put together something of their story. One, written to Anne Catharine by one of her cousins, outlined a family story: In 1711 their great-grandfather, leaving France, had been captured by the British and dumped as a prisoner in New Haven, Connecticut. He thus became the founder of an American family. These people were called Cossit.

And so, in a mood of loyalty (defend little Illinois towns), defiance (I do too know something about our history), curiosity (who were these people anyhow?), and nostalgia, I knew I would have to go revisit these scenes and try to find out something about the people who first came there.

It's not hard to get to downstate Illinois—you can fly to Moline's Quad City airport or rent a car in Chicago and drive. I had no logistical excuse for putting off my visit. (When I was a child, of course, there were trains to such places. The romantic engines whistled through at all hours; they took people to Chicago, carried cattle, hobos and runaways hid on them, or so went the stories. I heard their sounds in the night, never without wishing to be on one. There are no trains to these towns now.) Still, I put it off for a decade, and finally went to visit twice, once with my brother, once with two of my children and my niece.

BUT FIRST, HOMEWORK. When my mother died, we had scrupulously put the contents of her "family" drawer into a big plastic box to be stored by my daughter Darcy, who works at the Archives of American Art in Washington, D.C., and hence, is our family archivist. These papers comprised old photos of unidentified people and letters written in old-fashioned handwriting difficult to read and crossed as well, with two overlapping sets of handwriting, one going in one direction, the other on top of it at right angles—an enigmatic nightmare. No one

Connections

The two young women standing next to a chair and wearing Civil War uniforms are my grandmother and her sister, dressed up in men's clothes for their photo, probably around 1880. The uniforms probably belonged to their father, Charles Stuart Elder. The chair, now in my California living room, was recovered at some point, by some later ancestress, in brown needlepoint with flowers in the center of the seat and back.
—Diane Johnson

Autumn paints the landscape of America's Midwest.

THE STORY STARTED with an ancestor of a slightly different name, René Cossét. During the North American French and Indian Wars with the British that lasted until 1713, René was captured at sea. Perhaps he had intended to claim or rejoin some family estate in Canada. I found the forlorn French traveler via military records of 1713 in Alice C. Baker's *True Stories of New England Captives*. His British captors wanted to include him in a prisoner exchange with the French and their Indian clients for some Puritan settlers from Deerfield, Massachusetts. But René—"Ranna" to American ears—refused to be traded back to the French, a fact that's noted in letters by a Colonel Partridge, in charge of the exchange, to Governor Dudley in Montreal. For some reason, René said he would prefer to remain a prisoner his whole life than to go with the others to Canada. Perhaps appreciating his newfound loyalty, the British let him stay in the United States. He later settled in Connecticut

and married a Ruth Porter, and there he and his descendants lived quietly for a few generations, until we come to the Revolutionary War.

Wars are wonderful luck for someone looking up her roots—the military always documents itself. Who was in what regiment and on which side? In addition to the French and Indian Wars, my family search would involve the Revolutionary and Civil Wars, making it easy enough to find out about the men.

For Revolutionary War family history, I consulted the Daughters of the American Revolution (DAR) archives online. When I was growing up, the DAR had been tarred with Eleanor Roosevelt's reproach. Addressing them one time she is said to have said, "Thank you, fellow immigrants." She was reminding them of something they had preferred to forget. They were also criticized because they had objected to Marian Anderson, the great African-American soprano, singing in Washington's Constitution Hall, which belonged to them. Since then they have bent over backward to honor her, and the DAR archive is open and a great resource if you suspect an ancestor had fought for independence in 1776.

Some of mine had, but some, I discovered, had been among the considerable number of people who stayed loyal to King George III and were obliged by their angry patriot neighbors to flee to Canada, where they settled along the border between Quebec, Vermont, and New Hampshire, many around Lake Memphréma-gog. These were known as United Empire Loyalists. They were Protestant, and many were Anglican clergymen, torn between New World enthusiasms and their vows to the Church of England.

The letters and diaries I already had allowed me to pinpoint where and when my forebears had

> The letters and diaries I already had **allowed me to pinpoint where and when my fore-bears had moved.**

moved, starting in Stanstead, Quebec, and Derby, Vermont. They straddled the border and didn't think of themselves as Canadian or American. Starting in 1827, the younger Anne Catharine and her husband moved west, along with hordes of other Americans, on the heels of new land grant legislation. These particular ancestors weren't farmers but doctors, who would be needed by the new settlers clearing land for the big midwestern farms to come. They spent some years in Bloomingburg, Ohio, and became active in the abolitionist movement there. Then, for unknown reasons, they moved to Bloomington, Illinois, before the Civil War. I learned by chance that a young lawyer, Abraham Lincoln, came to their daughter's wedding. She was marrying a local doctor, Charles Stuart Elder. Googling him turned up the information that he had founded the Thirty-Third

Signs of an Illinois spring

Prairie home rainbows over Illinois

Illinois Volunteer Regiment Band and served with it in the Civil War. It was this musical group, still in existence, that published on its website the detail about Lincoln, something I had never heard. Charles Stuart was my great-grandfather.

Here a childhood memory could be updated. Maybe most children have seen a mystery house in their neighborhood, where some strange person lives or that has a sinister quality or reputation for ghosts. As a child, I was always drawn to a ramshackle, empty house sitting on a flat lot in Chenoa, not far from where my uncle's grand house stood (he was the town banker). My brother and I would peer into the empty rooms and think about who'd lived there. Now I wonder if there isn't a strange pull from places you are connected to, some house DNA that recognizes your own. Years later, our aunt told us, "Your great-great-grandfather lived in that house after the Civil War."

I was afraid the house was doomed—sagging, falling apart. It could be bought for a few thousand dollars but probably would get torn down, and I was

resigned to the idea that this bit of my family history would surely be lost. Fortuitously, the family of Adlai Stevenson, the statesman and presidential candidate, saved it. His ancestors had lived there too, in the 19th century. Prompted by some historian impulse, Stevenson's sister, Elizabeth Stevenson Ives, bought it in the 1980s.

Mrs. Ives set up a charming little museum, called the Matthew T. Scott House after the first owner, the founder of Chenoa. Finally, with the place now cozily restored, I could see what it was like inside. I knew my aunt Henrietta Elder had willed it a sofa that must have lived there with her great-grandparents. There it was. I found myself

Letters from the author's ancestors

Farmlands still reign over the Illinois countryside of the author's childhood.

wondering what happened to the little clock that sat on a table near the sofa when it was still in the Elder family house in Watseka. Inside its glass door lay a cushion, and on the cushion lay the winding key, the whole emitting a particular, unpleasant, rancid odor unforgettably associated with that clock. I hope whoever has it will bring it to the Matthew T. Scott House someday.

WHY WAS I SO MOVED and delighted to find the traces of my family, and the places and things I remembered from childhood? Memory is something we each have for ourselves. Almost more moving than memories, though, was the feeling of belonging, through the accidental connection of our modest family to history—via a president who came to a wedding and a vice president who lived in a house where my great-great-grandfather had lived too, of me to the small towns of Illinois, and so on—for some connectedness to our country and our history.

It's the feeling that motivates the members of the Chenoa Historical Society to pitch in with money and time to preserve things; Mrs. Ives to come up with funds to rescue a tumbledown house; others to call to witness and the corollary that we each matter. To feel that each of us is part of an effort, an identity, must be a natural human impulse but is too often diluted into tastelessness or manipulated for bad ends.

Anyhow, Moline, Chenoa, Watseka, and the surrounding Illinois cornfields filled me with strange

Diane Johnson

joy and consciousness of the beauty I had never noticed before. Maybe this is just called growing into your personal spot in the big picture.

I wish I could meet my French friend again, to tell her how I have come to appreciate her scolding about knowing about my family history. Alas, she has died and her children moved to America, where their French heritage could come to seem remote to them. I hope they will have learned from their mother the preciousness and fragility of memory and traditions, lessons she taught me.

DIANE JOHNSON is the author of *Flyover Lives: A Memoir, Le Divorce, The Shadow Knows,* and other novels and divides her time between Paris and San Francisco. She grew up in Moline, Illinois.

GET TO KNOW ILLINOIS HISTORY

• TOUR
Rock Island Arsenal near Moline, a key supply depot for Union forces in the Mississippi Valley, is home to two poignant Civil War–era cemeteries—**Rock Island National Cemetery** and **Rock Island Confederate Cemetery** (*www.cem.va.gov/cems/nchp/rockisland.asp*). See row upon row of marble headstones: round top for Union soldiers, pointed for Confederate.

• CRUISE
Roll down the mighty Mississippi aboard the ***Celebration Belle*** (*celebrationbelle.com*) paddle wheel boat on a narrated lunch cruise to learn about the symbiotic relationship the Quad Cities (Moline, East Moline, and Rock Island, Illinois; and Bettendorf and Davenport, Iowa) have with the river. The tour cruises past Rock Island Arsenal and the site of the first railroad bridge to span the river.

• TOUR
Whether to spark childhood memories of farm life or to learn how the state's rural lifestyle has evolved since 1850, spend an afternoon touring the four-acre **Illinois Rural Heritage Museum** (*illinoisruralheritage museum.org*) in Pinckneyville. Exhibits include a walk-through red horse barn, a model general store, and an antique tractor collection.

GENEALOGY 101

A general guide for planning your own extraordinary "journey home"

Every "journey home" begins at home. The search to learn more about your ancestors—who they were, where they came from, what happened to them and why—starts in conversations with older relatives, in the attic or storage boxes riffling through old family photos and documents, at the local library or archives researching vital records, or online mining family genealogy websites.

The payoff for all this detective work is nothing less than time traveling through your personal family history. You will get to know your ancestors in a more intimate and meaningful way. Megan Smolenyak, author of six genealogical books and the sleuth who uncovered Barack Obama's Irish ancestry, describes visiting one's ancestral home as one of life's few "universally moving experiences."

"No matter how successful you are or what you have seen, you can't be jaded when you walk in your ancestors' footsteps," Smolenyak says. "There's something powerful about seeing your surname on cemetery stones in some remote town, or sitting in the church where your great-grandparents were married. Getting there requires a great deal of patience and detective work, but I can assure you, it's well worth it."

To help you make your journey home a success, we've assembled this ten-step action plan based on expert input from Smolenyak; Loretto Szucs, vice president of community relations at Ancestry.com (who has traveled the world on her own family history adventure); Spencer Wells, Genographic Project director and National Geographic explorer-in-residence; and Marion Hager, owner of Hager's Journeys (*hagersjourneys .com*), a luxury tour operator offering custom genealogical adventures.

Review the tips, start researching, and get ready to "go home" for the very first time.

1. GET ORGANIZED

Before you dive in the deep end of your family's history, equip yourself with some essential tools of the genealogy trade. Although most smartphones perform all the basic functions you'll need to input and store the information you find, it's helpful to have some more basic equipment, such as a notebook and pen, a digital audio and/or video recorder, and a camera. These old-school tools will prove invaluable when you don't have a cell signal, cannot access the Internet, or need to recharge your phone.

Chances are good that the early weeks of your search will bear abundant fruit, since it's often easiest to gather facts about close relatives, such as parents, aunts and uncles, and grandparents. To save and organize everything you find, choose an online genealogical database now, before you actually start conducting research. Of course, there are also blank pedigree or family tree paper charts you can fill in with a pen, as well as genealogical software programs allowing you to build a family tree on your computer. The online option is the most convenient and flexible, however, because you can access your stored information and update your chart from any computer or mobile device.

Multiple free and fee-based online genealogical databases are available, including Ancestry.com, the world's largest online family history resource. Since Ancestry .com's 2.1 million subscribers have created more than 60 million family trees, some of those existing branches might prove valuable in your own search.

Helpful features to look for when choosing any online genealogical database include: easy-to-use programs to build, update, and share your family tree; tutorials and webinars presented by genealogy experts; the ability to upload photos, digitized documents, and video and audio files; an integrated line of genealogical products (to avoid duplicating efforts if you want to enhance and expand your family tree); and unlimited storage.
Tip: To manage and view your family tree on the go, choose a genealogical software program or online databases with a companion mobile app, such as those of **RootsMagic** or **Ancestry.com.**

2. TREASURE HUNT AT HOME

Professional genealogists are seasoned detectives: They look for clues, notice patterns, conduct research, and collect data to methodically solve mysteries and uncover family histories. And, like detectives, these ancestry experts know that some of the most valuable clues in any quest often are hiding in plain sight—at home.

"I know how tempting it is, but resist the urge to start your family history search online," says Smolenyak, chief genealogical consultant to the popular television series *Who Do You Think You Are?* Anything that could be part of the paper trail connecting you to your ancestors will help make your search more efficient and successful when you are ready to go online. "Instead, I begin with a treasure hunt at home. And, not just your home, but, if possible, your grandparents' and parents' homes too."

Smolenyak suggests focusing your hunt in the attic, basement, and drawers (like that junk drawer in the kitchen) where photos, documents, and personal correspondence may be stored. Items with dates are especially helpful. Family memorabilia to look for (and photograph if you do not have permission from the owner to take the item) include old family photos, military records, diplomas and report cards, and of course diaries, postcards, and letters. **Tip:** If your hunt involves searching through artifacts in relatives' homes, involve them in the process, if possible. Explain what you are doing and why, invite them to participate, and respect their wishes for how any item you discover will be handled, copied, or stored.

3. TALK TO YOUR ELDERS

"Your older relatives—even those who are just 20 minutes older than you—are living libraries," says Smolenyak. "The family histories stored in their brains can save you so much trouble down the road."

Even if you've heard family facts—and legends—your entire life, really taking the time to interview your elders armed with a digital recorder and specific questions will refresh your memory and reveal new details. Plus, if you treasure hunt first and interview second, you will have artifacts to talk about with your relatives. Asking them to identify people or places in old photos, for example, can be a catalyst for stories and leads you've never heard before.

And although older relatives are an obvious resource, even family members your age or younger may know family stories that are new to you. Use your interviews to establish essential facts, as well as those vivid details that only are preserved in your relatives' memories.

Because the information you gather will help you conduct a more effective online search, you'll want to ask questions about your parents, grandparents, and, if possible, great-grandparents and beyond that will reveal foundational knowledge. Basic information to ask about includes full names and names of siblings, birthplaces and birthdates, locations or even addresses of family homes, nationality and ethnic background, occupations, trades, and/or special skills, education, military service including nation and branch of service, and where relatives are buried.

Tip: Don't let your eagerness to gather facts override basic courtesy and respect. If a relative appears hesitant or outright refuses to share specifics about a certain event or person, move on to another topic. By speaking with multiple relatives and following up with your own research, often you can fill in the blanks without upsetting or alienating anyone.

4. GO ONLINE

This is the moment you've been waiting for—the chance to finally use all the information you've been gathering to search online. New resources, services, and options are added regularly on popular genealogy sites including **FamilySearch.org, Ancestry.com,** and its offshoots, **RootsWeb.com** and **Archives.com.**

Smolenyak suggests starting with the Mormon Church's free, nonprofit FamilySearch, the world's largest genealogical organization. They are in the process of digitizing an astounding 6.9 billion historic records now on microfilm. "They have been collecting records from around the world for about 100 years and are digitizing their collection at a pace of tens of millions of records a week," Smolenyak says.

Browse the FamilySearch catalog of genealogical materials (including books, online materials, microfilm, microfiche, and publications), and request a free loan to the closest Family History Center (typically at a public library) where you can view the items in person (family search.org/catalog-search).

You can also visit the church's **Family History Library** in Salt Lake City to take a family history research class; conduct online searches; and use the library's collection of printed, film, and digital resources (familysearch.org/locations/saltlakecity-library).

On Ancestry.com you'll find a one-stop shop for researching and writing your family story. Whether you want to create a basic family tree or actively collaborate with amateur and professional genealogists around the world, Ancestry.com has every conceivable resource you would need: family tree–building tools; expert guidance (such as webinars and live-stream video tutorials); digitized records (including census and voter lists; birth, marriage, and death; military; and immigration); and an integrated product line including photo books and posters created from your family history.

Many libraries offer the **Ancestry Library Edition,** providing free access to the bulk of the site's Immigration and Travel collection of six databases: Border Crossings and Passports, Citizenship and Naturalization Records, Crew Lists, Immigration and Emigration Books, Passenger Lists, and Ship Pictures and Descriptions.

In addition, comprehensive genealogical indexes such as **Cyndislist.com** and **Linkpendium.com** include categorized listings of current online resources related to family history research. (Note that it can take a lot of time to click down through the categories and sub-categories of these lists to find information specifically related to your research.)

Tip: Subscribe to the free, standard **Eastman's Online Genealogy Newsletter** (blog.eogn.com) or purchase an annual Plus Edition subscription ($19.95) to receive daily genealogy-related tips, articles, book and website reviews, and industry updates. Professional genealogist Dick Eastman curates the newsletter.

5. BE SOCIAL

Now that you've officially moved your genealogy search online, don't forget to use your favorite social networking and social media sites, such as Instagram, Reddit, Twitter, Facebook, and Pinterest. In addition to searching for and connecting with people who share your ancestral surname, look for local organizations, public resources (including libraries and archives), tour guides, and genealogy-related services in your ancestor's hometown or region.

"When I started researching family history, I had to correspond via snail mail letters and get them translated," Smolenyak says. "But now, even before you manage to connect the dots and realize exactly where your family started out, you can find people who are from the region where you think your ancestors came from. Even if they aren't related to you, often they will be helpful and go talk to the local priest or officials and ask if they can see the records for you."

Tip: You're more likely to get free, local help from random strangers who share your surname if they haven't been bombarded with requests from people tracing their family histories. Smolenyak who is half Irish, half eastern European says that although many Irish may be inundated with inquiries, family roots research remains somewhat of a novelty in eastern Europe.

6. GET A DNA TEST

Cutting-edge DNA ancestry testing kits like **National Geographic's Genographic Project** (genographic .nationalgeographic.com), **Family Tree DNA** (family treedna.com), and **AncestryDNA** (ancestry.com) can lead you to places and people you never may have found simply by following a paper trail.

National Geographic Society Genographic Project scientists work to determine deep ancestry. Although not primarily a genealogy testing service, "Participants will discover the migration paths their ancient ancestors followed thousands of years ago and will learn the details of their ancestral roots—their branch on the family tree," says Spencer Wells, Genographic Project director and National Geographic explorer-in-residence. Tests can demonstrate a genetic link between two people who never realized they were related. Says Wells, "It is an opportunity to participate in a real-time scientific research effort and connect with other participants to see how we are all related."

Public participants can transfer their results to **Family Tree DNA,** a National Geographic partner, to learn more about their own ancient origins. "You can find out if you are related to another family with the same surname and gain a deeper understanding about your ancestor's homeland," Wells says.

AncestryDNA "merges your results with 300,000 other people who have taken the test, and the 60 million family trees on Ancestry.com bring a new depth to your family history," says Ancestry.com's Loretto Szucs.

When choosing a DNA testing service specifically for ancestry research, look for one with a large database of people tested, as well as free DNA sample storage (in case you want to order a different test at a later date), and online support and tutorials.

Tip: Although DNA results can be helpful in your research, the decision to get tested shouldn't be taken lightly. Tests can reveal family paternity and maternity secrets kept hidden by your ancestors or immediate family members.

7. PLAN AHEAD BEFORE YOU GO

If you have the time and financial resources, booking a custom genealogical tour is one the best ways to get the most out of your journey home. Genealogy travel specialists such as Hager's Journeys (hagersjourneys.com), European Focus (europeanfocus.com), Ancestral Attic (ancestralattic.com), P.A.T.H. Finders (pathfinders.cz), Roadtrips Worldwide Ltd.'s Ancestors in Europe (ancestors ineurope.com), and Ancestors in England (ancestors inengland.com) take roots travel to the next level.

The trip-planning process typically begins with professional genealogy research to pinpoint exactly where you should travel and, possibly, identify any relatives who live in or near your ancestral home place.

Fees and options vary widely for guided "roots travel" experiences. Research what each company offers (some focus on a specific country or culture), and choose the trip that fits your budget and goals. Hager's Journeys is a luxury travel company that works with local tour operators to arrange a special family gathering of any relatives and contacts local genealogists to gain entry to view documents in archives. Ancestral Attic, which specializes in eastern European genealogy travel, can translate documents from Polish, Russian, Latin, and German to English, either in preparation for your trip or while traveling. Post-trip, Czech travel experts P.A.T.H. Finders can translate (for a fee) any correspondence resulting from a family reunion and can help you maintain contact with newfound relatives by sending cards, flowers, and even gifts to them (from you) on special occasions.

But planning your own trip can yield rewarding, and surprising, results.

"For some people, the thrill of just being there is enough," says Hager's Journeys owner Marion Hager. Here's how she says you can get the most of out a trip:

• **Use a local tour operator.** If you are going to a country, or an area of a country, where English is not widely spoken, be sure to use a reliable tour operator at the destination and arrange for a car and driver/guide. "This way, you will get the most from the time you spend there," Hager says.

• **Call the relatives.** When you find people you believe are living relatives, try to contact them prior to your travel. "It would be fun to meet them and have them show you around and tell you what they know about their ancestry."

• **Find a local genealogist.** It will be much easier to gain access to view documents and records in archives through a local genealogist. "They also can help you contact living relatives you discover," Hager says.

• **Bring printed copies of your family tree.** You never know who you may connect with. "On a trip to Würzburg, Germany, we visited with a 13th-generation pretzel baker who unrolled a huge chart to show us his U.S. relatives," Hager recalls. "He never knew he had an American family until they found him in their research, visited, and brought a copy of the family tree. He was so excited to show it to us."

• **Make appointments.** Records offices, churches, cemeteries, and other locations that might keep ancestral records may not be open to the public without an appointment, have very limited hours, or be closed due to holidays. To avoid disappointment, Ancestry.com's Szucs advises, make specific (day and time) appointments before you make final travel arrangements.

• **Do your homework.** No matter what kind of roots travel trip you book, do your homework in advance, "To appreciate the journey more, read up on the place where your ancestors grew up," adds Ancestry.com's Szucs. "What was the culture like? What were their traditions?

What may have caused them to leave their homes, loved ones, and all that was familiar to them to cross the sea to the unknown?" Plus, she says, "You don't want to find out about a family farm still in operation after the journey is over."

Tip: Don't wait too long to plan your ancestral journey. Although the geographical location of your ancestral home won't change over time, chances are the landscape and ambience will.

"On that first trip, our group raised $10,000 to help restore the church, which was great," Smolenyak recalls, "but I am so glad I got to see it in its original, slightly decayed state. It was easier to envision what it was like for my ancestors who had to live with the head-bumping ceiling in the church. I could really see what my great-grandfather saw before he came to America, which was cool."

8. MANAGE YOUR EXPECTATIONS

Celebrity family history search stories on TV unduly raise expectations that every genealogical search will uncover some famous (or infamous) ancestor, such as actor Sarah Jessica Parker's tenth great-grandmother who escaped death at the Salem witch trials. For most people, including celebrities, cautions Szucs, the ancestors discovered and the lives they led will be more mundane.

"Most of us came from ordinary people—people who made a difference in the kind of life we are able to enjoy today," she explains. "There is a wonderful satisfaction in working out our own family stories. Each record we find represents something seemingly insignificant, but sometimes these events were life-changing experiences for our ancestors and therefore for us."

Through her own experiences researching family history, Szucs says she knows firsthand how rewarding it is to connect to your personal past—the people, places, and events that have shaped your life in ways you never would have imagined. She adds, "There is nothing more enjoyable than finding and putting all the family puzzle pieces together. Each piece has a story and a clue of its own."

Tip: Use the historical information you've collected to write an engaging page-turner version of your family's story. Guides such as *You Can Write Your Family History* by Sharon DeBartolo Carmack (Genealogical Publishing Company, 2009) and *For All Time: A Complete Guide to Writing Your Family History* by Charles Kempthorne (Heinemann, 1996) include techniques, helpful tips, and sample formats designed to help non-writers bring their ancestors' stories to life.

9. KEEP GOING

In many ways, traveling to the place where your ancestors came from will be the reward for all of your hard work. By putting in the time and research, persevering through roadblocks and detours, and being open to accepting whatever you discover, you've earned this trip like no other you've ever taken before.

If possible, however, view your journey home as a beginning, not the end of your genealogical research, advises Smolenyak.

"One of the questions I often get in regard to tracing one's family history is: 'How long is it going to take?'" she says. "Well, the farther back you go, the more ancestors you have, so it could be a never ending game. This is your own personal history mystery. You don't want the book to ever end. You can quit at your great-great-grandparents, but I bet you won't. There's always another ancestor to chase and another home place to see."

Tip: Blogging about your genealogy research experiences (and following blog posts by other family tree detectives) can help sustain enthusiasm over the long haul. The free *GeneaBloggers.com* maintains nearly 3,000 blogs. Add yours to the collection and get inspired to update regularly using the more than 40 daily prompts listed on the site.

10. CRUISE THE LIBRARY

Dozens of helpful genealogical books are designed specifically for amateur family historians. Here's a sampling:

• HOW-TO

The Complete Idiot's Guide to Genealogy by Christine Rose and Kay Germain Ingalls (3rd edition, Alpha Books, 2012) covers the family history research basics: from where to start and finding and deciphering documents, to sharing your discoveries and using online sources.

The Family Tree Problem Solver: Tried-and-True Tactics for Tracing Elusive Ancestors by Marsha Hoffman Rising (F+W Media, 2011) offers alternative routes to pursue when historical documents are scarce and there isn't an extensive paper trail to follow.

• GENERAL GENEALOGY

In *Hey, America, Your Roots Are Showing,* noted genealogist Megan Smolenyak (original edition, Citadel, 2012) shares the stories and detective work behind some of her more intriguing family history finds, such as the familial connection between President Barack Obama and actor Brad Pitt.

Each chapter in *The Family Tree Guidebook to Europe* by Allison Dolan and the editors of *Family Tree Magazine* (Family Tree Books, 2013) focuses on a specific European region or country.

• ONLINE

Discover Your Family History Online by Nancy Hendrickson (Family Tree Books, 2012) includes detailed descriptions of the top online databases for researching family genealogy, as well as special resources to trace American Indian, African-American, and Jewish ancestors.

In addition to the online tools including mobile apps and social networks discussed in *Genealogy Online for DUMMIES* by Matthew L. Helm and April Leigh Helm (Family Tree Books, 2012), readers can access bonus features at *dummies.com/cheatsheet/genealogyonline*.

• ADOPTEES

Finding Family: My Search for Roots and the Secrets in My DNA by Richard Hill (CreateSpace Independent Publishing Platform, 2012) is an adoptee's personal story of piecing together the puzzle of his long-hidden past using DNA and genetic genealogy.

• DNA

Deep Ancestry: Inside the Genographic Project by scientist and National Geographic explorer Spencer Wells (National Geographic, 2007) is a reader-friendly introduction to genetic anthropology explaining the science and research behind human evolution and the landmark Genographic study.

Trace Your Roots With DNA by Megan Smolenyak (Rodale Books, 2004) discusses both the benefits and limitations of DNA testing in family genealogy research.

Tip: Additional genealogy books, as well as online tools, are listed on the U.S. National Archives and Records Administration's "Resources for Genealogists" page (*archives.gov/research/genealogy*).

COUNTRY-SPECIFIC INFORMATION
Research tips and details for featured countries

IRELAND

The key to unlocking your Irish history is pinpointing your ancestors' county and townland (the Irish equivalent of a U.S. neighborhood). Both often were included on tombstones and in birth, marriage, and death certificates with the townland listed first.

WHERE TO LOOK

rootsireland.ie
A not-for-profit site created by the Irish Family History Foundation (IFHF) to preserve and share genealogical records collected by IFHF Heritage Centres.
What You'll Find: Ireland's largest family database—20 million records, and growing. Most counties have IFHF Heritage Centres, where records are collected.
Tip: If visiting Ireland, contact the appropriate county IFHF Heritage Centre in advance. Many can arrange a consultation with a genealogist.

WHERE TO VISIT

National Archives of Ireland, Bishop Street, Dublin 8, Ireland, *nationalarchives.ie*
You'll need a Reading Ticket (photo ID and proof of address required) to view public records (such as censuses, wills, and marriage licenses). First-time researchers are encouraged to consult first with an archives genealogist (free; available weekdays, 10 a.m. to 3:30 p.m.).
Tip: The 1901 and 1911 censuses are fully searchable for free on the National Archives of Ireland website.

National Library of Ireland , Kildare Street, Dublin 2, Ireland, *www.nli.ie*
Onsite resources include Catholic parish registers, property records, directories, and area newspapers dating back to the 1600s, as well as published family histories. In addition, visitors have free access to helpful subscription websites while conducting research in the library.
Tip: Free genealogy advisers are available weekdays; no appointment necessary.

WHAT TO READ

The updated ***Tracing Your Irish & British Roots*** by W. Daniel Quillen (2nd edition, Cold Spring Press, 2013) includes helpful tips on finding and accessing Irish records online and in person.

ANGOLA/VIRGINIA

Although Africans began arriving in Jamestown in 1619, African Americans weren't listed by name in the federal census until 1870. If you are a descendant of a free black who lived in Virginia (or migrated to North and South Carolina) during the colonial period, you can search for your ancestor in vital records (birth, death, marriage), wills, "Free Negro Registers," and land purchase documents.

WHERE TO LOOK

Family Search: Virginia African Americans
familysearch.org/learn/wiki/en/Virginia_African_Americans
What It Is: The FamilySearch guide to African-American genealogy in Virginia
What You'll Find: Historical data (such as property tax lists, court records, and marriage registers), images, maps, cemetery overviews, genetic testing information, and helpful resources for researching African-American ancestors living in Virginia from 1619 through the 20th century.
Tip: For additional information related specifically to free African Americans in colonial Virginia, visit freeafricanamericans.com, the genealogical website created by award-winning African-American researcher Paul Heinegg.

WHERE TO VISIT

Library of Virginia, 800 E. Broad St., Richmond, Virginia *lva.virginia.gov*
What You'll Find: A large collection of printed, digital, and microfilm African-American family histories, area histories, abstracts of state and local records, genealogical how-to books, and genealogical and historical periodicals
Tip: Before visiting, download the library's PDF guide to African American Genealogical Research *(lva.virginia .gov/public/guides/aa_genealogical_research.pdf)*.

WHAT TO READ

Leading African-American professional genealogist Tony Burroughs shares case histories, documents, and helpful guidelines and resources for researchers in ***Black Roots: A Beginner's Guide to Tracing the African American Family Tree*** (Touchstone, 2001).

ARGENTINA

Lured by the promise of free land, tools, and livestock in return for a five-year commitment to work the land, millions of European immigrants flooded into Argentina between 1825 and the early 1900s. The earliest settlers were Scottish, Irish, and French Basque, followed by Swiss, Russians, Germans, and, in the largest numbers, Italians and Spaniards. The late 1800s also brought a large migration of Jews fleeing tsarist Russia. Begin your search for Jewish Argentine ancestors at JewishGen (*jewishgen.org/infofiles/argentina.html*).

WHERE TO LOOK

FamilySearch: Argentina
familysearch.org/learn/wiki/en/Argentina
What It Is: The portal to free Argentina genealogical information from FamilySearch
What You'll Find: Tutorials on where and how to conduct Argentina genealogical research and the digitized 1869 and 1895 Argentina national censuses
Tip: The BYU Research Outline for Argentina link (under "Research Tools") gives quick, practical advice on where to search for specific documents.

WHERE TO VISIT

Registro Civil (Registry Office), Uruguay 753, C.P. 1018 Buenos Aires, Argentina, *registrocivil.gov.ar*
What You'll Find: If you know your ancestor's first and last name, as well as the issuing year of the document (birth, death, or marriage certificate) you desire, you can request (in Spanish) a search and photocopy.
Tip: Since searches take a few days, contact the Registry Office ahead of time.

WHAT TO READ

Exile From Argentina: A Jewish Family and the Military Dictatorship (Information Age Publishing, 2008) provides insight into the Argentine Jewish experience through the stories of author Eduardo Faingold and his ancestors.

The indelible impact of European immigration on Argentine identity, economic policies, and international relations is a major theme of Latin scholar David Rock's sweeping history ***Argentina, 1516–1987: From Spanish Colonization to Alfonsin*** (University of California Press, revised edition, 1987).

CAMBODIA

Few Cambodians lived in the United States before 1975. The genocide carried out by Pol Pot and the Khmer Rouge coupled with Vietnam's invasion of Cambodia in 1979 brought an estimated 75,000 refugees to the United States between 1980 and 1984. Since most refugees fled with few possessions, it's unlikely that immigrants who resettled in the United States during this time brought many, if any, historical documents.

WHERE TO LOOK

Cambodian Community History & Archive Project (CamCHAP), *www.camchap.org*
What It Is: A multimedia resource hub for information about the Long Beach, California, Cambodian community, one of the largest Cambodian populations outside Southeast Asia
What You'll Find: Photographs, videos and audio recordings, and historical documents specific to the Long Beach community, as well as information about Cambodian arts, religious practices, and sports
Tip: If visiting Long Beach, schedule an appointment to view the CamCHAP collection archived at the Historical Society of Long Beach (*hslb.org*).

WHERE TO VISIT

Cambodia
Plan a custom itinerary with Southeast Asian custom travel specialist **Journeys Within Tour Company** (*journeys-within.com*).
What You'll Find: Cambodia-based Journeys Within can arrange a visit to your ancestor's town, local guides and English-speaking hosts, and volunteer experiences.
Tip: Book a couple of nights at the Journeys Within bed-and-breakfast in Siem Reap.

WHAT TO READ

Based on long-term research among Cambodians living in Boston, ***Khmer American: Identity and Moral Education in a Diasporic Community*** by Nancy J. Smith-Hefner (University of California Press, 1999) provides a detailed look at the Khmer-American experience.

Survivors: Cambodian Refugees in the United States by Sucheng Chan (University of Illinois Press, 2004) traces the Cambodian-American path from the horrors of the Khmer Rouge regime and the hardships faced in Thai refugee camps, to the challenges of resettlement in the United States.

BRITISH COLUMBIA

Since 1971, the British Columbia Genealogy Society (*bcgs.ca*) has been researching, preserving, and publishing the histories of its members and other British Columbia families. Membership is about $42 a year, and includes a variety of helpful benefits including genealogy education sessions, borrowing privileges (items can be mailed) at the BCGS Walter Draycott Library and Resource Centre, and opportunities to collaborate with others researching their own BC family trees.

WHERE TO LOOK

CanGenealogy: British Columbia
cangenealogy.com/bc.html
What It Is: The BC portal of CanGenealogy, the free family history site created by Dave Obee, editor in chief of the *Times Colonist,* western Canada's oldest daily newspaper
What You'll Find: Helpful shortcuts and links to access dozens of British Columbia and Canadian genealogy databases, plus listings of BC genealogical societies, archives, cemeteries, and libraries

Tip: The CanGenealogy home page (*cangenealogy.com*) lists upcoming family history events throughout Canada.

WHERE TO VISIT

British Columbia Archives, Royal BC Museum Corporation, 675 Belleville Street, Victoria, BC
bcarchives.bc.ca
What You'll Find: The official archives of the government of British Columbia including published and online government and personal records, family histories, cemetery listings, maps, newspapers, phone directories, sound recordings, and guides to conducting genealogy searches
Tip: Conduct an online search of the BC Archives genealogy databases before your visit to identify the records you want to see in person.

WHAT TO READ

The practical tips for accessing Canadian library and archives information included in *Finding Your Canadian Ancestors: A Beginner's Guide* by Sherry Irvine and Dave Obee (Ancestors.com, 2007) can save time and result in a more productive search.

FIRST NATIONS—MOHAWK

Eastern upstate New York is the ancestral homeland of the Mohawk, known as the "Keepers of the Eastern Door" of the original five-nation Iroquois Confederacy. When the American Revolutionary War and subsequent creation of the U.S.-Canada border (1783) geographically divided the Mohawk Nation, some members remained in New York State, while others fled north to Quebec and Ontario, or, in lesser numbers, to Ohio, and, subsequently, Oklahoma. Tracing the migration and forced relocations of the Mohawk should help yield more results as you search for ancestors.

WHERE TO LOOK

NativeWeb, *Nativeweb.org*
What It Is: An international, nonprofit, indigenous peoples online community and resource index
What You'll Find: Links to Mohawk and other First Nations organizations, databases, and periodicals (such as the *MNN: Mohawk Nation News* daily newsletter), plus a NativeWeb News Digest featuring current news stories about indigenous peoples
Tip: Another helpful site is the **FamilySearch Canada First Nations Genealogy Research Facebook page** (*facebook.com/CanadaFirstNationsGenealogy*).

WHERE TO VISIT

Library and Archives Canada, 395 Wellington St. Ottawa, Ontario, 613-996-5115, *bac-lac.gc.ca*
What You'll Find: Department of Aboriginal Affairs and Northern Development historical records (mainly from 1867 on) documenting aboriginal peoples' (including First Nations peoples') interactions with the federal government, such as births, deaths, and school and land records.
Tip: Before visiting, read the archives' **Aboriginal Peoples—Guide to the Records of the Government of Canada** (*collectionscanada.gc.ca/the-public/005-1143-e.html*).

WHAT TO READ

The lineage charts, memoir excerpts, reference footnotes, and other background information included in *Turtles, Wolves, and Bears: A Mohawk Family History* by Barbara J. Sivertsen (Heritage Books, 1996) can prove helpful in a Mohawk ancestry search.

Although written for students (grades 6 and up) *The Mohawk: The History & Culture of Native Americans* by Samuel Willard Crompton (Chelsea House Pub, 2010) offers a basic introduction to Mohawk history and traditions, details modern-day Mohawk experiences and issues, and includes photographs and reference resources.

CROATIA

Deciphering Croatian family records can be a challenge since historical documents can be written in any of a number of languages including Croatian, Glagolitic (a Croatian dialect script), Italian, Hungarian, and German. Joining a multiethnic genealogy group, such as the Croatian Heritage and Genealogy Facebook Group is an easy way to connect with others who have experience interpreting Croatian documents and who are interested in sharing their knowledge and family trees. To access, go to *facebook.com/browse groups,* enter "Croatian Heritage and Genealogy" in the search box, and click "Join Group."

WHERE TO LOOK

FamilySearch, *familysearch.org/learn/wiki/en/Croatia*

What It Is: The FamilySearch guide to researching Croatian genealogy

What You'll Find: A beginner's guide to Croatian research, links to historical records (such as church records of births, baptisms, marriages, and deaths) and other genealogical resources, and a helpful Bosnian/Croatian/Serbian word list

Tip: The Croatia websites section includes a number of additional resources, such as *croatia-in-english.com* and *croatian-genealogy.com.*

WHERE TO VISIT

Croatian State Archives, Marulićev trg 21
10000 Zagreb, Croatia, *www.arhiv.hr/en/index.htm*

What You'll Find: Millions of archival state records (print, microfilm, and scans) from the tenth century to the present, as well as Croatian heritage film and audiovisual materials from Croatia and international sources

Tip: The **U.S. Embassy in Zagreb** *(zagreb.usembassy.gov)* maintains a list of certified translators who could prove useful in translating archival documents into English.

WHAT TO READ

Revised and updated in 2005, American journalist Robert D. Kaplan's ***Balkan Ghosts: A Journey Through History*** (Picador, 2005) is a combination travelogue and insightful historical analysis detailing the ethnic conflicts, complex history, and contemporary challenges of the Balkan Peninsula.

CUBA

Only specially licensed operators, including National Geographic Expeditions *(nationalgeographic expeditions.com),* can lead U.S. Treasury Department–sanctioned tours from the United States to Cuba. Itineraries focus on personal encounters with Cuban musicians, artists, and other locals. For up-to-date information on traveling to Cuba, visit *treasury.gov.*

WHERE TO LOOK

Cuban Heritage Collection, *CubaGenWeb.org*

What It Is: A not-for-profit site created in 1996 by Ed Elizondo, a Cuban American who emigrated from Cuba as a child in the 1960s, to share what he learned while researching his own family history

What You'll Find: Helpful resources including passenger lists (both arriving and departing Havana) and links to Cuban family trees

Tip: Choose the "Telephones and Addresses" link to look for your ancestors' names in digitized copies of the 1949 Cuba and 1958 Havana phone directories.

WHERE TO VISIT

University of Miami Libraries, Cuban Heritage Collection, 1300 Memorial Dr., Coral Gables, Florida *library.miami.edu/chc*

What You'll Find: Considered to be the most important body of resources outside of Cuba documenting the island and the Cuban diaspora from colonial times to the present, the collection includes rare photographs, manuscripts, and documents. A free Aeon Research Account (preregister online at *library.miami.edu/chc*) is required to request materials.

Tip: Before visiting, review the website's Collections Overview to see what's available. Then, using your Aeon account, prerequest materials you would like to view.

WHAT TO READ

Follow the tips of Spanish-language genealogist George R. Ryskamp in ***Finding Your Hispanic Roots*** (Genealogical Publishing Company, 2009) to conduct Hispanic research in LDS Family History Centers.

Take Me With You: A Secret Search for Family in a Forbidden Cuba (Atria Books, 2009) is an evocative memoir by award-winning journalist Carlos Frias, a first-generation Cuban American who visited his parents' homeland for the first time in 2006.

CZECH REPUBLIC

Tremendous interest in Czech ancestry has resulted in six-month waiting periods on requests made to the State Central Archives in Prague. Since the Embassy of the Czech Republic in Washington, D.C., has historically referred all U.S. genealogy queries to the Central Archives, embassy staff researched alternative options. The result is the helpful resource guide Genealogical and Family History Research in the Czech Republic (*mzv.cz/washington/en/culture_events/cz_us_community/genealogy*).

WHERE TO LOOK

Czechoslovak Genealogical Society International (CGSI)
www.cgsi.org
What It Is: A resource site for Czech, Slovak, Moravian, Bohemian, Rusyn, and German-Bohemian genealogy created by the CGSI
What You'll Find: Advice on how and where to search for historical documents from the former Czechoslovakia, message boards to connect with other researchers, and information about Czech language classes and genealogy travel
Tip: CGSI maintains an updated list of professional genealogists who specialize in Czech and/or Slovak research.

WHERE TO VISIT

Library of Congress: European Reading Room
Thomas Jefferson Bldg, Room LJ-249, 101 Independence Ave. S.E., Washington, DC, 202-707-4515
loc.gov/rr/european
What You'll Find: Perhaps the best collection of Czech and Slovak books and periodicals outside of the Czech Republic and Slovakia. It includes more than 5,000 English-language resources (books, essays, articles, dissertations) on Czech and Slovak history.
Tip: The collection includes a variety of Czech and Slovak telephone directories dating back to 1921.

WHAT TO READ

Prague Winter: A Personal Story of Remembrance and War, 1937–1948 (Harper, 2012) couples former Secretary of State Madeleine Albright's vivid recollections of growing up in Czechoslovakia during the Nazi occupation with her meticulous historical research and thoughtful analysis.

Czech American Timeline: Chronology of Milestones in the History of Czechs in America by Miloslav Rechcigl, Jr. (AuthorHouse, 2013) explores when, why, and how Czechs immigrated to the Americas.

ENGLAND

Begin your records search at the National Archives website's "Start Here" page (*nationalarchives.gov.uk/records/start-here.htm*). The National Archives is the United Kingdom's official archive, but what makes this site particularly valuable to family genealogists isn't the 1,000 years of records (although those are helpful), but the one-stop guide for where and how to start your research.

WHERE TO LOOK

United Kingdom General Registrar Office (GRO)
www.gov.uk/research-family-history
What It Is: The GRO's online resource for researching family history
What You'll Find: Records of every birth, marriage, and death registered in England and Wales, starting from July 1837, and a free, downloadable 24-page *Discover Your Family History* guide
Tip: Find the GRO index reference numbers you'll need to locate and order vital records on the GRO site at *freebmd.org.uk*.

WHERE TO VISIT

Guildhall Library, Aldermanbury, London
cityoflondon.gov.uk
What You'll Find: Biographical and genealogical resources (particularly for former Londoners but also for the wider British Isles), including trade and telephone directories, apprenticeship and marriage records.
Tip: If you'd like to snap photos of records with your smartphone, stop at the Enquiry Desk first to consult with staff and complete an application form.

WHAT TO READ

The 896-page ***Ancestral Trails: The Complete Guide to British Genealogy and Family History*** (2nd edition, Genealogical Publishing Company, 2006) by London Society of Genealogists' member Mark D. Herber is a comprehensive resource for beginner and veteran researchers.

In ***Far From "Home": The English in New Zealand*** (Otago University Press, 2012), researchers weigh in on why the English have been immigrating to New Zealand for nearly 200 years.

GERMANY

Before Germany consolidated into 39 states in the early 1800s, it consisted of hundreds of microstates. Start your family search by brushing up on German political history basics to become familiar with names and places that may no longer exist on a map. Once you determine your ancestral village name, go to Ancestry.com and use the *Meyers Orts- und Verkehrs-Lexicon des Deutschen Reiches* (a 1912 guide to German places) to pinpoint where your relatives lived.

WHERE TO LOOK

Germany/Prussia Genealogy Research Facebook page *facebook.com/GermanyGenealogy*

What It Is: The FamilySearch genealogy research Facebook community

What You'll Find: Regularly updated research tools and advice for people researching German ancestry, as well as a forum to collaborate with other researchers, ask questions, share and find helpful advice, and get translations

Tip: Check the FamilySearch page regularly as more collections of German records are available for indexing and will be added to the site in the future.

WHERE TO VISIT

BallinStadt Emigration Museum, Veddeler Bogen 2 Hamburg, Germany, *ballinstadt.net*

What You'll Find: Housed in the former Emigration Halls where emigrants stayed before boarding ships bound for the United States, the museum includes interactive exhibits, as well as a free, in-house research center open to the public.

Tip: The research center staff is available to assist visitors from 1:30 to 3:30 p.m., Monday through Friday.

WHAT TO READ

Figure out exactly where your ancestors came from and then find out how to access records from that village or town using the practical suggestions in James Beidler's *The Family Tree German Genealogy Guide* (Family Tree Books, 2014).

Finding Your German Ancestors by Kevan M. Hansen (Ancestry.com, 2001) includes sample illustrations of German documents, making this practical guide particularly helpful in identifying and interpreting vital records online and in German archives.

INDIA

A trove of records documents the lives and deaths of all who worked with or for the East India Company from 1600 to Indian independence in 1947, including those who served in the British military, and civilian government employees such as police, postal service, railway, or civil service workers. For Hindus, family records spanning several generations, handwritten on palm leaf and paper scrolls, are maintained in the northern India city of Hardwar. The living documents are updated with the latest births, deaths, and marriages each time a family member makes a pilgrimage to the holy city. (FamilySearch has transferred the 1194–2012 Hindu pilgrimage records to microfilm; however, at present the collection only can be viewed by members of the Church of Jesus Christ of Latter-day Saints.)

WHERE TO LOOK

Families in British India Society (FIBIS), *Fibis.org*

What It Is: A resource for people of all nationalities researching ancestors who lived in British India between 1600 and Indian independence in 1947

What You'll Find: Nonmembers can access a helpful "Beginners' Guide" with links to free India genealogical websites including the **FIBIS database** (*search.fibis.org/frontis/bin*), **FamilySearch India** (*familysearch.org/learn/wiki/en/India*), and the British Library Board's **India Office Family History Search** (*indiafamily.bl.uk/UI*).

Tip: FIBIS membership is about $30 annually, and includes research services and access to members-only files.

WHERE TO VISIT

The British Library, St. Pancras Reading Rooms 96 Euston Rd., London, *bl.uk*

What You'll Find: Biographical, military, church, and occupational records for the British and other Europeans living in India between 1600 and 1947

Tip: Ask the library's Reference Enquiry Desk staff for help identifying and accessing the most relevant databases for your research.

WHAT TO READ

If your India ancestors were British or emigrated from the Indian subcontinent to Great Britain between 1600 and 1947, *Tracing Your British Indian Ancestors* by Emma Jolly (Pen and Sword, 2012) offers helpful strategies for finding your family's historical records.

JAPAN

The **Japanese American National Museum** (*janm.org*), an affiliate of the Smithsonian in Los Angeles's Little Tokyo neighborhood, contains over 80,000 artifacts, records, and artworks chronicling 130 years of Japanese-American history. Learn about the Japanese-American experience through the oral histories, home movies, and family photographs of first-generation immigrants, or issei.

WHERE TO LOOK

U.S. National Archives and Records Administration National Archives
archives.gov/research/japanese-americans
What It Is: The National Archives' introductory portal to Japanese-American records from the World War II era to the present
What You'll Find: Helpful information about what items (such as World War II internment and relocation records of Japanese Americans) and online search tools are available, and how to access documents and order copies
Tip: Teaching With Documents (*archives.gov/education/lessons/japanese-relocation*) has helpful background information, documents, and other resources related to the relocation of Japanese Americans during World War II.

WHERE TO VISIT

National Japanese American Historical Society (NJAHS), 1684 Post St., San Francisco, California *njahs.org*
What You'll Find: Programs, exhibits, and research resources including personal advice from the staff of this nonprofit organization dedicated to collecting and interpreting historical information related to the Japanese-American experience
Tip: Visit the separate **MIS (Military Intelligence Service) Historic Learning Center** (*njahs.org/640*) at the Presidio to learn about the Japanese-American soldiers secretly recruited by the U.S. Army before the attack on Pearl Harbor and assigned to World War II combat units in the Pacific.

WHAT TO READ

Don't let the title fool you. ***A Student's Guide to Japanese American Genealogy*** by Yoji Yamaguchi (Oryx Press, 1996) is a helpful, information-packed primer for anyone interested in Japanese immigration to the United States and tracing Japanese-American family history.

LAOS AND VIETNAM

By 1900, French Indochina included Cochinchina (the southernmost part of modern Vietnam), Cambodia, Annam-Tonkin (in modern Vietnam), Laos, and Kouang-Tcheou-Wan (on the southern coast of China). Any historical documents related to French citizens living in Indochina in the late 1800s through 1945 are maintained in France. Vietnamese and Lao genealogy resources are limited.

WHERE TO LOOK

Vietnamese American Heritage Project
vietnam.ttu.edu/vahp
What It Is: An outreach project of the Vietnam Center and Archive (VNCA) at Texas Tech University
What You'll Find: Materials documenting the experiences and contributions of Vietnamese Americans including the Families of Vietnamese Political Prisoners Association Collection, plus links to resources
Tip: The **VNCA's Virtual Vietnam Archive** (*vietnam.ttu.edu/virtualarchive*) includes millions of scanned pages (personal photos, maps, letters home) donated by U.S. veterans and others with personal Vietnam War–era experiences and artifacts to share.

WHERE TO VISIT

Archives Nationales d'Outre-Mer (Overseas Archives Centre), 29 chemin du Moulin de Testa, Aix-en-Provence, France, *archivesnationales.culture.gouv.fr/anom/en/index.html*
What You'll Find: Historical documents related to the administration of French Indochina including the archives of the admirals and governors general (1848 to 1945) and the general staff for troops (1880 to 1899)
Tip: A colonial personnel file may be available if you can provide the name, birthdate, position, and Indochina location where your French ancestor served.

WHAT TO READ

Duong Van Mai Elliott's ***The Sacred Willow: Four Generations in the Life of a Vietnamese Family*** (Oxford University Press, 2000) presents 130 years of Vietnam's history from the rarely heard Vietnamese point of view.

MEXICO

Mexico is made up of 32 states, each divided into *municipios* **(similar to counties). You'll have more luck locating your ancestors if you know both the name of the town or village where they lived and the name of the municipio. Typically, civil records are collected and stored by municipio offices, and church records are kept in the town or village.**

WHERE TO LOOK

Family Search: Mexico Records and Research
familysearch.org/mexico-genealogy
What It Is: The FamilySearch portal to Mexican historical record collections
What You'll Find: Select church and civil registration vital records (birth, marriage, and death) dating back to 1539, as well as the fully indexed 1930 federal census—the only Mexican census available to the public—and tutorials on how to read Spanish-language handwritten records
Tip: Check the FamilySearch page regularly as more collections of Mexican records are available for indexing and will be added to the site in the future.

WHERE TO VISIT

Archivo General de la Nación (National Archives of Mexico) or AGN, Col. Penitenciaria Ampliación, Deleg. Venustiano Carranza, Mexico City, Mexico, *agn.gob.mx*
What You'll Find: Hundreds of Mexican and Latin American printed and microfilm document collections (in Spanish only), including church, civil, court, land, and military records; emigration lists, maps, and photographs
Tip: Before visiting, use the Guía General link (choose Fondos, Expedientes y Documentos) on the website to see what collections are available.

WHAT TO READ

Ancestry.com's ***Finding Your Mexican Ancestors: A Beginner's Guide*** by George and Penny Ryskamp (2007) offers easy-to-follow instructions for finding and interpreting Mexican historical documents. It includes helpful illustration, charts, case studies, and a Spanish-English glossary.

In ***Replenished Ethnicity: Mexican Americans, Immigration, and Identity*** (University of California Press, 2009), social scientist Tomás Jiménez examines how the continual influx of immigrants to the United States from Mexico shapes and impacts people of Mexican descent whose families have been in the United States for decades.

NORWAY

From the 16th to 19th centuries, official Norwegian documents typically were written in Danish. Other records may be written in one of Norway's two official languages, Norwegian *Bokmål* **(book language) derived from Danish, and Norwegian** *Nynorsk* **(new Norwegian). Although Norway's National Archives doesn't provide translation services, the staff maintains an updated list of local, fee-based genealogy research and translation services.**

WHERE TO LOOK

National Archives of Norway, *arkivverket.no/eng*
What It Is: The official Digital Archives of Norway
What You'll Find: Government records and parish registers, some dating back to the 1600s; includes church books, censuses, emigration registers, military rolls, and probate records
Tip: Check the Most Recent 100 page to see the latest digitized records added to the site.

WHERE TO VISIT

Norwegian American Genealogical Center & Naeseth Library (NAGC & NL), 415 W. Main St., Madison, Wisconsin, *nagcnl.org*
What You'll Find: Thousands of Norwegian and Norwegian-American genealogy books, microfilms, and other resources; select Norwegian-American cemetery and church records, obituaries, family histories, and an 1825–1850 index of the first 20,000 Norwegian immigrants in the United States
Tip: An affordable associate membership ($40 a year) provides discounts on NAGC & NL, fee-based research, staff assistance, and translation services.

WHAT TO READ

Updated in 2013, ***A Research Guide for Norwegian Genealogy,*** published by the NAGC & NL (and available in the *nagcnl.org* E-Store), includes specific tips for locating and interpreting historical documents found in the library, in Norway, at home, and online.

In ***Their Own Words: Letters From Norwegian Immigrants*** (University of Minnesota Press, 1991) is a collection of letters written between 1870 and 1945 by nine Norwegian immigrants to friends and family in Norway.

PERU

Peru doesn't have a nationwide index of vital records, so tracing your roots requires knowing the name of the village, town, or city where your ancestors came from. From there, you can search for the corresponding department (similar to a county) and municipal office where marriage, death, and census records typically are collected and stored.

WHERE TO LOOK

Family Search: Getting Started With Peru Research
Familysearch.org/learn/wiki/en/Peru
What It Is: The Peru portal for FamilySearch resources
What You'll Find: Links to FamilySearch digitized Peru document collections, such as baptisms, deaths, and Catholic Church records, and civil registration records for specific provinces including Amazonas, La Libertad, and Lima
Tip: Scroll down to the Peru Research Outline link for practical tips about where and how to search.

WHERE TO VISIT

Biblioteca Nacional (National Library)
Av. Abancay Cdra, 4 s/n
Cercado de Lima, Lima, *www.bnp.gob.pe/portalbnp*

What You'll Find: A Hall of Research where you can access large collections (primarily in Spanish) of interest to family historians including military records, land grants, judicial and chaplaincy records, parish registers, town council minutes, and notary registers from Lima, Arequipa, and Cusco
Tip: Two photographs, a letter of recommendation, a nominal fee, and attendance at an informational session (in Spanish only) about using the library's collections are required to conduct research.

WHAT TO READ

Although genealogy isn't the focus of ***The Peru Reader: History, Culture, and Politics*** (Duke University Press Books, 2005), this 600-page deep dive into the country's complex history provides a detailed look at the civilizations, traditions, and events that have shaped Peru.

If your Peruvian ancestral surname is Spanish, ***Finding Your Hispanic Roots*** by George R. Ryskamp (Genealogical Publishing Company, 2009) is a helpful resource for locating and deciphering Spanish-language documents in South America and Spain. It includes a glossary and directory of Hispanic genealogical societies in the United States.

WORLD WAR II PHILIPPINES

Military history travel specialists at Valor Tours (*valortours.com*) lead an annual April group expedition to the Philippines to commemorate the anniversary of the Fall of Bataan, and have offered other World War II–focused Philippines trips. For information about upcoming Philippines itineraries, visit *valortours.com.*

WHERE TO LOOK

Bacepow.net
What It Is: Bay Area Civilian Ex-Prisoners of War (BACEPOW) serves—and preserves the histories of—civilians who were imprisoned in East Asia by the Japanese during World War II.
What You'll Find: BACEPOW databases and archives are available for relatives of civilian and military POWs imprisoned in the Philippines.
Tip: The BACEPOW monthly online newsletter includes helpful background information for family genealogists.

WHERE TO VISIT

National Archives and Records Administration
Philippines Archive Collection, 8601 Adelphi Rd.

College Park, Maryland, *archives.gov/research/military/ww2/philippine*
What You'll Find: Among the records documenting life in World War II Philippines are civilian prisoners' personal histories, journals, and medical records.
Tip: Before visiting, use the "View Online Exhibits" search at archives.gov to identify documents of interest. Then contact the National Archives to confirm that what you want to see is located at the College Park facility.

WHAT TO READ

Based on prisoner diary entries, medical records, and other primary resources, author Frances B. Cogan's ***Captured: The Japanese Internment of American Civilians in the Philippines, 1941–1945*** (University of Georgia Press, 2000) is a detailed account of daily life in five civilian internment camps.

Terry: The Inspiring Story of a Little Girl's Survival as a POW During World War II (Outskirts Press, 2002) is author Terry Wadsworth Warne's personal account of her childhood in the Philippines during the Japanese occupation.

WORLD WAR II POLAND

Launch your genealogy research at JewishGen (*jewish gen.org*), a nonprofit organization affiliated with the Museum of Jewish Heritage. The site's "First Timer" primer offers helpful hints for researching thousands of databases including the combined JewishGen Poland Database (*jewishgen.org/databases/Poland*) featuring more than five million records.

WHERE TO LOOK

db.yadvashem.org/names/search.html?language=en
What It Is: Yad Vashem's (the Holocaust Martyrs' and Heroes' Remembrance Authority) Central Database of Shoah (Holocaust) Victims' Names is the single largest computerized database of Jews murdered in the Shoah.
What You'll Find: The names of an estimated 4.3 million (as of January 2014) Jewish Holocaust victims, some 2.5 million of who are commemorated with "Pages of Testimony" (one-page, mini-biographies)
Tip: Visit the site's **"Transports to Extinction"** (*db.yad vashem.org/deportation*) page to search for information about how and when your ancestors were deported from their homes and moved to another country or to concentration camps.

WHERE TO VISIT

Galicia Jewish Museum, ul. Dajwór 18, 31-052 Krakow, Poland, *en.galiciajewishmuseum.org*
What You'll Find: Located in Kazimierz, Kraków's Jewish quarter, the museum honors Holocaust victims and celebrates the Jewish culture of historical Polish Galicia (a former Polish province split post–World War II between Poland and Ukraine). During the war, Galician Jews were primarily sent to the Belzec concentration camp.
Tip: The museum houses Poland's largest Jewish bookshop; all books can be ordered online.

WHAT TO READ

Suzan Wynne's quest to learn more about her European Jewish ancestors resulted in *The Galitzianers: The Jews of Galicia, 1772–1918* (Wheatmark, 2006), which includes helpful historical background and genealogical research information.

The comprehensive *Jewish Heritage Travel: A Guide to Eastern Europe* by award-winning writer Ruth Ellen Gruber (National Geographic, 2007) provides a detail-packed tour of synagogues, cemeteries, villages, and other ancestral sites.

RUSSIA

Russian state archives are cataloged and stored under modern-day administrative divisions. Those placenames, as well as the borders of towns, districts, and provinces (oblasts), may be different from when your ancestors lived in Russia. To identify where to look for historical genealogy documents, you'll first have to determine who was in charge (e.g., imperial Russia, Soviet Union, Russia Federation) and what your ancestral home place was called during that period.

WHERE TO LOOK

Russian Life, *russianlife.com/blog/genealogy-online*
What It Is: The *Russian Life* magazine genealogy blog
What You'll Find: Continually updated genealogy research and resource links including helpful books, websites, organizations, databases, and contact information for firms specializing in Russian family history research
Tip: To research Russian records, you will need to know some Russian or hire a translator to help you.

WHERE TO VISIT

Family History Library, 35 North West Temple St. Salt Lake City, Utah

familysearch.org/locations/saltlakecity-library
What You'll Find: The collection's ever growing Russian genealogy materials (microfilm, microfiche, digital, and publications) plus research consultants and volunteers to answer basic questions and direct you to the most appropriate sources
Tip: If you cannot visit in person and need a Russian microfilm that has not yet been digitized, copies can be sent to your local **Family History Center** (*familysearch .org/locations/centerlocator*).

WHAT TO READ

In Their Words: A Genealogist's Translation Guide to Polish, German, Latin, and Russian Documents: Russia by Jonathan Shea and William Hoffman (Avotaynu, 2014) includes helpful tools for non-Russian speakers, such as 88 translated Russian-language historical documents and a Russian letter-writing guide.

The Family: Three Journeys Into the Heart of the Twentieth Century (Viking Adult, 2013) is author David Laskin's sweeping and spellbinding history of his own Russian-Jewish ancestors and how the choices they made shaped his life.

SCOTLAND

Online Scottish records are plentiful and easily accessible; however, they can be difficult to decipher. To help genealogists and other researchers read documents handwritten between 1500 and 1700, National Records Scotland created the free Scottish Handwriting Site (*www.scottishhandwriting.com*). Use the tutorials, weekly lessons, and coaching tips to learn how to read Scottish handwriting and interpret specific historic documents.

WHERE TO LOOK

ScotlandsPeople, *scotlandspeople.gov.uk*

What It Is: The official online directory for genealogical data from National Records of Scotland, General Register Office, and Court of the Lord Lyon (heraldry)

What You'll Find: More than 50 million records, such as civil registrations, wills, and census records, from the 1500s to the 1900s, plus free research tools to help conduct a more productive search

Tip: Most of the content is fee-based, so start with the FAQ section to pinpoint what documents are worth purchasing.

WHERE TO VISIT

ScotlandsPeople Centre, General Register House
2 Princes St., Edinburgh, *scotlandspeoplehub.gov.uk*

What You'll Find: The brick-and-mortar component of ScotlandsPeople, which offers more resources than what's available online including images of recent records (less than 100 years old), unlimited image views for a single day-use fee, and a research library

Tip: The Centre's gift shop has a wide selection of general and Scottish genealogy books.

WHAT TO READ

The National Archives of Scotland's ***Tracing Your Scottish Ancestors: The Official Guide*** (6th edition, Birlinn Ltd., 2012) offers a step-by-step guide to its printed and digitized documents available to people researching their Scottish family history.

 The Scottish Family Tree Detective: Tracing Your Ancestors in Scotland by professional genealogist Rosemary Bigwood (Manchester University Press, 2006) is a practical guide to locating, evaluating, and using historical documents stored in local and central Scottish archives and online.

SICILY

The Greeks, Romans, Arabs, Normans, Spaniards, and others who colonized or conquered Sicily left lasting imprints on the island, autonomous from Italy for most of its 10,000-year history, including its distinct surnames, such as "Salemi" from the Arabic word *salam* or *salem* (meaning "peace"). So, even if your ancestors' name sounds like it is from another place, it's likely the result of historical linguistic influences, not migration from other shores.

WHERE TO LOOK

ItalianAncestry.com

What It Is: A nonprofit, one-stop resource compiled by Italian Americans who share a passion for family genealogy research

What You'll Find: Dozens of links to Italian genealogy and cultural websites, as well as information about Italian-American history, organizations, and events

Tip: Look for records from your ancestors' Sicilian town using the "Transcribed Vital Records of Italian Towns" link (*sersale.org/comunes.htm*).

WHERE TO VISIT

Archivio di Stato di Palermo (State Archives of Palermo), Corso Vittorio Emanuele, 31, Palermo, Italy
archiviodistatodipalermo.it

What You'll Find: All of Sicily's existing vital documents (such as church records, civil registrations, censuses, court records, and military records) are stored in the Palermo archives.

Tip: Family Search (*familysearch.org*) has a wealth of Sicilian vital records searchable online. Enter "Palermo" (not Sicily) in the "State or Province" search box.

WHAT TO READ

Monte Etna's Children: A Story of Sicilian Immigration to America, by Mary Linda Miller (CreateSpace Independent Publishing Platform, 2011) includes a descendants chart, photographs, maps, a Proper Name Index, and other helpful research resources.

 Genealogists Guide to Discovering Your Italian Ancestors: How to Find and Record Your Unique Heritage by Lynn Nelson (F+W Media, 1997) offers step-by-step instructions for beginner family genealogists.

TAIWAN

If your ancestor has a Chinese surname, chances are you'll hit one or both Chinese genealogy jackpots: *Zong Pu* (clan genealogy) and/or *Jia Pu* (family genealogy). Zong Pu is a detailed record of the history and lineage of people who come from the same village. Jia Pu traces a specific family's history.

WHERE TO LOOK

Taiwan Family Genealogy Catalogue Database *nclcc.ncl .edu.tw/ttsweb/nclfamilyeng/index.html*

What It Is: The database works as the card catalog for all the genealogical titles contained in Taiwan libraries.

What You'll Find: Entering your family name or a specific location (such as an ancestral county) into the search box generates a list of written sources (either in traditional or simplified Chinese) where the name or location is mentioned. Viewing the material requires visiting the Taiwanese library where the volume is stored.

Tip: Try to determine the proper Chinese surname of your ancestor before getting started. For example, one of the most common surnames in China is Zhang, an ancient surname whose variations include Chang, Cheung, Jong, and Chong.

WHERE TO VISIT

Taiwan Family History Centers, various locations in Taiwan, *familysearch.org/learn/wiki/en/Category:Taiwan_ Family_History_Centers*

What You'll Find: Order any of the films and fiche available through the Family History Library Catalog and get free, personal help (in Mandarin) conducting a family history search.

Tip: Many centers have organized and searchable paper clan genealogies (in traditional or simplified Chinese) available to visitors who want to search physical records.

WHAT TO READ

Chinese-American journalist Frank Ching meticulously traces 900 years of his family's history in **Ancestors: The Story of China Told Through the Lives of an Extraordinary Family** (Random House UK, 2010).

TANZANIA AND AFRICA

Tracing your African ancestry using a DNA testing service such as National Geographic Geno 2.0 kit, its partner *FamilyTreeDNA.com, AfricanDNA.com,* or *AfricanAncestry.com* can leapfrog your family tree back to its African origins. (For more information on National Geographic Geno 2.0, see page 264. If you discover your ancient roots lie in northern Tanzania's Rift Valley and want to travel there, choose a custom cultural tourism outfitter, such as Africa Odyssey *(africaodyssey.com),* with experience procuring access permits to protected zones.

WHERE TO LOOK

African American Biological Database *aabd.chadwyck.com*

What It Is: A database thought to be the largest digitized collection of biographical information about African Americans living between 1790 and 1950

What You'll Find: Biographies of over 30,000 African Americans including former slaves and religious leaders; thousands of historic photographs; obituary files; and slave narrative collections

Tip: Access to this subscription-only database is available to students at most university libraries and at many public libraries.

WHERE TO VISIT

National Archives and Records Administration Bureau of Refugees, Freedmen, and Abandoned Lands (the Freedmen's Bureau), 700 Pennsylvania Ave. N.W. Washington, D.C.

What You'll Find: Post–Civil War (1865–1872) federal records documenting African-American births, marriages, deaths, and military service, as well as names and addresses of former slave owners

Tip: Another free, public resource is **"Voices From the Days of Slavery"** *(lcweb2.loc.gov/ammem/collections/ voices),* a U.S. Library of Congress oral history project preserving the audio recordings of several former slaves.

WHAT TO READ

Black Roots: A Beginner's Guide to Tracing the African American Family Tree by Tony Burroughs (Simon & Schuster, 2001) includes tips for researching African-American genealogy and planning a genealogy trip.

Help Me to Find My People: The African American Search for Family Lost in Slavery by Heather Andrea Williams (University of North Carolina Press, 2012) details the heartbreaking separation of African-American families during the slave era and the frustrating attempts of families to reunify following the Civil War.

NORTHERN IRELAND

The Public Record Office of Northern Ireland, or PRONI *(www.proni.gov.uk)*, the official archive of Northern Ireland, is the place to start tracing your Ulster roots. Key resources include church records (baptisms, marriages, burials, and even pew registers), the 1901 census, and records documenting who owned and lived in every property in Northern Ireland from 1828 to 1993.

WHERE TO LOOK

nidirect.gov.uk/archive-for-family-and-local-history

What It Is: The official website of the government of Northern Ireland

What You'll Find: The "Archives for Family and Local History" page has lots of helpful links to online government genealogy resources, as well as suggestions to help you conduct a more effective search.

Tip: The Irish Family History Foundation (IFHF) ROOTS IRELAND.ie database includes family records for Northern Ireland. Insert the county name before the URL *(e.g., derry.rootsireland.ie)* to find out what records are available for that county.

WHERE TO VISIT

Centre for Migration Studies, Ulster American Folk Park 2 Mellon Rd., Castletown, Omagh, , County Tyrone, Northern Ireland

nmni.com/uafp/Collections/Centre-for-Migration-Studies

What You'll Find: A free Irish Emigration Database containing over 33,000 primary source documents (including personal letters and passenger lists), an extensive collection of books on Irish migration history, and, for a small fee, copies of any documents you want to take home

Tip: Before your visit, complete the short "Ask the expert" form on the center's website to ask the curator about items in the archives that might be particularly helpful in your family history research.

WHAT TO READ

Get helpful advice on navigating the comprehensive collections available at the Public Record Office of Northern Ireland in Ian Maxwell's ***Tracing Your Northern Irish Ancestors*** (Pen and Sword, 2010).

ILLINOIS, UNITED STATES

If your roots run deep in the American heartland, some of the most enlightening historical documents can be found in the local public libraries of the towns, cities, and counties where your family lived, and may still live today. Ask the reference librarian for help locating printed resources, such as local histories, city directories, Old Settlers' files, tombstone surveys, scrapbooks, and voting registries.

WHERE TO LOOK

Illinois State Genealogical Society (ISGS), *ilgensoc.org*

What It Is: The website for ISGS, a not-for-profit, volunteer organization dedicated to collecting, preserving, and promoting Illinois local and family histories

What You'll Find: Links to free genealogy databases, current and archived ISGS newsletters, lists of Illinois research resources, and upcoming events hosted by ISGS and other Illinois genealogical groups

Tip: The second Tuesday of each month, ISGS hosts educational webinars—free when accessed live—and archived for on-demand viewing by members only.

WHERE TO VISIT

Midwest Genealogy Center (MGC), 3440 S. Lees Summit Rd., Independence, Missouri , *mymcpl.org*

What You'll Find: The nation's largest public freestanding genealogy library featuring 52,000 square feet of research and resource space containing more than 17,000 circulating and 85,000 reference genealogy titles, as well as periodical, newspaper, microfilm and microfiche records; maps; and online database collections

Tip: The center offers a variety of free genealogy classes each week. Preregistration is required.

WHAT TO READ

The Distancers: An American Memoir (Vintage, 2013) is author Lee Sandlin's personal, quintessentially midwestern story. It begins in 1850 with his German immigrant great-great-great-grandparents and chronicles multiple generations of his family life in rural Illinois.

Although ***Find Your Chicago Ancestors: A Beginner's Guide to Family History in the City of Chicago*** by Grace DuMelle (Lake Claremont Press, 2005) focuses on a specific city, the recommendations for using Chicago-area resources and research facilities are helpful for any midwestern genealogy researcher.

ILLUSTRATIONS CREDITS

Cover: (UP LE), Lisa-Blue/iStockphoto; (UP RT), LiliGraphie/Shutterstock .com; (CTR LE), Bettmann/Corbis; (CTR RT), Heinz Wohner/Getty Images; (LO LE), Catherine Karnow/National Geographic Creative; (LO RT), Alison Wright; Back Cover: (LE), Peter McBride; (CTR), Dave Yoder; (RT), Stanislav Horaček; 2-3, Land and Light/Getty Images; 4, Estea/ Shutterstock; 6, Timothy Allen/Getty Images; 8-9, Dave Yoder; 10, Dave Yoder; 11, Dave Yoder; 12, Phil Sheldon/Popperfoto/Getty Images; 13, Dave Yoder; 14 (UP & LO), Dave Yoder; 15, pawel.gaul/iStockphoto; 16-17, Dave Yoder; 18-21, Dave Yoder; 22, Hoffmann Photography/age fotostock; 23-33 (all), Dave Yoder; 34-35, guenterguni/iStockphoto.com; 36, Joe Mozingo; 37, Alfredo D'Amato/Panos Pictures; 38, Jiro Ose/Redux Pictures; 39 (UP & LO), Joe Mozingo; 40, Luis Sinco/Los Angeles Times; 41, Joe Mozingo; 42-43, Javier Pierini/Redux Pictures; 44, van der Meer Marica/age fotostock; 45, Heeb Photos/eStock Photo; 46, Claudia Uripos/eStock Photo; 47, Luis Davilla/age fotostock; 48 (UP), Alex Bellos; 48 (LO), Tim Makins/ Lonely Planet Images/Getty Images; 49, Alex Bellos; 50-51, Philippe Body/ age fotostock; 52, Dave Stamboulis/age fotostock; 53, Martha Kendall; 54, Stuart Dee/Robert Harding World Imagery/Corbis; 55, Holger Mette/ iStockphoto; 56, Timothy Allen/Getty Images; 57 (UP), Martha Kendall; 57 (LO), Daniel Osterkamp/Getty Images; 58 (UP), MORANDI Bruno/ Hemis/Corbis; 58 (LO), Martha Kendall; 60-61, jonmullen/iStockphoto; 62, Joyce Maynard; 63, meunierd/Shutterstock.com; 64, Sergio Ballivian/ TandemStock.com; 65 (UP), Aaron Huey/National Geographic Creative; 65 (LO), Michael Wheatley/Alamy; 66, Joyce Maynard; 67, Aaron Huey/ National Geographic Creative; 68, Wikimedia Commons; 69, Aaron Huey/ National Geographic Creative; 70-71, Glenn Davy/All Canada Photos/ Corbis; 72, Tiffany Thornton; 73, Marilyn Angel Wynn/Nativestock/ Corbis; 74 (UP), Gaertner/Alamy; 74 (LO), Marilyn Angel Wynn/ Nativestock.com; 75, Marilyn Angel Wynn/Nativestock .com; 76, Sebastian Santa/Getty Images; 77, Tiffany Thornton; 78 (UP), Tiffany Thornton; 78 (LO), Terfili/Wikimedia Commons; 79, Tiffany Thornton; 80-81, Wild Wonders of Europe/Biancarelli/Nature Picture Library/Corbis; 82, Stanislav Horaček; 83, Jennifer Wilson; 84 (UP & LO), Jennifer Wilson; 85, Stanislav Horaček; 86, Stanislav Horaček/Pixoto; 87-89 (all), Jennifer Wilson; 90-91, Desmond Boylan/Reuters/Corbis; 92, Juan Jose Valdes; 93 (UP), John Birdsall/age fotostock; 93 (LO), Juan José Valdés; 94, JayKay57/iStockphoto; 95, tunart/iStockphoto; 96, Ingolf Pompe/age fotostock; 97 (UP), Juan José Valdés; 97 (LO), Bruno Morandi/ Hemis/Corbis; 98, Christian Kober/Robert Harding World Imagery/ Corbis; 99, David Montgomery; 100-101, 145/Tom Bonaventure/Ocean/ Corbis; 102, Nikada/iStockphoto; 103, Christer Fredriksson/Lonely Planet Images/Getty Images; 104, Joe Hurka; 105, Yadid Levy/age fotostock; 106, Pietro Canali/SIME/eStock Photo; 107 (UP), alanphillips/iStockphoto; 107 (LO), Joe Hurka; 108 (UP), David Epperson/Getty Images; 108 (LO), Joe Hurka; 109, Joe Hurka; 110-111, Peter Adams/age fotostock; 112, Greg Balfour Evans/Alamy; 113, Jon Bower/Loop Images/Corbis; 114 (UP & LO), Jim Eagles; 115, Dennis MacDonald/age fotostock; 116, Detail from the Bayeux Tapestry—11th century. Musée de la Tapisserie de Bayeux; 118-119, Heinz Wohner/Getty Images; 120, Joe Yogerst; 121, Martin Siepmann/ imageBROKER/age fotostock; 122-124 (all), Joe Yogerst; 125, Raimund Kutter/imageBROKER/age fotostock; 126, Joe Yogerst; 127 (LE & RT), Joe Yogerst; 128-129, Bob Krist/Corbis; 130, Danny Lehman/Corbis; 131, Peter Adams/Getty Images; 132 (UP), Taka/age fotostock; 132 (LO), Roberto A Sanchez/iStockphoto; 133, f9photos/Shutterstock; 134, Frank Bienewald/ imagebroker/Corbis; 135, Alison Wright/Corbis; 136, Kaushik Saha/ National Geographic Your Shot; 137, Pico Iyer; 138-139, Christian Goupi/ age fotostock; 140, Robert Essel NYC/Corbis; 141, Joao Maia/Alamy; 142 (UP), JTB Photo/age fotostock; 142 (LO), Herb Dreiwitz/Los Angeles Times; 143, MIXA/age fotostock; 144, Richard Cummins/Robert Harding

World Imagery/Corbis; 145, Robert Churchill/iStockphoto; 146, Jason Arney/Getty Images; 147, Edward Iwata; 148-152 (all), Eric Melzer; 153 (UP), Thomas Fuller; 153 (LO), Katie Garrod/Getty Images; 154 (UP), Eric Melzer; 154 (LO), xPACIFICA/age fotostock; 155, Eric Melzer; 156-162 (all), Peter McBride; 164-165, Holger Leue/age fotostock; 166, Tom Wallace/ Minneapolis Star Tribune/ZUMAPRESS.com/Alamy; 167 (UP), Gonzalo Azumendi/age fotostock; 167 (LO), Dave Hage; 168 (UP), Gonzalo Azumendi/age fotostock; 168 (LO), Dave Hage; 169, jenifoto/iStockphoto; 170, Tumar/Shutterstock.com; 171, Dave Hage; 172-173, Ira Block/National Geographic Creative; 174, William Albert Allard/National Geographic Creative; 175, Florian Kopp/imageBROKER/age fotostock; 176 (UP & LO), Marie Arana; 177, Kim Schandorff/Getty Images; 178, HUGHES Herv/ hemis f/age fotostock; 179, Michael DeFreitas/Robert Harding World Imagery/Corbis; 180 (UP & LO), Marie Arana; 181, Ira Block/National Geographic Creative; 182-183, JTB Photo Communications, Inc./age fotostock; 184, Barbara Noe; 185, Barbara Noe; 186 (UP & LO), Barbara Noe; 187, Steve McCurry; 188, Keystone/Stringer/Hulton Archive/Getty Images; 189, David Kennedy; 190-191, Henryk T. Kaiser/Getty Images; 192, Robert Haidinger/Anzenberger/Redux Pictures; 193, SIME/eStock Photo; 194 (UP), Nina Strochlic; 194 (LO), Henryk T. Kaiser/Getty Images; 195, Gerhard Westrich/laif/Redux Pictures; 196 (UP), Henryk T. Kaiser/Getty Images; 196 (LO), Nina Strochlic; 197, Nina Strochlic; 198-199, Leonid Serebrennikov/age fotostock; 200, Hilary Mandleberg; 201 (UP), Leonid Serebrennikov/age fotostock; 201 (LO), Hilary Mandleberg; 202, Hilary Mandleberg; 203, Hilary Mandleberg; 204, RIA Novosti/Alamy; 205, Wikipedia; 206 (UP), Ocean/Corbis; 206 (LO), Hilary Mandleberg; 207, Jane Sweeney/JAI/Corbis; 208-209, Jim Richardson/National Geographic Creative; 210, Claudio Divizia/Shutterstock; 211 (UP), Alice/ Getty Images; 211 (LO), Peter Ribbeck/Getty Images; 212, Mary Evans Picture Library Ltd./Library of Congress/age fotostock; 213, DEREKMcDOUGALL/iStockphoto; 214, munro1/iStockphoto; 215, Andrew Evans; 216 (UP), rechitansorin/iStockphoto; 216 (LO), Carmelyn Ramos/National Geographic Your Shot; 217, Andrew Evans; 218-219, Matthew Williams-Ellis/Robert Harding World Imagery/Corbis; 220, Universal Images Group/DeAgostini/Alamy; 221 (UP), Katja Kreder/ imageBROKER/Corbis; 221 (LO), Renée Restivo; 222 (UP), Renée Restivo; 222 (LO), Christophe BOISVIEUX/hemis.fr/Getty Images; 223, Alessandro Saffo/Grand Tour/Corbis; 224, Kevin Galvin/imageBROKER/age fotostock; 225, Renée Restivo; 226-227, Jung-Pang Wu/Getty Images; 228, Michael Wolf/laif/Redux Pictures; 229, jeeaa.CHC/Shutterstock; 230 (UP), Top Photo Group/Corbis; 230 (LO), Mei-Ling Hopgood; 231, xPacifica/ National Geographic Creative; 232 (UP), Imagemore Co., Ltd./Corbis; 232 (LO), Mei-Ling Hopgood; 234-235, ranplett/Getty Images; 236, Ruan Boezaart/Getty Images; 237, Steve McCurry/National Geographic Creative; 238, Ariadne Van Zandbergen/Lonely Planet Images/Getty Images; 239 (UP), Huber/Sime/eStock Photo; 239 (LO), Donovan Webster; 240, Steve McCurry/National Geographic Creative; 241, Mitsuaki Iwago; 242, Fred Ward/Corbis; 243, Steve McCurry/National Geographic Creative; 244-245, Chris Hill/National Geographic Creative; 246, Andrew Hetherington/Redux Pictures; 247 (UP), Hans van Rhoon/Hollandse Hoogte/Redux Pictures; 247 (LO), Canadian Pacific Railway Archives; 248 (UP), Canadian Pacific Railway Archives; 248 (LO), Gareth Wray/Getty Images; 249, Liz Beatty; 250, Chris Hill/National Geographic Creative; 251, Liz Beatty; 252-253, AgStock Images, Inc./Alamy; 254, RWP/Alamy; 255, Library of Congress Prints & Photographs Division, LC-D4-42296; 256 (UP), Lynn Stone/age fotostock; 256 (LO), Diane Johnson; 257, Jennifer Byron/Getty Images; 258, Jason Ross/age fotostock; 259 (UP), Nick Suydam/Alamy; 259 (LO), Diane Johnson; 260, PVstock.com/Alamy; 261, Gamma-Rapho via Getty Images.

INDEX

Journeys
HOME

Published by the National Geographic Society

Gary E. Knell, *President and Chief Executive Officer*
John M. Fahey, *Chairman of the Board*
Declan Moore, *Chief Media Officer*
Chris Johns, *Chief Content Officer*
Keith Bellows, *Senior Vice President and Editor in Chief,*
  National Geographic Travel Media

PREPARED BY THE BOOK DIVISION

Hector Sierra, *Senior Vice President and General Manager*
Janet Goldstein, *Senior Vice President and Editorial Director*
Jonathan Halling, *Creative Director*
Marianne R. Koszorus, *Design Director*
Barbara A. Noe, *Senior Editor*
R. Gary Colbert, *Production Director*
Jennifer A. Thornton, *Director of Managing Editorial*
Susan S. Blair, *Director of Photography*
Meredith C. Wilcox, *Director, Administration and*
  Rights Clearance

STAFF FOR THIS BOOK

Lawrence M. Porges, *Editor*
Carol Clurman, *Project Editor*
Elisa Gibson, *Art Director*
Uliana Bazar, *Illustrations Editor*
Linda Makarov, *Designer*
Maryellen Kennedy Duckett, *Contributing Writer*
Marshall Kiker, *Associate Managing Editor*
Judith Klein, *Production Editor*
Galen Young, *Rights Clearance Specialist*
Katie Olsen, *Production Design Assistant*
Hannah Lauterback, Marlena Serviss, *Contributors*
George Bounelis, *Manager, Production Services*

The National Geographic Society is one of the world's largest nonprofit scientific and educational organizations. Founded in 1888 to "increase and diffuse geographic knowledge," the member-supported Society works to inspire people to care about the planet. Through its online community, members can get closer to explorers and photographers, connect with other members around the world, and help make a difference. National Geographic reflects the world through its magazines, television programs, films, music and radio, books, DVDs, maps, exhibitions, live events, school publishing programs, interactive media, and merchandise. *National Geographic* magazine, the Society's official journal, published in English and 38 local-language editions, is read by more than 60 million people each month. The National Geographic Channel reaches 440 million households in 171 countries in 38 languages. National Geographic Digital Media receives more than 25 million visitors a month. National Geographic has funded more than 10,000 scientific research, conservation, and exploration projects and supports an education program promoting geography literacy. For more information, visit www.nationalgeographic.com.

For more information, please call 1-800-NGS LINE (647-5463) or write to the following address:

National Geographic Society
1145 17th Street N.W.
Washington, D.C. 20036-4688 U.S.A.

For information about special discounts for bulk purchases, please contact National Geographic Books Special Sales: ngspecsales@ngs.org

For rights or permissions inquiries, please contact National Geographic Books Subsidiary Rights: ngbookrights@ngs.org

ISBN: 978-1-4262-1381-6

Printed in the United States of America

14/QGT-CML/1